WOBBLIES ON THE WATERFRONT

PETER COLE

Wobblies on the Waterfront

INTERRACIAL UNIONISM IN PROGRESSIVE-ERA PHILADELPHIA

UNIVERSITY OF ILLINOIS PRESS

URBANA AND CHICAGO

© 2007 by the Board of Trustees
of the University of Illinois
All rights reserved
Manufactured in the United States of America
C 5 4 3 2 1

∞ This book is printed on acid-free paper.

Library of Congress Cataloging-in-Publication Data
Cole, Peter, 1969–
Wobblies on the waterfront : interracial unionism in
progressive-era Philadelphia / Peter Cole.
p.   cm. — (The working class in American history)
Includes bibliographical references and index.
ISBN 978-0-252-03186-1 (cloth : alk. paper)
1. Industrial Workers of the World—History.
2. Stevedores—Labor
unions—Pennsylvania—Philadelphia—History.
3. Labor unions—Social aspects—Pennsylvania—
Philadelphia—History.
4. Philadelphia (Pa.)—Race relations—History.
I. Title.
HD8055.I5C63   2007
331.88089'0097481—dc22   2007005059

Contents

Abbreviations

ALU   American Longshoremen's Union
BLMOHP   Blacks in the Labor Movement Oral
           History Project
CIO   Congress of Industrial Organizations
GEB   General Executive Board
ILA   International Longshoremen's Association
ISU   International Seamen's Union
IWW   Industrial Workers of the World
LDOHP   Labor on the Delaware Oral History Project
MTW   Marine Transport Workers
ONI   Office of Naval Intelligence
UNIA   Universal Negro Improvement Association
USSB   United States Shipping Board

Acknowledgments

Though we historians are encouraged to view the past as a process that evolves over the *longue durée*, I confess that I never imagined how long this project would take! Over the past decade, I have been fortunate and am grateful that I have so many people to thank for helping me make this book a reality. Alas, there are simply too many to name.

The numerous institutions where I conducted research must be noted. No single cache of records exists, so I navigated collections across the land. In Philadelphia, the Independence Seaport Museum, Free Library, Urban Archives at Temple University, and Pennsylvania Historical Society proved invaluable. In Washington, D.C., I spent many months in the unsurpassed collections of the Library of Congress and at National Archives' branches downtown and in Suitland and College Park, Maryland. Howard University's Moorland-Spingarn Library is home to a few of those proverbial golden nuggets that historians always dream about. In New York City, the excellent Tamiment Institute Library at New York University and collections at the New York Public Library proved useful. Of course, countless labor historians owe debts of gratitude to the Walter P. Reuther Library at Wayne State University in Detroit, and I am no different, though I must be one of the few researchers to have spent a week sleeping at a Catholic old age home in the city. Both Ann Arbor's Labadie Collection and Madison's State Historical Society of Wisconsin are pleasures to do research at, as is the Chicago Historical Society.

I have had conversations, in person and via e-mail, with literally dozens of fellow historians, scholars, and activists who care about U.S. history, race relations, the labor movement, Philadelphia, maritime history, and the IWW. Perhaps we are not quite the beloved community but there truly is a deeply caring group of human beings who support scholarly research, and I am proud to be a part of such a fellowship. I want nothing more than to thank them all, but would be remiss if I did not single out a few. Jim Barrett has read my manuscript more times than he would care to, no doubt, and probably only I have spent more time with it. I envision Jim as the consummate editor. David Roediger, Joe McCartin, Eric Arnesen, Bruce Nelson, and Marcus Rediker each have provided sage advice and/or read portions of my work. Various current members of the IWW also have proved quite supportive. I only wish I could have actually talked to a member of Local 8; the closest I got was Ellen Doree Rosen, who, alas, does not remember her father, though our conversation brought me closer to him and the rest of Philadelphia's longshoremen than otherwise would have been possible.

In my years at Western Illinois University, I received a faculty summer stipend to fund a research trip. Even more important, I deeply appreciate the emotional support of my colleagues in and outside of my department. You folks have made Macomb feel like home, even if there aren't any mountains in the land of Lincoln.

What can I say? I am blessed with tremendous friends too numerous to name but who have provided endless support. You make life worth living. An extra shout out to my cousin, brother, and mother. My father "crossed the bar" before this project was finished, but if there is a heaven he is there smiling a big, toothy grin. To him, I owe my love of history and humanity.

WOBBLIES ON THE WATERFRONT

Introduction:
In Search of Local 8

One of the IWW's favorite slogans was "All for one and
one for all." I haven't heard that slogan used as much as
I did with the IWW. It was true then, and each day I live
I see the truth of it more and more.
—James Fair, *Philadelphia Inquirer*, April 6, 1980,
"Today," 4

Jake had just gotten a job unloading rotting pineapples. Most
of Jake's coworkers were black, along with a few white men who were
not regulars on the New York City docks. Although told to stay inside
the pier's gates for the entire shift, Jake went out for lunch anyway. As
soon as he walked off the pier, a white man approached Jake and started
talking. The white man belonged to the union that had struck the pier
and wanted Jake to join his union. Jake declined.

> "Nope, I won't scab, but I ain't a joiner kind of a fellah," said Jake. "I ain't
> no white folks' nigger and I ain't no poah white's fool. When I longshored
> in Philly I was a good union man. But when I made New York I done finds
> out that they give the colored mens the worser piers and holds the bes'n
> a' them foh the Irishmen. No pardner, keep you' card. I take the best I
> k'n get as I goes mah way. But I tells you, things ain't none at all lovely
> between white and black in this heah Gawd's own country."[1]

Typically, as W. E. B. Du Bois and many others report, race relations
in early-twentieth-century America were awful, white racism making
the lives of African Americans a struggle merely to survive. Jake, the
protagonist in a novel written by the Jamaican-born author and Ameri-

can Communist Claude McKay, tells us a great deal about race and labor relations along America's waterfronts. Throughout America's ports, longshoremen worked in racial and ethnic (as well as gender) segregation, with African Americans forced into the worst jobs and denied access to white-dominated labor unions except during strikes, when white workers feared blacks as strikebreakers more than as unionists. The situation in Philadelphia that Jake referred to differed greatly, however, for there black and white longshoremen worked side by side, on the docks and in their union. Local 8 was, quite likely, the strongest interracial union of its time. Who were these workers who shockingly broke the racist traditions firmly in place along waterfronts, shop floors, offices, and stores in Philadelphia and nationwide? How did their organization manage to bridge ethnic, national, and racial divides that few other unions dared cross?[2]

Thousands of Philadelphia longshoremen belonged to Local 8 of the Industrial Workers of the World (IWW), whose members also were called Wobblies. Founded in 1905 as a radical alternative to the American Federation of Labor (AFL), the IWW simultaneously embraced collective action via industrial unions as well as anarchist notions of freedom from and hostility to government. The IWW advocated the overthrow of capitalism but did not think socialism could be achieved through the political process, instead focusing its energy where workers held their greatest power, on the job. These men and women believed that those who toiled on the docks, underneath the earth's crust, in the forests, and in the mills deserved to control the wealth, and they were not shy about sharing their vision. Hundreds of thousands joined the proudly militant and flamboyant left-wing organization, and millions more were influenced by it, while employers and government officials alike targeted it for destruction.[3]

Philadelphia's longshoremen were doubly unusual, in that they joined the radical IWW and forged an interracial alliance. Given the ongoing fascination for the IWW as well as the nation's tortured history of race relations, these facts alone justify an investigation of this Philadelphia story. Atypically, these black and white,[4] native-born and immigrant longshoremen successfully seized and maintained long-term power due to their allegiance to the IWW. The IWW's ideological commitment to what I call radical egalitarianism allowed the dockers to maintain a united front against their employers, government, and rival unions.

Most notably, Benjamin Harrison Fletcher, a Philadelphia-born black man, came to represent Local 8 in the eyes of many. Ben Fletcher was one of the great African Americans of his generation, yet was and still is almost entirely unknown. Surely he stands in the top echelon of black labor leaders of his time, alongside A. Philip Randolph and Hubert Harrison. By all accounts, Fletcher was the most important leader in Local 8. For a decade he helped lead the union, a man respected by thousands of African American, European immigrant, and European American waterfront workers.[5]

Wobblies on the Waterfront seeks to rescue Local 8 from historical obscurity. After all, Local 8 was arguably the most powerful mixed-race union of its era. It deserves to be remembered and studied, but Local 8's fascinating and instructive story largely has been ignored. In 1933 the first historian to examine Local 8, John S. Gambs, did not consider its diversity to be worth exploring: "The race question, however, though dormantly existing, does not concern us." In his 1971 review of what is still the last major wave of writing on the IWW, William Preston commented that despite its "notable success" Local 8 was "rarely drawing much historical emphasis." Slowly, the compelling story of Local 8 has attracted a few chroniclers in the last quarter century, most importantly historical sociologist Howard Kimeldorf. However, scholars have yet to integrate the experience of Local 8 into recent discussions of either the IWW or interracial unionism. This book reclaims Local 8's story from the proverbial dustbin of history.[6]

Local 8 was one of only a handful of unions in Progressive-Era America to organize across racial and ethnic divides. The U.S. working class always has been diverse, far more so than the classes above it, yet most unions remained white only and white dominated at least into the 1930s and, for many, well beyond. Similarly, for much of the twentieth century most scholars ignored the fundamental way in which race shaped labor relations. In recent years, though, many more labor historians have given race, central to all of U.S. history, its proper place. This book is my attempt to enter this discussion by examining the union that demonstrated the limits of what was possible in the Progressive Era.[7]

In this period a few unions organized black workers, but even among these organizations Local 8 was unusual. Many unions that organized blacks were biracial—keeping black and white members in separate groups that collaborated. Moreover, even when blacks were the majority in the labor force and union, they often were compelled to accept white leadership and a less-than-equal share of the work. However, Local 8 was committed to being completely interracial and egalitarian. Blacks were allowed in on equal terms and worked, for the first time on the city's piers, in integrated gangs. African Americans also made up a major portion of the leadership cadre.[8]

Local 8 committed itself to full and total equality for both ideological and pragmatic reasons, and the union rose and fell on this crux. The IWW's commitment to overthrowing capitalism resulted in a union that defied American society in another important way: the IWW proudly organized African Americans. To the IWW, never overly concerned with theories, there were but two groups of people—workers and bosses—and they shared nothing in common. By the same token, all workers were just that: workers first. Hence, regardless of a worker's ethnic or racial heritage, he or she belonged in what Wobblies called the One Big Union. Of course, as a few other unions also realized, in those fields with large black workforces, unions simply could not succeed without blacks. When Local 8 was founded, upon the bedrock principles, tactics, and passion of the IWW—along with what Brian Kelly calls "pragmatic interracialism"—Philadelphia's diverse longshoremen finally achieved some control on the docks. To African Americans, European Americans, and European immigrants, a union that advocated equality must have been astounding, given mainstream America's obvious biases. By the same token, when Local 8 was torn asunder along racial lines during a bitter 1922 lockout, sure enough the union was defeated. While Local 8's interracialism is central to this book, a second, equally vital, theme intricately weaves throughout, too.[9]

Race matters aside, Local 8 was among the most successful IWW branches, dominating labor relations on the Delaware River for a decade and seemingly providing a model for how the IWW simultaneously could advocate revolutionary ideals while meeting the more immediate, "bread and butter" needs of workers. Local 8's durability is remarkable considering its affiliation with the IWW, whose national reputation drove fear into the hearts of many an employer but whose ranks included far fewer members than the more mainstream AFL and whose branches often emerged and disappeared in the course of a single job action. Working on both pork chops and revolution was no easy task, and Local 8 often suffered from criticism that illustrates this dilemma: how to form a strong, well-organized union fighting for important albeit not revolutionary gains (e.g., higher wages, less abusive foremen) while striving to overthrow the economic system. For all its fame, or notoriety, few IWW branches were durable, representing workers' interests day in and day out, before the much hoped-for revolution. Of course, this problem is inherent in all organizations seeking major change (the Communists come to mind). Yet Local 8 organizers Ben Fletcher, E. F. Doree, and Walter Nef did not see the question as either/or, though Local 8 frequently battled a central leadership that did. Especially during the postwar Philadelphia Controversy, Local 8 clashed with many in the IWW over how to maintain its dominance on the Delaware while remaining true to revolutionary principles. Seeing that Local 8 succeeded for a decade—combining IWW tactics and ideals, while also dealing pragmatically on issues like hours and the labor supply—surely other IWW branches could have done the same. Thus, Local 8 seems to offer a "path not taken" not just in regards to its almost unique interracialism but also in its hybrid of radical and not-so-radical methods of improving workers' lives. These two themes are the heart of this project, but a few other, related matters percolate throughout the book as well.

Although its heyday is eighty years past, the IWW continues to fascinate people the world over. Many unionists, activists, students, anarchists, environmentalists, and others appear to understand, perhaps better than academic historians, that the IWW was something special. Few scholars study the Wobblies of late, but this book grapples with the historiography of the IWW. One of the key factors that contributed to the decline of the IWW, in addition to external repression, was internal dissent over centralization. Those interested in this matter will find much here; before, during, and particularly after World War I, Local 8 clashed with the national leadership over the issue of local control. Ultimately, this dispute exploded into the Philadelphia Controversy, one of the most interesting and complex chapters in the story of Local 8 and the IWW. The longshoremen's quest to maintain local control, while acknowledging their commitment to and need for the larger body, is an important theme here. A second topic laid bare is how vital the leaders were to Local 8's successes and failures. Clearly, the wartime repression of Local 8 weakened the union. Though others stepped into the breach, poor leadership in the postwar era contributed to the union's decline, just as tremendous prewar leadership helped it gain traction. While not meaning to belittle the rank and file, this book makes apparent how large a role leadership plays in a social movement. Finally, the story of Local 8 provides ammunition to those who decry the notion that wartime repression utterly destroyed the IWW; seeing that Local 8, and other outposts, remained vibrant into the 1920s, it begs the question of whether external repression deserves as much blame (or credit) as it receives.

In some ways this book has more in common with the "old" labor history than the "new," in that its gaze is fixed firmly upon the workplace organization that the longshoremen created. As Howard Kimeldorf argues, it is necessary to study unions, for they are "the central institutions of American labor," both setting the tone for all of America's workers and acting as shock troops for the entire working class. Yet, given the tumultuous history of racial and ethnic relations in the United States, to study Local 8 while ignoring the workers themselves and their identities is impossible. Thus, this book examines the issues of racial and ethnic identity and, to a lesser extent, gender—but, again, particularly as it played out in the union. The need to take into account race and ethnicity seems all the more important in the history of American work, where the heterogeneity of the nation's labor force often has divided and/or been used to divide workers. However, this study is not about the Philadelphia waterfront as a community, nor can it be an exploration of the personal views of the thousands of rank-and-file members of Local 8. I would love to know what ordinary members of Local 8 thought about their union, fellow workers/union members, leaders, employers, government, and society. Alas, that is impossible. Rather, the actions of Philadelphia's longshoremen, I suggest, are indicative of what they believed. Incorporating the best of the old and new variants of labor history, this book examines the institutional history of Local 8, for it was through their union that Philadelphia's longshoremen made their most dramatic mark.[10]

Some historians shrink from the notion that history should be "usable." I vigorously disagree. In a nation whose ideals are so explicitly egalitarian, the United States' shameful history of prejudice (against American Indians, African Americans, other people of color, immigrants, women, homosexuals, and others) is possibly the nation's greatest paradox. I purposefully explore an example, admittedly all too rare, of an organization that lived up to the promise of America. Of course, the history of organized labor in the United States is replete with racism. But acknowledging that central fact, to me, only makes it more important to examine the people, places, and times where diverse unions thrived. It is vital for people today to know that almost a century ago a group of ordinary workers, black and white, native-born and immigrant, citizen and noncitizen, Protestant, Catholic, and Jewish achieved something truly remarkable: they not only preached but tried hard to practice equality. It goes without saying that these men did not fully eradicate prejudice from their actions and minds. In fact, racial divisions, among other factors, played a pivotal role in the union's demise. Still, when it came to racial equality, Local 8 and the IWW often stood alone, at least until the rise of the Congress of Industrial Organizations (CIO) in the 1930s, which obviously was inspired by the Wobblies. So, if some people find the story of Local 8 usable, if others are inspired to live a life more committed to equality because of this book, then I will be pleased.

Of course, there are historical arguments and analysis of the literature threaded throughout this book, but it is also a story, a narrative.

Human beings write, study, and talk about history to share such stories. History defines who we are, tells us where we have been, and suggests possibilities for where we might go. This book simultaneously attempts to satisfy the cravings of academic historians and ordinary people in seeking to explain why things are the way they are.

Almost a century has passed, but these longshoremen still seem remarkable, which indicates how far we still have to go. First, we must learn about the work of longshoremen, something about race and labor relations in Philadelphia generally and on the Delaware River specifically, and a bit about the city. Then the story of Local 8 can be told, beginning with IWW organizing efforts in the city and among maritime workers and followed by Local 8's founding strike. After it was established, the union dramatically reshaped labor and race relations on the waterfront and continued doing so for a decade. This book delves deeply into the union's history, focusing upon the power it achieved, its combative relations with employers and the government, and its interaction with the larger IWW, before, during, and after World War I. The men of Local 8 took seriously Philadelphia's proud nickname, the City of Brotherly Love. Though, ultimately, their efforts failed, as longshoreman James Fair reminds us, Local 8 and the IWW still provide lessons for all of us to ponder.

1   Philadelphia:
"The Workshop of the World"

In 1842 African Americans marching to celebrate Jamaican Independence crossed into the heavily Irish Southwark section of Philadelphia. Irish Catholics attacked the black revelers but, not coincidentally, fighting quickly moved westward to the Schuylkill River docks, where native-born blacks and immigrant whites competed for jobs. By 1850 the black-dominated docks had been taken forcibly by the Irish, who controlled waterfront work for fifty years. Yet by the late nineteenth century African Americans had returned to the riverfront and East European immigrants also had carved themselves a niche. By 1900 Philadelphia had perhaps the most diverse longshore workforce in the nation, which meant, among other things, that it would be a real challenge to organize a union.

This chapter will tackle a number of important questions to set the stage for the rest of the book. What was it about longshoring that made the work so hard and the workers so weak? Why was the city's waterfront so diverse? Why were race relations in the so-called City of Brotherly Love so poor? How come a stable union did not emerge in Philadelphia, as it had in nearly every other port in the nation? To answer these questions, we must act like longshoremen prior to the days of containerization, namely, carry some very heavy and varied loads. First, the chapter will examine Philadelphia's vibrant industrial economy and its maritime sector, at both the macro level and from the perspective of longshoremen. Philadelphia was among the nation's leading manufacturing and trans-

9

portation centers, which explains why so many European immigrants and African Americans moved there in the Gilded Age and Progressive Era. Then this chapter will explore the ethnic and racial identities of those who worked dockside prior to Local 8's emergence. Job competition, notably for river work, was central to but not the only reason for the racial and ethnic conflicts the city periodically suffered. Employers' hiring decisions and the failure to create a strong union also contributed to the dockers' diversity and their weakness. By this chapter's conclusion, a picture of Philadelphia's business, ethnic, labor, and racial history, and their intersections, should come into focus.

Philadelphia: The Port and "the World's Greatest Workshop"

Located where the Delaware and Schuylkill Rivers converge, eighty-eight nautical miles from the Atlantic Ocean, Philadelphia was an important port since its founding in 1682. The harbor of Philadelphia includes more than twenty miles of shoreline along the Delaware River and eight miles along the Schuylkill and was the largest freshwater port on America's Atlantic seaboard. During the colonial era, Philadelphia was the second busiest port in the entire Atlantic world, London being the first. Until 1830 Philadelphia was *the* leading commercial and manufacturing city in the United States, as well as the easternmost link in the agricultural trade of the old Northwestern states—which depended on Philadelphia's maritime connections to the Atlantic. Through the mid-1900s Philadelphia served as a major port for anthracite coal, steel, and oil. Philadelphia also was a leading builder of ships, first wooden sailing vessels and later metal steamships, both merchant and naval.[1]

The port has played a central role in the city's identity from its founding. In recognition, a three-masted vessel at full sail and an emblazoned anchor held prominent places in the city's official seal. Philadelphia's maritime significance is evident in how it entered into sailing culture. One windlass shanty, sung to raise sails, included the following stanza, apparently referring to the wave of Irish migration to Philadelphia in the 1840s:

> Now I'm in Philadelphia an' workin' on the Canal,
> To go home in one of them packet-boats I'm sure I never shall.

A sailor who knew the Maritime Code, that is, the rights of seamen, extremely well was called a "Philadelphia Lawyer." The port also lent its name to the "Philadelphia Catechism," which referred to the hard lives of sailors: "Six days shalt thou labor, and do all thou art able, and on the seventh thou shalt holystone [clean] the decks and chip the rusty cable."[2]

Throughout the nineteenth century and well into the twentieth, the port played an important part in the urban and regional economies. Although self-consciously in the shadow of New York City, in the early 1900s Philadelphia still was the nation's second busiest port and housed the third largest population, with more than a million and a half residents. Philadelphia actively traded with many East and West Coast cities as well as numerous destinations in Asia, Europe, and Latin America. Emil P. Albrecht, president of the Philadelphia Bourse (a major local business association), wrote that "the Port is the city's biggest asset" and boasted, "As a base for export and import operations it is unexcelled elsewhere." In fact, the Bourse's slogan was "Buy, Sell and Ship via Philadelphia." The Philadelphia Chamber of Commerce had a column entitled "Business of the Port" in its monthly newsletter.[3]

In contrast to ports like New Orleans that specialized in a few commodities, Philadelphia shipped a great variety of products. Grain from the Midwest along with coal and oil from western Pennsylvania joined textiles, locomotives, and other manufactured goods produced in the city. Ships brought in agricultural commodities, including unrefined sugar from Cuba and bananas from Central America along with cotton from the American South. While the Pennsylvania, the Baltimore & Ohio, and the Philadelphia & Reading Railroads all had large holdings, none of the railroads exerted much influence beyond their own piers, clustered mainly in North Philadelphia at Port Richmond. In 1913 several dozen shipping firms and stevedoring agents, many of them locally owned, contributed to the port's decentralization of power.[4]

Away from the waterfront, Philadelphia possessed a diverse manufacturing base, the local Chamber of Commerce boosting its city as "The World's Greatest Workshop." As American industrialization advanced, Philadelphia maintained its position, along with New York and Chicago, as one of the nation's three premier cities. Historian Howell Harris notes, "The value of the goods that Philadelphia produced exceeded that of forty-five states and territories." Philadelphia workers generally did not toil in mammoth factories mass-producing their wares. Instead, with the exceptions of the Baldwin Locomotive Works and the William Cramp Ship and Engine Building Company, Philadelphia's manufacturers maintained smaller workshops and factories where highly skilled workers produced specialty items. Along with the two largest industries—textile and garment manufacturing and metal production—marine transport, streetcar building, printing, tool and machine, furniture, railroad, oil and sugar refining, and chemical industries ranked among the city's most important. In short, well into the Cold War era Philadelphia possessed a thriving and varied industrial base, "everything from buttonhooks to battleships," as Harris quotes one booster.[5]

Working along the Shore

Longshore work involved the heaviest of manual labor, for long hours under very difficult, often dangerous, conditions, with abusive bosses. A longshoreman never knew how long his job would last or if he would find another, fully aware that his employers controlled his fate, that labor surpluses made job competition fierce, and that no union protected his interests. Philadelphia's longshoremen and the other folks who inhabited this world struggled simply to stay out of poverty.[6] But before further discussing this world, a quick note about terminology is in order. Some people use the words *stevedore* and *longshoreman* interchangeably. In this study, the term *longshoreman* is reserved exclusively for someone who actually loads and unloads vessels. The terms *stevedore* and *employing stevedore* will be used for those who hire longshoremen to perform manual labor.

Philadelphia's waterfront districts, like maritime areas across the seven seas, were places of commerce and chaos. The well-known Progressive Era writer Ernest Poole described this world in his 1915 novel *The Harbor,* "There stretches a deafening reign of cobblestones and asphalt over which trucks by thousands go clattering each day. There are long lines of freight cars here and snorting locomotives. Along the shore side are many saloons, a few cheap decent little hotels and some that are far from decent. And along the water side is a solid line of dock-sheds." Though spread along many miles of shoreline and across the Delaware River around Camden, New Jersey, Philadelphia's maritime heart remained in the district first platted by William Penn, hard along the Delaware and on the south side of the city, still referred to as South Philadelphia.[7]

The men who toiled on the piers, atop the decks, and deep inside the holds were casual laborers, meaning that they did not have a regular job with a salary or contract. On some days and at certain times of year, the port of Philadelphia boomed, while in other times, especially winters, little work occurred. Thus, the labor market fluctuated according to the number of ships in port, commodities, weather, and season. Typically, workers were hired for a shift, a day, or the duration of a job, lasting at most four or five days. If work was delayed for whatever reason (e.g., broken equipment or bad weather), the foreman could tell the men to "knock off" and later rehire them without paying for the time spent waiting. Generally, there was a core of experienced, regular longshoremen who worked at a certain pier or for a certain stevedore. Some longshoremen regularly rotated into other lines of work, black men often as hod carriers in construction, Poles to dockside sugar refineries. Despite the many challenges, most longshoremen remained committed to this line of work and, accordingly, passed the trade on to their sons, nephews, neighbors, countrymen, and fellow churchgoers; that is, ethnic, family, gender, neighborhood, and religious connections determined who entered this line of work. However, given the work's casual nature, there always were additional men with little or no experience hoping to get hired.[8]

The combination of the casual, unskilled nature of the work, employers' fluctuating needs, and workers' movements into and out of the industry led to chronic and often huge labor surpluses. Most importantly, the nature of the work—loading, lifting, carrying, pulling, and unloading—ensured that any man could perform the tasks. This reality was most apparent during hard times, when the number of men looking for longshore work exploded. Philadelphia longshoreman Bob Callan explained, "Every time there would be a big lay-off in the city or anything, you would go down there." True, as Walter Licht writes, "Unemployment and irregular employment were constant features of working-class existence in Philadelphia in the Progressive era." Still, the working lives of longshoremen were more insecure than most.[9]

The hiring method on the waterfront was called the shape-up, or "shape." In Philadelphia men shaped-up at 7 A.M. for the morning, 1 P.M. for the afternoon, and 7 P.M. for the night shift. Longshoreman Richard Neill described Philadelphia's shape-ups: "Each company had a specific spot on Delaware Avenue where they hired, some hiring bosses wanted you to form a big circle. They would then walk around the inside, eyeing each man up before giving him a [work] ticket." Many longshoremen shaped "at the corner," the intersection of Front and Christian Streets, the heart of the waterfront district. Alternately, men lined up in a semi-circle around the head of the pier, additional men behind the first row, with the hiring boss in the middle. The foreman proceeded to pick out individuals for the shift. Writer Ernest Poole described a typical shape in which "the figures of dockers appear, more and more. . . . Soon there were crowds of thousands, and as stevedores there began bawling out names, gang after gang of men stepped forward, until at last the chosen throngs went marching in past the timekeepers."[10]

Employers benefited the most from the shape-up. Employers ensured that there always were men available in case more workers were needed—without paying for these men's time while waiting at piers and waterfront bars. As Philadelphia dockworker John Quinn declared: "Even if they [employers] knew their ship wasn't coming in, they'd order you down there just so they'd have more manpower. Obviously if you went down there you couldn't go up there [to another shape] so you would be available whenever their ship came in." The combination of the method of hiring and labor surpluses resulted in bosses commanding near total control of the hiring process. It also contributed to many a longshoreman's alcoholism and saloon's prosperity, as men awaited the next shape.[11]

Not surprisingly, longshoremen hated the shape-up. Henry Varlack, a second-generation Philadelphia longshoreman whose father had immigrated from St. Thomas, called the shape, "an evil form of hiring . . . a slave market [where employers] play one guy against the other." Furthermore, this system of hiring was open to tremendous abuse. A boss often demanded a bribe in exchange for selecting a worker. Where the hiring boss had so much control and labor surpluses were so common, men could not refuse kickbacks. Thus, longshore unions often attempted to regulate the method and amount of hiring. Ironically, though, the International Longshoremen's Association (ILA), the IWW's rival, benefited from the shape; according to Bruce Nelson, the shape "swelled the number of union members, kept their dues flowing into the ILA treasury, and offered ILA officials numerous ways to pad their pockets via kickbacks and other forms of graft."[12]

Stevedores sought even greater control over the labor supply by encouraging ethnic and racial divisions among workers. As noted by W. E. B. Du Bois and other scholars, workers labored in segregated groups in most, if not all, of the city's workplaces. They also toiled in racially segregated areas—on the docks that meant all-black or all-white gangs. Employers used ethnic and racial divisions to their workers' detriment. African American longshoreman Abe Moses understood that foremen (all of whom were white in this era) encouraged segregated gangs to compete with each other in unloading ships, simultaneously increasing company profits and fomenting animosity among the workers. Irish American John Quinn seconded Moses's claim, "It was not uncommon that the gangs would be pitted against each other, white against black, Irish against the Polish. It made no difference to the companies." Philadelphia's waterfront employers also used the timeworn tactic of hiring black strikebreakers. White strikers, native-born and immigrant, often transferred their hatred from white employers to *all* black workers, thereby allowing white employers to use white supremacy to deter white workers from forming interracial unions.[13]

Philadelphia's waterfront workers, though, also had to contend with their own prejudices. A riot that erupted in June 1898 between African American and Italian longshoremen was only one conflict in an ongoing struggle between whites and blacks to find jobs on the waterfront. A 1928 Urban League survey of the Philadelphia waterfront confirms the conclusion; when asked about the relations between black and white members, the ILA secretary (clearly, not a friendly source concerning IWW matters) referred to the "intense race hatred that existed between whites and blacks on the water front prior to 1913 [when Local 8 emerged], in the community and among longshoremen as a result of keen competition between the workers." As for unions, most excluded blacks entirely, while so-called progressive ones segregated them in black-only locals. For their part, black workers felt little loyalty to white co-workers and white unions that actively and often openly excluded blacks. Black leaders like Booker T. Washington insightfully noted that white racism caused black strikebreaking.[14]

As if the shape was not bad enough, longshoring was brutal manual labor. Charles Barnes, author of perhaps the best book on longshoremen, contended in 1913, "It is probable that there is no other heavy physical work which is accompanied with so much overtime and such long stretches of toil without interruption." Local 8 leader John J. Walsh testified that

> the man has got to pull from five to eight and ten hundred pounds on hand trucks, down the hold of a ship; it is nothing new for a man to haul—well, they don't haul in hand trucks, they carry the freight down the hold of the ships, you carry anything from a two hundred pound bag of potatoes, 280 pound bags of flour, and 380 pound bags of San Domingo sugar, carried right on their backs, handle big cases of bacon weighing about 500 pounds, and got to go right up against the list of the ship with it sometimes.[15]

In an era where ten-hour days were common, longshoremen regularly toiled far longer. Philadelphia longshoreman John Ushka recalled, "Sometimes the ship would work, maybe two or three days, sometimes be about thirty-six hours. That was continuous work. You didn't go home or nothing." Powerless, longshoremen complied with their bosses' demands. Docker Francis Brennan complained: "The shift might have lasted 48 hours and you had to stick with it because the man would ask you, 'if you are tired, go home!' and you wouldn't get picked for the next boat." If a man refused to work a longer shift, at night, or on weekends, an employer simply no longer hired that man again.[16]

The motivation behind the longshoremen's feverish pace and heavy burdens was maximizing employer profit. It was in the shipowners' and stevedores' interests to load and unload ships as quickly as possible, as they paid their workers on an hourly basis, paid daily dock fees to the pier owner, and needed to move perishable commodities as quickly as possible. Moreover, the faster a cargo was stowed or unloaded, the more voyages a ship could make and, hence, further profits. According to the 1914 report of the Philadelphia Department of Wharves, Docks, and Ferries, "Delay in disposing of cargo on piers is tremendously expensive." Thus, longshoremen typically worked through nights, meal breaks, Sundays (Saturday being a normal workday in this era), and holidays. Again, Ernest Poole captures the ethos:

> For in this long sea station, under blue arc-lights, in boxes, barrels, crates, and bags, tumbling, banging, crashing, came the products of this modern land. You could feel the pulse of a continent here. From the factories, the mines and mills, the prairies and the forests, the plantations and the vineyards, there flowed a mighty tide of things—endlessly, both day and night—you could shut your eyes and see the long brown lines of cars crawl eastward from all over the land, you could see the stuff converging here to be gathered into coarse rope nets and swept up to the liners. The pulse beat fast and furious. In gangs at every hatchway you saw men heaving, sweating, you heard them swearing, panting. That day they worked straight through the night. For the pulse kept beating, beating, and the ship must sail on time!

Unlike unionized ports, though, Philadelphia longshoremen were not paid a higher wage for working exceptional hours, nights, weekends, or holidays.[17]

Though classified as unskilled labor, longshore work required strength, dexterity, and keen awareness. Barnes details the longshoreman's "ever present" risk of accident:

> Cargoes are handled amid a tangle of ropes, gear, spans, masts, derricks, and swinging booms. On deck, the whistles and calls of command, the rattle and whir of winches, the creaking of booms and drafts, the noise of chains, are confusing to ear and brain. Buckets of coal are dumped into the portholes with a roar, amid flying dust. Huge loads of goods jerked from

the hold or pier, sway and twirl as they rush through the air and swing past the heads of the men. Spans of steel wire sag and sway. In the hold below, the work goes on amidst the rolling and tumbling of boxes, bales, and barrels, or out in the "square of the hatch" under the ascending and descending loads. On the pier packages are trucked back and forth, bags are carried on the back, boxes and bales tiered up amid the confusion of horses and wagons, the cries of teamsters, the swinging of drafts.

Employers knew that certain aspects of longshoring were skilled work and hired accordingly. For instance, working in the cargo hold required great skill, to maximize the amount of cargo loaded, ensure that the cargo would not break, and guarantee that the ship was evenly loaded—front-to-back and side-to-side—to prevent a ship at sea from listing. "Green hands" were used for simpler, dockside tasks. More experienced men were hired to work ships sailing for foreign ports of call, labeled the deep-sea trade, while less skilled and irregular workers shaped for jobs loading and unloading ships plying the nation's Atlantic seaboard and were called coastwise longshoremen.[18]

The heavy loads, long hours, and perilous conditions led to high rates of workplace injuries and deaths. Of course, hauling weighty loads for hours on end could be backbreaking—literally—but doing so aboard a ship greatly complicated the task. Philadelphia longshoreman George McKenna complained in 1898 that "hundreds of longshoremen have been crippled or maimed for life," just as James Fair recalled nearly a century later that working on the docks was "very rough . . . had no safety regulations or safety rules. People were getting hurt. Getting hurt one after another. Just going to the hospital." The Baltimore *Afro-American* once reported that when a barge capsized off Philadelphia's South Street wharf, three hundred tons of sulfur and ten longshoremen were dumped into the Delaware River; as many dockworkers could not swim, drowning was not uncommon. Displaying the gallows humor that many a macho worker used, Ernest Poole quoted one foreman, "That's what's the matter with a good many boys on the docks. Their wives are always becoming widders [widows] and I don't know anything that can annoy a man more."[19]

Although perhaps not educated, longshoremen well understood the issues that affected their livelihoods and lives. As James Fair discussed, "We had no medical [benefits and] no safety rules or anything like that." Combining the dangers of the job with the powerlessness of the long-shoremen, Bob Callan claimed, "I've seen some cases where people get killed. Their parents, wives never got a dime. They just bluffed them out. Jarka [a large stevedoring firm in Philadelphia] was great for that in them days." Linking the risks of longshoring with a critique of capitalism, Local 8 organizer Jack Walsh explained that "plenty [of accidents happen] to the longshoremen. It is quite a dangerous job. Of course, that don't count. Men are cheap."[20]

If for this dangerous and backbreaking work, Philadelphia's longshoremen were paid well, there would have been less cause for complaint. In the early twentieth century, unionized deep-sea longshoremen in New York City received thirty-three to thirty-five cents per hour, fifty cents per hour for night and holiday work, and sixty cents per hour for Sundays, holidays, and working through meals. Longshoremen in Boston earned thirty-five cents per hour as their standard rate, in Baltimore twenty-five cents, and Newport News (the South had lower wages and costs of living) twenty cents—all with time and a half for night work and double time on Sundays and holidays. After their 1898 strike, Philadelphia longshoremen briefly received higher rates for overtime, Sunday, and holiday work, but employers quickly rolled back that gain. In May 1913 longshoremen forced their wages *back* to thirty cents per hour after years at twenty-five cents and still did not receive higher rates for overtime, night, Sunday, or holiday work.[21]

Due to the labor surplus and irregularity of work, the great majority of longshoremen were quite poor. Second-generation docker Bob Callan recalled his father's precarious situation, "He'd have a ship. Sometimes a month, three weeks would go by before he got another one." Moreover, the wages of Philadelphia longshoremen had remained flat for fifteen years while the cost of living had risen almost 40%. Figures on Philadelphia longshoremen's annual wages in the 1910s do not exist, but there is no reason to suppose that they would have differed much from Charles Barnes's estimates for New York longshoremen, who earned a higher hourly wage than Philadelphia's. Barnes reports that a steadily employed deep-sea longshoreman averaged less than $12 per week, with many earning below $10. Barnes also cited a 1903 study of average wages of American occupations in which longshoremen earned $340 a year, which rated ninety-seventh out of one hundred occupations surveyed. For perspective, one study at the time estimated that a family of three needed at least $800 a year to maintain a meager but sufficient lifestyle. Therefore, despite a decent hourly wage rate, most if not all of Philadelphia's longshoremen struggled to subsist.[22]

Their hardships and work culture encouraged longshoremen to develop a job- and class-based identity. The abusive and authoritarian stevedores, strenuous work, low pay, and life-threatening conditions—all were experienced by every single longshoreman, regardless of ethnicity, nationality, race, or religion. Crucially, the work required coordinated activity on the part of many men; no individual longshoreman could load or unload a vessel by himself, so he identified as part of a gang. Even the most basic tasks demanded working together for long periods of time, thus becoming very familiar with each other. David Montgomery writes, "Longshoremen usually lifted heavy burdens in pairs and became so accustomed to each other's movements that they needed no verbal communication to coordinate their efforts." Or, as put into verse in 1995 by John Fern, recalling a former work partner who recently had "crossed the bar":

> Salvaging barrels working side by side
> Working hip to hip, watch it partner
> Careful don't slip.
>
> Linseed oil drum's shaken loose by
> A raging sea, we righted, lifted
> And smiled, him and me.

In particular, the many inherent dangers caused workers to bond because they needed each other to perform the job and, literally, survive. Thus, as in many industries, longshoremen developed a system to take care of "their own" through collections every payday for fellow workers who had been injured or killed on the job that week.[23]

Even when not working, longshoremen (and sailors) identified with each other as part of a brotherhood. Of course, the brute manual strength required and inherent dangers reinforced a common sense of masculinity—as did the complete lack of women in the trade, hence the term *longshoreman*. Many of them shared ethnic and religious ties, especially as most gangs were segregated by ethnicity. Moreover, family ties—fathers and sons, uncles and nephews, cousins and brothers—were deeply interwoven on the docks, helping each other find jobs and work partners. These bonds were cemented further by the fact that most longshoremen lived in the same waterfront districts near the Delaware River, drank at the same saloons, and attended the same fraternal societies and churches. All of these factors contributed not just to a shared identity but also encouraged a particularly militant brand of unionism.[24]

The Peoples of Philadelphia

Longshoremen defined themselves by their work but also as members of distinct racial and ethnic groups. In the 1910s African Americans were the largest group of longshoremen in Philadelphia, and their numbers increased to well over half the workforce with the onset of the Great

Migration in the World War I era. Significant numbers of East European immigrants and their sons, in particular Catholics from Russian-controlled Lithuania and Poland, along with some native-born Americans, especially Irish Americans, worked the riverfront, too. In addition, the significance of maritime commerce guaranteed that conflicts elsewhere in the city reverberated on the waterfront. By tracing the city's intersecting ethnic, labor, and racial relations, the rise of Local 8 can be placed in the proper context.

Despite Philadelphia's racist climate, Philadelphia remained the premier Northern city for blacks in the late nineteenth century. While its total population almost doubled from 1870 to 1900, Philadelphia's black population trebled, to 63,000. By 1910 the city housed almost 85,000 blacks, although New York's black population had surpassed Philadelphia's. Most of Philadelphia's black migrants arrived from the Upper South states of Maryland, North Carolina, and especially Virginia. This exodus preceded the Great Migration of 1915–40 but shared the same fundamental causes: an eroding situation for blacks in the South and the hope of better economic, educational, judicial, political, and social conditions in the North. In the South the great majority of blacks remained sharecroppers and tenant farmers. Southern blacks were politically powerless, impoverished, and under the oppressive system of segregation known as Jim Crow. Drawing on their understanding of the Old Testament, black migrants saw Northern cities such as Philadelphia, New York, and Chicago as the Promised Land, a chance for a new start and better future for their children.[25]

In the early twentieth century, African Americans flocked to Philadelphia, not yet fully defined by racial ghettoes. Though, in subsequent decades, North and West Philadelphia became very heavily black, in the Progressive Era most African Americans still lived in the central part of Philadelphia, William Penn's original settlement. Charles Hardy, who

Table 1. Philadelphia Population Statistics, 1900–1930

Year	Philadelphia Population	Native-born	Immigrants	Irish	African
1900	1,293,697	998,357	293,669	98,427	62,613
1910	1,549,008	—	382,578	83,187	84,459
1920	1,823,779	1,290,253	397,927	64,590	134,229
1930	1,950,961	1,359,833	368,624	31,359	219,599

Source: United States Historical Census Data Browser. http://fisher.lib.virgina.edu/census

conducted extensive oral histories of black Philadelphians of this era, notes that "blacks inhabited several large districts in South, North, and West Philadelphia, and were lightly scattered throughout the city." That is, blacks lived throughout the central business districts, the teeming working-class neighborhoods of South Philadelphia, and along the banks of the Delaware River—not far from jobs at docks, shipyards, and rail depots. W. E. B. Du Bois's pioneering sociological study, *The Philadelphia Negro*, chronicles the Seventh Ward, the city's largest black neighborhood, which also was its oldest, poorest, and most crowded section (for blacks). Even there, however, blacks did not live in total racial segregation, though many blocks were racially homogeneous. Philadelphia was less segregated than many of its Northern counterparts and less segregated than it would become.[26]

Although conditions for blacks in Philadelphia clearly were superior than in the rural South, race relations in the City of Brotherly Love were far from ideal. The city's high number of native-born white citizens is only one of its similarities to Southern locales. As Jim Crow consolidated its grip in the South, Philadelphia followed. In the early twentieth century, the city's schools and neighborhoods slowly became more segregated. Concurrently, blacks were excluded from or segregated in most public spaces, restaurants, theaters, and hotels, as "public" became code for "white only." The rise of Jim Crow in Philadelphia was highlighted in 1913 when the NAACP held its annual convention there; just one month before Local 8's birth, the nation's premier civil rights organization was forced to find private lodgings for its black delegates since no hotel accepted them. Race relations continued to deteriorate over the next few decades. Kenneth Jackson notes that the Northeastern stronghold of the resurgent Ku Klux Klan was eastern Pennsylvania, and Philip Jenkins contends that Philadelphia was a national center for far-right-wing and racist political activism through the 1930s.[27]

Black Philadelphians suffered most egregiously at work. During the Progressive Era, scholars such as Du Bois and organizations like the National Urban League's Armstrong Association arrived at the same conclusion: African Americans' options for work in Philadelphia were severely limited due to racism. Du Bois argued that job discrimination was the single greatest cause of black poverty in the city. The mainstream daily *Public Ledger* concurred, "In brief, the negro is denied the opportunity to earn an honest living in most of the big industries and commercial enterprises of this city." Historian Charles Hardy contends that blacks were excluded completely from most of the city's workplaces, notably the city's many industrial plants, thereby forcing African American men, regardless of skill, to work as domestics or casual, unskilled labor (such as longshoring).[28]

In Philadelphia custom demanded that workers labor in segregated groups and that unions exclude blacks. Employers used segregated gangs, which also kept wages down: bosses forced white gangs to accept the lower wages given to black gangs or else not work at all. Where they had organized union (and therefore exerted some power), white workers acted no differently than white employers. Excepting the American Longshoremen's Union (ALU) in 1898 (discussed in chapter 2), Philadelphia's lily-white unions excluded blacks and readily colluded with employers. As a result, skilled blacks could not get work, and less than two hundred blacks in the entire state of Pennsylvania belonged to labor unions in 1911. Although Du Bois does not cite it specifically, it is highly probable that conditions for longshoremen were no different than for other black workers. After analyzing the inability of black men to get work as conductors on Philadelphia's street cars, historians Lorenzo J. Greene and Carter G. Woodson concluded, "And so it is through the entire field of desirable labor in the North—there is no place for the colored man."[29]

The Irish understood prejudice quite well, too, but over the course of the nineteenth century, as their numbers grew, Philadelphia's Irish Americans and Irish immigrants rose tremendously in economic and political power. The plight of Irish immigrants, especially in antebellum Philadelphia, is well chronicled. Though founded by Quakers seeking peace, the Irish were not welcomed in the City of Brotherly Love. Instead, as almost 100,000 arrived prior to 1860s, teeming Irish ghettoes became the norm: Southwark (one of the largest), along the Delaware River in South Philadelphia; Port Richmond, along the Delaware in North Philadelphia; and Grays Ferry, along the Schuylkill River in South Philadelphia. As the Irish arrived, often utterly destitute, they established the precedent for subsequent waves of immigrants (Italians, Poles, Jews) by living in ethnic ghettoes and battling for jobs. Through hard work and ever-growing numbers, the Irish fought, often literally, their way into better jobs and political power. By the Progressive Era, the Irish American Vare brothers led the powerful Republican machine in Philadelphia.[30]

As will be discussed below, in the late antebellum era Irish men fought for and soon dominated the city's unskilled labor market, including dockwork. Thus began the long, intimate relationship that Irish had with longshoring in Philadelphia—as in Boston and New York City as well as London and Liverpool. However, by the late nineteenth century, many Irish Americans had moved into the middle class—and postfamine immigrants were not as desperate—so competition between Irish and African Americans for unskilled work diminished. Similarly, Irish-black social conflict decreased somewhat; between the frequent, brutal clashes in the antebellum era and the rising racism that accompanied the Great Migration in the late 1910s, only the Election Riot of 1871, in which Irish mobs murdered several blacks, revealed the depth of Irish-black conflict. Still, in the early twentieth century there remained a goodly amount of Irish American longshoremen fiercely loyal to each other, reinforced by ethnic, familial, neighborhood, and religious ties. Instead, blacks found new competitors for work.[31]

Between the Civil War and World War I several hundred thousand Southern and East European immigrants flocked to Philadelphia, seeking to better their lives and those of their children. Starting in the 1870s Poles, Lithuanians, Slovaks, Russians, Magyars, Croatians, Slovenians, Jews, and Italians began moving in large numbers to Pennsylvania. Poles (Catholics and Jews) made up the largest immigrant group until 1901, when Italians eclipsed them. More than two million people arrived in the state between 1899 and 1914. In this era 85% of America's immigrants arrived from Southern and Eastern Europe, called "new" immigrants to distinguish them from older immigrant groups of Northern and Western Europe.[32]

Poles and Lithuanians repeated the migration patterns of prior immigrant groups—choosing locales based upon job security and economic advancement. In 1910 about five thousand Catholic Poles lived in Philadelphia, in 1920, around eighteen thousand. Like other smaller immigrant groups of the period, the Poles settled throughout the city, with its decentralized industrial economy. As cars were beyond working-class Americans' means and mass transit was prohibitive, a great many Poles lived close to their jobs. Virginia Purul remembered that her father, Stanley Olszewski, "walked from home to Port Richmond and back every day. Everybody along the river front knew him." Many of the Poles who worked on the city's docks, including Olszewski, lived in Pennsport and Port Richmond along the Delaware or in Grays Ferry near the Schuylkill. The largest Polish neighborhood was in South Philadelphia, among Italians, Jews, Irish, and African Americans, and close to the riverfront sugar refineries. Lithuanians in Philadelphia, about which no scholarship exists, seem to have lived and worked in close proximity to the Poles, especially near South Philly's refineries.[33]

As with the Irish and blacks, ethnic culture and family networks were essential to the identities of new immigrants. The preservation of their familial and cultural ties to Europe took precedence. Many of the unions that new immigrants joined replicated such ethnic segregation. These values were one of the main obstacles that Local 8 faced in attempting to weld the city's diverse longshoremen into a unified group.[34]

Ethnic and Racial Conflict on and off the Waterfront

Philadelphia possessed a distinctly conservative, nativist, racist, and violent personality. Many, blacks included, might assume that Philadelphia was a progressive Northern city. It housed one of the nation's oldest and largest black communities, was the birthplace of the first African American Christian denomination, the African Methodist Episcopal Church, and headquartered the black fraternal order the Odd Fellows. The city's proud if tiny Quaker population also suggests racial liberalism. Instead, for the most part, Philadelphia has remained conservative and racist since the Revolutionary era. In 1903 the era's leading muckraking journalist, Lincoln Steffens, called Philadelphia the most "American" of the nation's large cities due to its conservatism and relatively high number of native-born white Americans, more like Atlanta than New York. From the Civil War through the New Deal, Philadelphia was the only large American city that consistently supported the more xenophobic and antiunion of the two main political parties, the Republicans. Yet despite their consistent support for the city's Republican machine, blacks had no political clout in Philadelphia. The editor of the local black weekly, *The Philadelphia Tribune*, blamed the city's white politicians who "openly show their Southern prejudice." Having adapted to Philadelphia's Republican politics, the Irish American Vare brothers machine took African American votes for granted. Further, as historian Elizabeth Geffen writes, "the Quaker city of brotherly love has throughout its history erupted again and again into bloody violence," both racial or labor related.[35]

In the mid-nineteenth century Irish immigrants supplanted blacks, long dominant among Philadelphia's unskilled workers, on the riverfronts. From the city's founding through the 1830s, blacks, slave and free, had performed most of the city's unskilled labor, including dockwork. However, this black monopoly was challenged by waves of Irish, fleeing English colonial oppression and the potato famines. By 1860 about one hundred thousand Irish lived in Philadelphia, almost 20% of the city's population. Prior to the Irish explosion, blacks and Irish lived in neighboring communities in relative peace. Yet increasing job competition in the 1840s did not bode well for African Americans. According to historian Bruce Laurie, "evidence abounds" that whites, especially Irish immigrants and native-born migrants arriving from the hinterlands, used violence against blacks and occasionally against employers literally to "muscle their way into jobs on the waterfront." The apparent justification for these attacks was that no black person deserved a job so long as a white one remained unemployed. Laurie contends that Irish immigrants identified blacks—in particular black longshoremen—as a direct threat to their ability to survive in the city. Historian Noel Ignatiev perceptively argues that it was in this same era that Philadelphia's Irish "became white." As the Irish immigrants and their children desperately fought for the privilege of being white (with all the rights and benefits, not simply material ones, that went along with whiteness), they developed an intense hatred for black African Americans, who shared poverty in common with the Irish if not ancestry or skin color. In his provocative book *Divided We Stand*, Bruce Nelson argues that, in their efforts to survive, Irish immigrants and Irish Americans consciously embraced whiteness and its concomitant antiblack racism to take control of the New York waterfront in the 1840s, just as in Philadelphia.[36]

Thus, Irish anger at blacks—fueled by their desperation for work and to become white—seems more comprehensible, especially riots in 1834 and 1842. Much of the fighting occurred along the Schuylkill River, where unemployed Irishmen joined with Irish gangs like the Schuylkill Rangers ("a savage gang of boatmen, [that] evidently grew out of crews on the Schuylkill") in attacking black dockworkers. For days after the 1834 riot, unemployed Irish men attacked black coal heavers. The 1842 riot began when blacks marched, as part of their celebration of Jamaican Emancipation Day, to a temperance hall in the predominantly Irish neighborhood of Southwark. Once the black parade reached the heart of Southwark, Irish onlookers—angered by the twin "evils" of temperance and abolition—broke up the parade and attacked blacks. Though job competition did not cause the riot, the next day Irishmen assaulted black longshoremen along the Schuylkill, where both Irishmen and African Americans looked for work. More than one thousand troops were needed to quell the Irish anger, including one posse that saved black dockers trapped in a warehouse set on fire by the Irish. The last major race riot in antebellum Philadelphia occurred in 1849 when the Killers of Moyamensing and the Stingers, two notorious Irish gangs, shot up a popular black tavern. The apparent cause was that the tavern owner, either a black or mulatto, married a white woman, perhaps an Irish woman.[37]

Irish Catholics also suffered, notably in 1844 riots, from the wrath of native-born white Protestants, who did not see Irish attacks of black people as sufficient proof of Irish commitment to a white republic. David Roediger cites a common antebellum assumption: "To be called an 'Irishman' had come to be nearly as great an insult as to be called a 'nigger.'" Thus, in May 1844, when Irish Catholics protested the teaching of the King James Bible to their children in public schools, a riot erupted. Three thousand soldiers were necessary to stop Protestants from murdering Irish Catholics and destroying their homes, stores, and churches. At least sixteen people died during four days of rioting, several more that July when Protestants attacked a Catholic church in Southwark. The twenty dead and hundred wounded make the 1844 riots the bloodiest street affair in Philadelphia history. The vicious 1844 attacks were caused, at least in part, by the debate over who would be accorded the "wages of whiteness"; in 1844, the Irish had not yet earned that status.[38]

Frequent and ferocious fighting was at least partially the result of intense job competition between Irish and blacks. These riots and other less dramatic but equally important actions resulted in the docks—once a black stronghold—becoming predominantly Irish. As one contemporary observed after the 1849 riot, "When a few years ago we saw none but Blacks, we now see nothing but Irish [longshoremen]." Using the 1850 U.S. Census, Theodore Hershberg of the Philadelphia Social History Project calculated that the number of black longshoremen decreased by several hundred percent over a three-year period. In short, a decadelong battle between the city's large and growing Irish Catholic population and an entrenched black community ended with the Irish displacing blacks from the docks, where they had found work for 150 years. The Irish maintained dominance for the second half of the nineteenth century and, even when their numbers diminished, remained a force on the waterfront well into the twentieth.[39]

The Colors of the Waterfront

By the Progressive Era, though, African Americans, excluded from most other lines of work, and East European immigrants, many of whom did not possess the skills needed in the city's specialized industries, dominated the city's waterfront. In his 1899 study, *The Philadelphia Negro*, Du Bois found that in the Seventh Ward, the largest concentration of African Americans in Philadelphia, nearly 9% of black males worked as longshoremen, who easily could walk to either river from their neighborhood. Some African Americans lived in the Delaware riverfront wards, along with Irish, Italians, Jews, and other groups. By 1910, according to the U.S. Census, there were 3,063 longshoremen in Philadelphia: 1,369 "Negroes," 844 immigrants, 440 native-born of immigrant parents, and

410 native-born of native parentage. The number of black longshore-men continued to grow after the inclusive Local 8 took control of the docks and Southern black migration increased. For instance, Abraham Moses, the Alabama-born son of freed slaves, moved from Mobile to Philadelphia in 1916 and quickly became a longshoreman and proud Local 8 member. When interviewed decades later about his efforts at organizing longshoremen in Philadelphia, Wobbly Jack Lever, a Russian immigrant, also referred to "the many Negroes from the South." By 1920 4,035 longshoremen worked in Philadelphia, with African Americans accounting for the entire increase since 1910. In 1920 there were 2,388 black longshoremen, 814 immigrants, 436 native-born of foreign-born parents, and 397 of native-born parents. Or, as Philadelphia longshore-man John Quinn poetically explained, "Longshoremen, the sons and grandsons of immigrants and freed slaves, were among the many of the other laboring groups to be exploited, driven, and bullied by powerful corporation policies and tactics."[40]

The explanation for the prevalence of black longshoremen is simple: racism. In perhaps no aspect of black Philadelphians' lives was discrimi-nation more severe than on the job. Barred from skilled, artisanal, and industrial work, African Americans had no choice but to work in the low-est-paid, least secure, most physically demanding, and dangerous fields, including longshoring. The city's riverfronts were simply too large and black numbers too great to keep them off the docks. Despite Irish ef-forts to preserve their preeminent status, blacks increasingly worked on the waterfront. Further evidence comes from the Dillingham Immigra-tion Commission; in a 1911 sample of households from an unidentified "poorer" district of Philadelphia, twenty-nine of the thirty-three men who identified as longshoremen were "Negro." Clearly, white waterfront em-ployers disregarded their white employees' desire to maintain a lily-white workplace (a goal of white workers nationwide) and hired blacks.[41]

Table 2. Philadelphia Longshoremen, 1910–20

Year	Total Longshoremen	Native Parentage	Foreign or Mixed Parentage	Foreign-born White	Negro
1910	3,063	410	440	844	1,369
1920	4,035	397	436	814	2,388

Sources: U.S. Census Office, *Thirteenth Census of the United States Taken in the Year 1910,* vol. 4: *Population 1910: Occupation Statistics* (Washington, D.C.: Government Print-ing Office, 1914) and *Fourteenth Census of the United States Taken in the Year 1920,* vol. 4: *Population 1920: Occupations* (Washington, D.C.: Government Printing Office, 1923)

The rising number of black longshoremen was, partially, the result of the *absence* of a union. The presence of black longshoremen declined nationwide in the Gilded Age and Progressive Era as white workers unionized, increasingly in the ILA. As Greene and Woodson perceptively note, "Along the wharves and rivers where the Negro had long been employed as deckhands, stevedores [longshoremen], and sailors, the organization of white longshoremen's unions, especially in the South, culminated in the Negroes losing their former positions in some instances even as a result of violent attacks." By contrast, in Philadelphia, where no strong union existed, employers hired increasing numbers of blacks, presumably because it was in their bosses' interests to do so and quite possibly to hinder unionization.[42]

The new immigrants who landed in "the world's greatest workshop" were mostly peasants with few industrial skills. Of the 155 Polish male heads of households in Philadelphia studied by the Dillingham Immigration Commission between 1907 and 1910, 93 reported their occupation in Poland as farmer. Immigrants such as these offered their strong backs and availability in large numbers. They moved where needed, especially the mining and steel industries in central and western Pennsylvania. Philadelphia, by contrast, was an older and more established industrial city that did not experience the rapid, heavy industrialization of newer locales like Pittsburgh or Chicago. Rather, Philadelphia's economy was highly diversified and required more skilled than unskilled workers. These skilled workers generally were native-born Americans of British, German, and increasingly Irish descent. New immigrants like Poles found work in Philadelphia as unskilled labor: construction and maintenance of roads, railroads, and bridges, cleaning streets, collecting garbage, as well as loading and unloading ships, barges, and railroad cars.[43]

Since Philadelphia was such a large port, thousands of workers were needed daily, and immigrants obliged. Three of the nation's largest railroads—the Pennsylvania, the Baltimore & Ohio, and the Philadelphia & Reading—all had major operations in Philadelphia, with hundreds of acres of rail yards and major terminals on the Delaware River, all of which demanded thousands of laborers. The oil refineries located on the Schuylkill, just above where it spilled into the Delaware, and the sugar refineries on the Delaware in South Philadelphia employed several thousand immigrants, especially Poles. While there is little documentation of Lithuanian life in Philadelphia, hundreds worked as longshoremen and in sugar refineries. Like Poles and other Slavs, far more Lithuanians toiled in western Pennsylvania's mills and mines rather than in Philadelphia's highly specialized economy. Thus, the city's Poles and Lithuanians competed for work with Irish and African Americans.[44]

Once Southern Italians, almost entirely of peasant stock, started arriving in America in large numbers, they also vied for unskilled jobs. Generally, Italians, despite their own dark complexions, were favored over blacks for the city's unskilled work: tens of thousands of Italians worked in textiles, construction, and railroads. A good deal of animosity existed between African Americans and Italians, who often competed for jobs and worked in segregated gangs; for instance, after the June 1898 waterfront strike, when black numbers on the waterfront increased, blacks and Italians came to blows. However, in contrast to blacks, who were excluded systematically, Southern Italians and East European Jews, who made up the bulk of Philadelphia's new immigrants, flocked to Philadelphia's largest industry, textile and garment manufacturing.[45]

Caroline Golab contends that there was an inverse relationship between new immigrants and native-born groups of Irish Americans and African Americans. Relatively fewer Poles, Italians, and other European immigrants moved to cities, where more blacks lived, one of the main factors in explaining why far fewer European immigrants moved to Southern cities. Since so many blacks lived in Philadelphia (the largest black population outside of the South in 1900) and since one of the few avenues open to blacks was unskilled work, there was far less need for new immigrant labor than in cities that possessed smaller black populations (before the Great Migration). Moreover, new immigrants also contended with the Irish, who continued to be the single largest immigrant group in the city and maintained a strong presence on the Philadelphia waterfront. The Irish tended to fill jobs first, so only if there were not enough of them available were new immigrants hired. What work was left over after Irish Americans and African Americans divided up the lion's share went to Poles and Lithuanians, who, in turn, made sure their families and friends got positions when possible, following the tradition of most jobs in the era. Evidence culled from the Labor on the Delaware Oral History Project (LDOHP) confirmed this conclusion: most Philadelphia longshoremen had relatives who had assisted them in securing work.[46]

Any effort to organize Philadelphia's longshoremen into a union, thus, faced numerous obstacles. In 1928 Thomas Dabney, a researcher at the Urban League's Armstrong Association of Philadelphia, noted the "intense race hatred that existed between whites and blacks on the water front prior to 1913, in the community and among longshoremen." With no established labor organization to protect them, Philadelphia's diverse waterfront workers were subject to the whims of their employers, who had demonstrated their determination to keep their workers as weak and divided as possible. Adding to the myriad difficulties involved in organizing were the conservatism, racism, and antilabor feelings of the city's majority population and government. Divided racially and ethnically, with no union, and living in a city actively opposed to them as workers, minorities, and immigrants, Philadelphia's longshoremen faced great obstacles.

2 Wobblies Take the Docks

On May 14, 1913, the longshoremen of Philadelphia walked out and "re-entered the Labor Movement after an absence of 15 years," according to the local African American leader, Ben Fletcher. The IWW quickly gained control of this unaffiliated group—despite competition from a rival union and an awful reputation in mainstream culture—and, as reported by the *Public Ledger*, "virtually tied up" the port. Fletcher noted that Local 8's victorious strike involved more than four thousand deep-sea longshoremen, grain trimmers, sugar-refinery workers, and coal heavers, from "Polish, Jewish, Negro and English speaking" backgrounds. Part of an international wave of labor militancy called the "new unionism," this strike ushered in an era of unprecedented power for these longshoremen, the likes of which never had been seen before in the city or almost anywhere else in the nation. This chapter explores the decades-long effort of Philadelphia dockers to unionize, the history of the IWW in the city and among maritime workers, and finally the 1913 strike. Momentous for both its commitment to industrial unionism and racial inclusiveness, Wobbly ideology and tactics proved more powerful than the divided and primarily local waterfront employers.[1]

Organizing Dockworkers in the "Black Pit of Unionism"

In addition to the city's troubled racial history, Philadelphia's waterfront periodically erupted in labor conflict throughout the nineteenth century. Although the longshoremen's impulse for unionism was strong, as labor historian David Montgomery argues, it also was episodic: "Unions in all the major ports were incessantly formed, broken, and reformed." Ethnic and racial issues complicated these efforts. Despite the workers' desire to have a voice, unionism never took firm root in Philadelphia until the arrival of Local 8.[2]

Not surprising given its prominent place in American and maritime history, Philadelphia waterfront workers played a crucial role in the most prominent strike of the young nation. In May 1835 Schuylkill River coal heavers, mostly Irish immigrants, formed a labor union and initiated a monthlong strike for higher wages and a ten-hour day. The coal heavers' actions sparked the Philadelphia General Strike of 1835, involving twenty thousand people, the apex of the greatest wave of labor unrest the nation yet had seen. The strike also was the most notable instance in antebellum Philadelphia of laborers crossing craft, ethnic, and religious divides—most remarkably, as quoted in the *United States Gazette,* "a procession of persons calling themselves stevedores [longshoremen]—some eight or ten white persons bearing banners, which we suppose rather belonged to the ships' carpenters. These were followed by about twenty blacks." In a few years, such a diverse labor parade would have been unthinkable.[3]

Of all the city's unskilled laborers, dockworkers were the most likely to organize. Historian Marcus Rediker perceptively argues that sailors and other maritime workers were among the first to experience the harsh realities of industrialization, large-scale capitalist enterprise, and gang labor in veritable open-air factories. Coal heavers and other waterfront workers toiled in gangs and so were accustomed to identifying their interests collectively; that is, worker solidarity, an essential component of any effort to unionize, arose directly out of the labor process.[4]

Ethnicity, especially Irish ethnic identity, also played an important role in labor organizing. In accordance with the job, the coal heavers worked in gangs; in keeping with desires to work with "their own kind," the gangs were ethnically homogeneous. In fact, some of the nation's most powerful unions have been based upon ethnic homogeneity and racial exclusivity. Bruce Laurie postulates that these waterfront gangs acted as "surrogate unions. . . . They controlled access to work, negotiated with employers, and enforced unity in strikes." The Schuylkill Rangers, for instance, determined who became a river boatman, and these Irish gangs acted as quasi-unions in the nineteenth century.[5]

Some labor activism occurred on Philadelphia's waterfront with the rise of the Knights of Labor, but nothing long-lasting. Founded in 1869 by Philadelphia garment workers, the Knights organized more than three hundred area locals, mostly skilled textile and garment workers. At the height of the Knights' power, the early and mid-1880s, some Philadelphia waterfront workers belonged to at least three assemblies. In contrast to efforts in Chicago and elsewhere, though, Philadelphia's Knights did not actively participate in the eight-hour movement; one labor observer reported that "the whole movement is dull as ditch water in Philadelphia." The Philadelphia-based national leadership of the Knights, led by the Irish American Catholic Terrence Powderly, condemned the events of 1886 as insurrectionary; his conservatism, no doubt, influenced local activity. Although belonging to the first white-dominated labor organization in the nation open to African Americans, Philadelphia Knights—skilled workers of Irish, German, and British ancestry—did not line up African Americans. This Philadelphia story was quite typical: the Knights rarely organized either unskilled workers or Northern blacks. The phenomenal growth of the Knights in the mid-1880s was followed by an equally rapid decline, largely due to intense employer and governmental opposition.[6]

Efforts to organize Philadelphia's waterfront workers recommenced in 1898. The Dockers' Union of England, under the direction of Tom Mann, dispatched Edward McHugh to organize American longshoremen to prevent them from scabbing during English dock strikes. When McHugh arrived in New York City in 1896 he established the ALU, rather than working through the AFL's ILA. Perhaps the radical English dockers considered the AFL too conservative. Within a year and a half McHugh had organized approximately fifteen thousand longshoremen. The ALU took for its motto "all men are brothers" and opened its membership to all, regardless of craft, ethnicity, or race.[7]

Building on this success, McHugh targeted Philadelphia. McHugh quickly organized Quakertown's dockers into an ALU local and on June 1, 1898, fifteen hundred of them struck. Although not mentioned, some African American longshoremen likely supported the union since the great majority of the port's longshoremen struck and blacks already made up more than 10% of the waterfront workforce (the exact racial and ethnic breakdown of Philadelphia's longshoremen in 1898 is not documented).[8] The union demanded wage hikes and more safety precautions. The local branch of the AFL's International Seamen's Union (ISU) refused to support the strike, but the New York ALU donated its entire treasury to the cause.[9]

The longshoremen won their strike within three days. Despite securing four hundred replacements, mostly from Philadelphia and Brooklyn, and police support, the stevedores quickly conceded defeat. ALU Secretary George McKenna addressed a victory meeting and "the enthusiasm was immense," according to the mainstream *Philadelphia Inquirer.* Employers agreed to ALU wage demands: time and a half for night work, double time for Sundays, and fractions of a day, when a long walk was required to get to the working pier, to be considered a half day's work. Another major concession the ALU gained involved safety; no union man would work a hatch unless safety devices in hauling cargo were employed. If these precautions were not met, all work would be suspended until the employer took the appropriate measures. McKenna considered this point of "great value" because longshore work regularly occurred without essential protection.[10]

The matter of race during the 1898 strike was complex: clearly, racial animosity existed on and off the Philadelphia waterfront, yet, crucially, one of the new work rules proclaimed that there would be "no distinction between white and colored men, and that they would be engaged on an equal basis." This demand conformed to the ALU constitution that prohibited discrimination based on "race, creed, color, or nativity." Aside from this contract provision, no other reference to race exists during the strike. It is well known that in the aftermath of the mammoth New York dock strike in 1887 employers brought in legions of Italians to weaken that Irish-dominated workforce. In this light, the *Philadelphia Inquirer's* mention that some replacement workers came from Brooklyn is noteworthy, as most of that borough's longshoremen were Italian, whereas few Italians worked the Philadelphia waterfront. Since the Philadelphia ALU demanded that "no distinction between white and colored men" occur in hiring, and given the widespread racism in the city's workplaces, it should be assumed that Philadelphia's black longshoremen had suffered from discrimination. After all, that same year, local white rail workers conducted an effective "hate strike" to prevent black men from operating streetcars. Yet, Philadelphia's white longshoremen were pragmatic enough to support black equality, likely attributable to a progressive union leadership, significant black numbers, and a strike victory that proved the efficacy of the ALU's interracial policy.[11]

One month later, though, the ALU collapsed. In July 1898 scandal rocked the New York local, after the general secretary looted the union's treasury. Shortly thereafter, the entire ALU dissolved. While New York's longshoremen quickly reorganized themselves into an independent union, no such thing occurred in Philadelphia. Quakertown's dockers had been organized by an Irishman in an English union based in New York. With the main base gone, the Philadelphia ALU disappeared and with it the possibility of harmonious race relations on the Philadelphia waterfront. Historian Roger Lane reports African Americans and Italian immigrants battling for work on the shores of the Delaware in the same month that the ALU imploded. Philadelphia's longshoremen remained nonunion until 1913.[12]

The only other attempt to organize Philadelphia's longshoremen was undertaken by the ILA. Founded in 1892 and affiliated with the AFL the following year, the ILA focused its early activity on the Great Lakes. Curiously, in 1913 ILA Atlantic District Secretary William Dempsey claimed that "this organization had a foothold in Philadelphia" in 1898; Dempsey reported that members of this phantom local struck but then left the ILA after feeling "grossly neglected." If there was a battle between the ILA and ALU, neither Charles Barnes in his seminal work nor the *Philadelphia Inquirer* mentioned it. Several other brief references exist, but if an ILA presence existed on Philadelphia's waterfront, its power was nil.[13]

When it organized on the Atlantic coast in the first decade of the twentieth century, the ILA took a very pragmatic approach to race matters. In Northern ports, the ILA conformed to existing patterns, meaning blacks were seen as inferior to whites and, accordingly, segregated. For instance, when it took over local longshore unions in Boston and New York in 1912, the Irish-dominated ILA maintained ethnically segregated locals and mostly excluded blacks. When asked in 1930 about black membership in the ILA, one black leader in Brooklyn replied, "We are in the union today because the white man had to take us in for his own protection. Outside the Organization the Negro could scab on the white man. Inside he can't." Blacks supported the ILA but were acutely aware of how the white leadership manipulated black longshoremen.[14]

The ILA's pragmatic approach to organizing blacks resulted in a varied, and at times inclusive, policy in Southern ports. In Atlantic ports south of the Mason-Dixon line, like Baltimore, Norfolk, and Hampton Roads, Virginia, the ILA chartered white-only locals; as IWW organizer Jack Lever put it, "The ILA came in [to Baltimore] and organized whites and left the Negroes out." Importantly though, in certain Gulf of Mexico ports, where large numbers of African American longshoremen meant that their inclusion was necessary to ensure union power, the ILA actively lined up black workers, albeit in segregated locals. Eric Arnesen points out, "Without exception, wherever and whenever Gulf longshore workers organized unions, they did so along racially separate lines, and those unions eventually established formal and informal relations with one another across the racial divide." Most notably, Arnesen documents the biracial unionism of the New Orleans waterfront; as in other industries where blacks made up a significant percentage of the workforce, like coal mining in Alabama and timber in Louisiana, white unions did, at times, line up blacks. Like Alabama coal miners, the ILA insisted on white leadership in organizations with black majorities.[15]

For the early twentieth century the ILA should be considered quite progressive, as it promoted "stomach equality." For example, ILA President T. V. O'Connor stated in 1911, "The black man has got to play fair with the white man and the white man will have to play fair with the black man. We are not going to attempt to take up the question of social equality, but we can, if properly and thoroughly organized, bring about industrial equality." Thus in New Orleans, where blacks made up a majority of the workforce and a powerful tradition of biracial unionism predated the ILA, the ILA preserved this system. By the same token, where blacks maintained some power, as in Galveston, Texas, the ILA leadership pushed white unionists to accept black workers, though in separate and lesser locals. Where white workers were in a position of unquestioned superiority, however, the ILA encouraged black subservience or exclusion from the union, as in Mobile and Gulfport. In all of these cases, pragmatism and not ideology motivated the ILA. In some instances, considerations of power and stability led to biracial unionism while in others these same factors led to the exact opposite strategy. The goal never was, in Arnesen's words, "to promote interracial collaboration."[16]

Regardless of its racial policy, the ILA never established itself in Philadelphia until the 1920s. As Maud Russell writes, "The Wobblies were entrenched on the docks of that city and they would not yield their waterfront jurisdiction without a long struggle. . . . Philadelphia was the last major port . . . to affiliate with the ILA."[17]

It was not only on the waterfront that Philadelphia's workers had difficulty organizing. Although home to one of the nation's first major strikes, Philadelphia workers consistently met fierce resistance to unionism. For instance, when textile workers joined the Knights of Labor in droves, textile factory owners formed the Philadelphia Manufacturers' Association, which successfully squashed the Knights. Similarly, the powerful and well-organized Metal Manufacturers' Association of Philadelphia eliminated the local metal trades unions for thirty years after "a united employer offensive," according to Ken Fones-Wolf, one of the few historians to study the AFL in the city. By the early 1910s Philadelphia was a well-known open-shop (i.e., nonunion) town, due to the close alliance forged between the city's businesses and the Republican political machine. In honor of its antilabor heritage, one organizer for the Amalgamated Clothing Workers of America labeled Philadelphia "the black pit of unionism," and an organizer for the International Association of Machinists called it "the 'Scab City' of the country." In 1905 about 10% of the city's wage earners belonged to unions, almost all of them to craft unions dominated by white, native-born, male skilled workers; of these, under two hundred were black. Moreover, employers consciously used their workers' diverse identities to decrease union power. Into the 1910s the rifts between skilled and unskilled, native-born and immigrant, man and woman, and black and white kept Philadelphia's workers divided and weak. As a result, Philadelphia—like many Northern cities—possessed a dual labor market. The first was reserved for native-born and old-stock immigrant men, the second market accommodated African Americans, new immigrants, and women. The latter group worked far less regularly, for lower wages, and typically was nonunion.[18]

The IWW in Philadelphia

Despite their deplorable conditions and collective identity, Philadelphia's longshoremen were not targeted by the IWW. Rather, the first IWW local was chartered in 1907 to Hungarian metal workers, and the IWW concentrated its efforts on the textile industry, as Philadelphia was among the largest textile centers in the world. In the early 1900s the textile industry employed 35% of the city's workers. Elizabeth Gurley Flynn, who later earned the nickname "the Rebel Girl" from Wobbly songster Joe Hill, regularly spoke in the city, including on the waterfront. In one speech, Flynn invoked the name of one-time Philadelphia resident Thomas Paine, claiming that workers needed another American Revolution.[19]

In September 1911 Philadelphia's Wobblies undertook their own free-speech fight. As in previous summers, the IWW held weekly open-air meetings on the City Hall Plaza. The police already had demonstrated their dislike of the IWW during a Baldwin Locomotive strike when some officers admitted to arresting Flynn solely because Baldwin's managers requested it. Philadelphia's police regularly arrested people on the arbitrary charge of vagrancy; one unlucky Wobbly was jailed for three months for it. So, it is not surprising that the police attempted to prevent the IWW from holding meetings before 10 P.M.; the police clubbed and arrested Wobblies for doing so. When arrests and beatings proved ineffective, the police chief rescinded the order and "permitted" the IWW to hold meetings. The IWW redoubled its efforts to organize bakers, tapestry and carpet workers, railroad workers, launderers, and button makers—all into Local 57, a mixed branch for workers in industries where there were not yet enough members to justify separate locals.[20]

The IWW held meetings throughout the Delaware River valley, some of which served as a training ground for the man who became Local 8's most prominent leader, Benjamin Harrison Fletcher. Like many black Philadelphians, Fletcher's parents had migrated from Virginia; supposedly, Fletcher's ancestors included both African Americans and American Indians, quite possible considering the history of mixing between these groups. In 1912 Fletcher was twenty-two years old, worked as a longshoreman, and lodged in South Philadelphia with other young black men who also worked as day laborers, typical for single men. Fletcher traveled among the Philadelphia Left for a year or two prior to Local 8's founding, possibly having met Joe Hill, the IWW's most famous bard, before he moved west. Fletcher also is reported to have known the soon-to-be prominent radical journalist, John Reed. Years later Fletcher referred to his membership in the Socialist Party; like Big Bill Haywood, he probably belonged to both organizations until the Wobblies broke with the Socialists in 1913. In 1912 Fletcher served as Local 57's corresponding secretary. Fletcher was obliged to join Local 57 since no longshoremen's union existed. Fletcher represented Local 57 at the annual IWW convention in Chicago that fall. His presence, as well as that of D. B. Gordon, a black man representing the IWW's Brotherhood of Timber Workers in Louisiana, was cited in *Solidarity* as "proof that we have surmounted all barriers of race and color." Fletcher was an active street speaker for the IWW; another local Wobbly reported that, at one meeting in Chester, Pennsylvania, Fletcher "certainly knows how to deliver the goods. . . . The crowd was very attentive, taking to everything the speaker had to say regarding the class struggle," the first of numerous references to his outstanding speaking abilities.[21]

Simultaneously, the IWW made a nationwide call in *Solidarity* for "Negro Workers" to unionize. The article noted that "YOUR RACE know[s] better than any about injustice, off and on the job." The open letter pointed out that employers kept black and white workers fighting each other by convincing white workers that "social equality," not greedy employers, was the greatest threat to white workers. As a result of employers' use of race, both white and black workers suffered. This article fit well within the socialist preamble of the IWW, which boldly declared that "the working class and the employing class have nothing in common!" That is, racial and ethnic differences should not deter workers from uniting against their shared foe.[22]

In keeping with such calls for solidarity, Philadelphia Wobblies put great effort into supporting IWW struggles elsewhere. During the summer of 1912 the IWW led its famous "Bread and Roses" strike among textile workers in Lawrence, Massachusetts. Philadelphia Wobblies took in dozens of children of the Lawrence strikers as part of a savvy strategy to help these kids and publicize the strike. Further, Philadelphia's Wobblies were active in the defense of strike leaders Joseh Ettor and Arturo Giovannitti, who were arrested on bogus murder charges. To raise publicity and money for the defense, the Philadelphians held weekly protests, the largest of which saw Big Bill Haywood speak before an estimated crowd of five thousand. Through Ettor-Giovannitti defense work, the union also made connections in the city's burgeoning Italian community.[23]

The following spring, twenty-five thousand silk workers struck in nearby Paterson, New Jersey. Philadelphia Wobblies raised money for the cause and repeated the Lawrence strategy by housing two thousand children during the strike. Philadelphia silk workers also struck, as part of IWW efforts to prevent manufacturers from subverting the Paterson strike. Wobbly railroad workers tried tying up Philadelphia rail lines in sympathy. Unlike Lawrence, though, the Paterson strike failed, partially because silk manufacturers shifted much of their production into neighboring factories, including in Philadelphia.[24]

For six years, then, the IWW had organized workers in Philadelphia. The greatest effort had been made among the city's textile workers—not surprising since that industry employed more Philadelphians than any other—and the IWW had some success in that field. The IWW organized in a wide assortment of industries—hotels, bakeries, laundries, and railroads—demonstrating a commitment to skilled and unskilled workers. Further, the IWW had expended effort at lining up native-born workers as well as Italians, Poles, Germans, Lithuanians, and others. Yet, the IWW had not acquired a solid foothold among any group of Philadelphians. That changed with the 1913 longshore strike, though Philadelphia was not the first place that the IWW had organized waterfront workers.[25]

Prior to the chartering of Local 8, the IWW targeted the marine transport industry because of its importance to the national and global economies. The IWW established branches of longshoremen and other maritime workers on the Pacific Coast from Nome, Alaska, through Vancouver, Canada, and as far south as San Pedro, California. In April 1913 the New York–based, anarchist-led, Spanish-dominated Marine Firemen, Oilers, and Watertenders' Union of the Atlantic and Gulf voted to abandon what they believed was a too-conservative AFL and join the IWW as the National Industrial Union of Marine Transport Workers. In response, the ISU, a conglomeration of the AFL's marine craft unions, chartered an "Anglo-Saxon" firemen's union in 1914. Still, Wobbly success in the marine transport industry was limited prior to Local 8.[26]

Strike! The Founding of Local 8

Despite oppressive conditions on the city's riverfronts, no major union drive had occurred for fifteen years. Still, the IWW could draw upon a century-old tradition of resistance. The difference between 1898 and 1913 was that in 1913 there was a labor organization that had been very active in lining up unskilled and minority workers, as opposed to the AFL, which ignored much of the U.S. working class. The IWW did not find Philadelphia's longshoremen, rather the longshoremen found the IWW. At a meeting in early May, Ed Lewis, a native Philadelphian "known in the labor movement as the king of mob orators," was assigned to organize longshoremen, but he could not find any interested ones.[27]

Concurrently, the IWW was conducting a strike at a sugar refinery located on the banks of the Delaware. Joseph Schmidt, a Polish organizer who also spoke Lithuanian, signed up more than four hundred sugar workers at the Spreckles Refining Company, a part of Theodore Havemeyer's American Sugar Refining Company trust. In response, Spreckles started firing union workers. This action led to a strike of eight hundred workers, mostly Poles and Lithuanians and some African Americans; in this strike, native-born whites were the scabs. No doubt, many longshoremen knew sugar-refinery workers and heard of the strike because they labored on nearby piers, lived in the same South Philly neighborhoods, and competed for the same jobs, since waterfront workers were primarily Poles, Lithuanians, and African Americans.[28]

Local 8's origins began with the sugar-refinery strike since contact between Philadelphia dockers and the IWW occurred amid that walkout. After one strike meeting, a group of longshoremen approached George Speed, one of the union's general organizers helping Schmidt run the sugar strike. At their request, Speed met with the longshoremen and helped draw up a list of grievances and demands. It was fortuitous that the longshoremen met with Speed because he was committed to a racially and ethnically inclusive labor movement. Speed's many experiences organizing in California, with the much-maligned Asian population there, and Louisiana, working with the interracial Brotherhood of Timber Workers, helped Speed to see the necessity of bringing minorities and immigrants into the IWW.[29]

Several days later, on May 14, 1913, the deep-sea longshoremen put down their cargo hooks and walked off their jobs. At that moment few if any could have envisioned that this action would usher in a decade of unprecedented power for Philadelphia longshoremen. Their demands included a pay raise to thirty-five cents per hour for *all* waterfront workers, a ten-hour day, time-and-a-half wages for night work, double time for Sunday and holiday work, no discrimination against strikers, and recognition of a committee of longshoremen representing the workers. Earlier in May, Stephen Shell, the International Mercantile Marine's (IMM) stevedore, refused his employees' demand for a raise. A little later, P. F. Young, IMM general manager, agreed to a wage increase from twenty-five cents to thirty cents per hour. Since June 1898 riverfront employers had dropped wages from thirty cents to twenty-five cents and ceased paying higher rates for night, Sunday, and holiday work. Those longshoremen who had pushed most forcefully for the raise in early May had suffered from a common—and, at that time, legal—employer strategy; the boss fired the leaders in the hopes of intimidating the rest. Wobbly organizer Ed Lewis cited Young, in particular, for discriminating against activist longshoremen, stating that "no sooner was the contract signed than Young and his men refused to employ those who were instrumental in getting the raise."[30]

The IWW-led strike began with fifteen hundred deep-sea longshoremen demanding higher wages, overtime pay, and the power to bargain collectively. As soon as the longshoremen walked, shipping companies and stevedores started losing money as ships were stranded, forced to leave with less than a full cargo to keep on schedule, or diverted from Philadelphia. Close to one thousand strikers already had joined the IWW, who were awarded a charter on May 17. IWW national organizers John J. McKelvey and Ed Lewis led the strike. In addition, George Speed and James Renshaw, secretary of the city's industrial council (IWW), served "the strikers with large doses of the straight stuff every day" at strike meetings held in South Philadelphia's New Academy Hall. Curiously, Ben Fletcher's name never appeared in either IWW or mainstream strike accounts, even though he was the IWW's first contact with Philadelphia's longshoremen and, no doubt, *the* crucial link to African American dockworkers. IWW historian Fred Thompson speculated in 1982 that Fletcher purposefully kept a low profile during the strike, "with the full knowledge of the [other] IWW organizers [hence, Fletcher] avoided giving the impression he was their [the union's] lone contact [to the longshoremen]."[31]

Even early on, the strike strove for the IWW principles of democracy and equality. To negotiate with employers, the strikers elected a committee of fifteen longshoremen with at least one member from each ethnic group among the workforce (as in the 1912 Lawrence textile strike). This policy ensured that every group had its interests represented, though those running the strike were Wobbly organizers. Such representation was essential since the four thousand waterfront workers included African Americans, European immigrants (especially Poles and Lithuanians) and their sons, Irish Americans, and a smattering of other groups.[32]

The strikers practiced industrial unionism—in which all workers in an industry, regardless of their job, belonged to one organization. By contrast and typically for an AFL union, the ILA formed locals strictly by craft. The Wobbly strike began with deep-sea longshoremen. Still, Local 8 demanded a universal wage rate of thirty-five cents per hour for "all hands on the waterfront." The demand was impressive, as deep-sea longshoremen were at the top of the dockside hierarchy and had the least to gain from leveling. Demanding equal wages for all marine transport workers required larger raises for the lesser-skilled, lower-paying trades and could break down traditional craft divisions in the industry. As the grain-shipping broker F. W. Taylor of the firm Charles M. Taylor's Sons wrote to his stevedore superintendent Eugene O'Neill, "We do not believe the [deep-sea] longshoremen are fools enough to unite with all kinds of labor for a uniform rate of pay, as they are not to be classed with watertenders, oilers, cooks, and waiters." Yet the longshoremen's attempt at uniting with other waterfront workers was arguably quite savvy.[33]

The strikers also attempted to expand the strike to other ports. Wobblies in Baltimore and New York City received telegrams informing them not to handle "hot cargo," goods handled by strikebreakers or management, on any ships coming from or going to Philadelphia. Ben Fletcher traveled to Baltimore to convince longshoremen there to respect Local 8's strike and leave hot cargo untouched. While anathema to the AFL, including the ILA, as violations of contracts, the IWW often encouraged sympathy strikes and categorically refused to sign contracts that might prevent such acts of solidarity—for they claimed that workers needed all the help they could get.[34]

The strikers not only squared off against their employers but also against Philadelphia's police department, which was well known for its vigorous efforts to crush strikes. The second night of the strike, IWW organizer McKelvey was beaten unconscious by a policeman and thrown in jail for over a day with no charge. Following his release, McKelvey warned a thousand strikers at a meeting not to get arrested, as "the most unsafe place for a workingman in this town is a police station." One magistrate condemned "the brutality and lawlessness of the police department of Philadelphia, which has rendered itself infamous from one end of the country to the other." Nevertheless, McKelvey was tried and convicted on an unknown charge and served two months in jail, thereby removing one of the IWW's best organizers. Police intimidation, beatings, and arrests occurred daily throughout the strike but accelerated in the second week. Hundreds of police, some on horseback, and squads of private detectives stationed themselves along the riverfront to prevent pickets from approaching strikebreakers.[35]

Police actions typified the city government's corruption and probusiness bias. In 1903 Lincoln Steffens, the famous muckraking journalist, wrote a scathing article entitled "Philadelphia: Corrupt and Contented." Steffens's opening sentence declared, "Other American cities, no matter how bad their own condition may be, all point with scorn to Philadelphia as worse—'the worst-governed city in the country.'" Steffens also discussed the city's smug aristocratic nature and labeled Philadelphia as "the most corrupt" city in the nation, based upon the disenfranchising of its citizens ("the honest citizens of Philadelphia have no more rights at the polls than the negroes down South"), total domination of the city's Republican machine, and plundering of the public's finances and trust. Thus, Local 8 was forced to contend with a city government that was corrupt and heavily antilabor.[36]

Of course, employers fiercely resisted the strike. Representatives of all of the steamship companies and employing stevedores immediately formed a committee, with P. F. Young as chair, to crush the strike and union. Young, who managed longshoremen for numerous shipping lines, maintained that the companies would fight the IWW for as long as it took and threatened to abandon Philadelphia rather than raise wages. Shipping companies diverted their vessels to other ports, most commonly Baltimore, hence Fletcher's trip. Shipping companies employed sailing crews to load and unload cargo. The shippers also received the active support of the city's mainstream press; one editorial in the *Public Ledger* declared that "the destructive organization [IWW] must be rooted out."[37]

Stevedore and shipping companies used spies and strikebreakers to defeat Local 8, thereby opening up the thorny issue of deploying black replacements to break a strike with many black workers. The employers hired several detective agencies to spy on the strikers and import strikebreakers. For these replacements, employers outfitted an entire pier with beds and a commissary, and later the Pennsylvania Railroad contributed sleeper and dining cars. By the strike's second week about four hundred strikebreakers tackled the backlog of ships on the Delaware. Warren C. Whatley, an economic historian of twentieth-century black labor, notes that blacks commonly broke longshore strikes, as in the novel by Claude McKay that introduced this book. Stephen H. Norwood's book on strikebreaking lists many reasons why blacks regularly did so: the racist and exclusionary practices of Northern industrial employers and most unions, advocacy of scabbing among black elites, and lack of familiarity with unionism.[38]

Typically, fighting erupted between strikebreakers and large crowds of strikers and their sympathizers, but racism did not appear to play into these conflicts. For instance, on the night of May 16 the police arrested three black strikebreakers and charged them with carrying concealed weapons (replacements often armed themselves). The three had opened fire when strikers attempted to prevent the replacements from getting to the docks; this incident and similar ones reveal that, at least during this conflict, divisions were between strikers and strikebreakers, rather than between black replacements and white strikers. Historian Stephen Norwood highlights that in other strikes during the era, black replacements were threatened with lynching by hostile white crowds, but no such thing occurred in this one. Of course, the union sought to discourage replacements, but notably, and atypically, the union never condemned the strikebreakers in racist terms and none of the striker-replacement clashes exploded into racial conflict.[39]

The Wobblies also combated a rival labor organization, the ILA. Several days into the strike, ILA organizers attempted to convince the men to forgo their recent IWW affiliation for an ILA button. The IWW claimed that ILA organizers tried to bribe rank-and-file longshoremen with alcohol and leaders with the promise of salaried positions. ILA official Dempsey later confirmed that "the I.W.W.'s have kept singing into the ears of these men that the A. F. of L. officials sell their organization out to the highest bidder." The longshoremen stuck with the IWW or, in the Wobbly vernacular, "Their [ILA] game did not work at that time as some of those approached told them in no mistaken terms that they were not wanted at this time and to get out of the city for the benefit of their health. They seemed to take the hint and beat it for a time."[40]

There is no direct evidence that the black community—business, political, or religious sectors—supported the strike, Local 8, or the IWW. Even though the IWW stood clearly against racism and had hundreds of black members, the strike received no mention in the local black newspaper, the *Philadelphia Tribune*. In fact, the newspaper did not mention work, strikes, or unions a single time the entire year. Despite Local 8's long presence in the community, middle-class black political and religious leaders apparently never supported unionism. When the National Urban League surveyed an ILA local in 1928, the secretary reported that "Negro churches [were] appealed to but no real help or encouragement [was] given by them." That black strikebreakers had to be recruited from neighboring Chester and Baltimore suggests that the local community supported the strike. After all, blacks did not need to resort to strike-breaking to enter the field in Philadelphia, and blacks, including Fletcher, helped found Local 8. And, of course, it is by no means clear if the black workers much listened to the black middle class, as both Robin Kelley and Brian Kelly convincingly argue. Furthermore, Robert Gregg, the author of a fascinating book on black churches in Philadelphia during the Progressive Era, notes that even before the Great Migration, the diversity in the black community along class, gender, region, and especially religious lines mitigated against the notion of a monolithic black community.[41]

The longshoremen received a little support from outsiders. When one crew was offered high wages to coal up a steamship stuck in port, the firemen, likely Spanish members of a union that recently had joined the IWW en masse, refused and convinced the rest of the crew to support the strike. This and similar acts testify to the new unionism spreading throughout the maritime industry, which identified all fellow workers as allies. The Reverend Dr. George Chalmers Richmond, rector of the Old St. John's Episcopal Church, quite vocally supported IWW; at an IWW rally in June 1913 Richmond declared, "The I.W.W. doesn't care for laws if by breaking laws, they can get righteousness. I'm not certain as to the value of that. But history shows that the great martyrs broke the laws of the church and now we erect memorials to them." After the strike ended, one minister of the African Methodist Episcopal Church reportedly said that he "liked the I.W.W. because it believed in the colored man." Further support came from neighborhood saloonkeepers who refused to sell liquor to replacement workers. The proprietors supported their neighbors—regular customers, relatives, and comrades—as opposed to outsiders brought in from Baltimore, Chester, or New York.[42]

As the workers remained firm, the strike shut down the port. The *North American*, quite hostile to the IWW, declared in its headline, "Cargoes Choke Docks; Strikers Won't Quit." Hundreds of "carloads of merchandise" and more than twenty ships were idled with more than 2.8 million bushels of grain piled high on the docks in Port Richmond and Girard Point. Between the longshoremen's and sugar-refinery workers' strikes, not a grain of sugar was touched. The longshoremen's ranks were solid, but to induce more men to join the strike and IWW, anyone striking did not have to pay the already low $1 initiation fee. Soon twelve hundred waterfront coal and iron-ore handlers walked off their jobs. Every picketer wore a red badge with "I.W.W." and "Longshoremen Striker" printed in black. Planning also started for a parade with the famous labor activists Mother Jones and Big Bill Haywood (but the strike ended before the event occurred).[43]

Despite the strike's effectiveness, employers refused to concede. Employer spokesman Young reiterated that the shippers would neither grant a raise nor recognize the IWW. The employers corresponded with counterparts in other ports, comparing wages and conditions, clearly adamant about resisting the IWW. Young blamed the strike on the IWW, claiming that, were it not for its "machinations," the longshoremen would work for thirty cents per hour. He contended that most of the men wished to return to work but feared reprisals. Young admitted that the strike was hurting the port considerably.[44]

With both sides refusing to back down, the tension along the waterfront erupted on the night of May 21, when groups of strikers attacked strikebreakers in numerous incidents. In the largest outbreak, the *Public Ledger* reported that "bricks, clubs, fists and revolver shots figured last night." The "melee" began when more than one hundred strikers met fifty strikebreakers, quickly degenerating from a shouting match to a brawl. In a huge show of community support, about one thousand people filled the streets, throwing missiles from nearby windows and alleys and preventing the police from interceding. As historian Montgomery notes, "The dense concentration of workers in class-segregated neighborhoods made economic struggles community mobilizations."[45]

In a second "riverfront riot" pitting seventy-five strikebreakers and their police escorts against six hundred strikers and sympathizers, women demonstrated that this strike was theirs, too. The police reported that women hurled "all sorts of vile epithets on the non-union party . . . [and] were more earnest in their attack than the men." A group of twenty policemen charged into the crowd, fired their revolvers above the protesters' heads, and drove the crowd west (away from the river) for blocks. Numerous locals were arrested. In this riot as in others, female sympathizers, most likely wives and daughters of strikers, were blamed by the newspapers for much of the violence. These protests regularly turned out hundreds, with women playing conspicuous roles, and testify to the community's strong support for the longshoremen. Parallels to Barcelona, as thoughtfully studied by Temma Kaplan, apply to Philadelphia: "Working women played a key role in certain aspects of political street life in early twentieth-century Barcelona because they felt they had special responsibilities and so demanded special rights to protect their families and communities against extinction."[46]

Due to the strikers' ability to shut down the port, on May 28 employers conceded to most of the Wobblies' demands. The deal was struck with Fred W. Taylor, who ran a family grain and shipping firm that had been active in the city since 1869. Taylor claimed to act on behalf of the city's shipping interests when a strike delegation consisting, tellingly, of a Polish immigrant, an Irish American, and an African American (their names lost to history), visited Taylor's office. The agreement worked out that day included a ten-hour day, time and a half for overtime and night work, as well as double time for Sundays and holidays. The basic wage rate, however, remained at thirty cents per hour, which had gone into effect just prior to the strike, rather than the thirty-five cents the strikers had wanted. In addition, the strikers were promised that there would be no discrimination against union men. The employers also agreed to negotiate with a committee representing the workers. The next evening the strikers voted unanimously to return to work. Local 8 had won its first strike.[47]

Employers ultimately conceded because the strike caused them major financial difficulties at a time when maritime interests were striving to expand the port's business. Young lamented, during the strike, that the port had increased its business by 40% in recent years and was poised for further expansion. Just prior to the strike, the *Philadelphia Inquirer* reported "the most favorable record made in exports by the port for many years" in the first four months of 1913, in part because numerous large European shipping companies had started using Philadelphia. Thus, the *Journal of the Philadelphia Chamber of Commerce* regretted that "the business of the port was handicapped to a great extent by reason of a strike." Additionally, the strike seriously hurt merchants and manufacturers as millions of bushels of grain, tens of thousands of gallons of petroleum, and thousands of tons of sugar, iron ore, and other cargo sat on the city's docks and wharves. The workers' standpoint, of course, was quite different. The city's longshoremen and other waterfront workers obviously noticed the increase in port activity and surmised that their own wage rates remained constant while employer profits had increased.[48]

A second financial reason for the employers' willingness to compromise was the "extraordinary expenses connected with the employment of strike-breakers and detective guards," according to grain dealer Taylor. Employing strikebreakers cost significantly more than paying their regular workers, as strikebreakers were provided with room, board, and medical care, the latter a benefit any longshoreman or other American worker of the era could only dream about. Moreover, the employers hired scores of detectives to guard the replacements. Perhaps these additional expenses would have been worthwhile had the replacements' work been decent. However, as Taylor wrote to an associate, "the daily work performed by them [strikebreakers] was extremely slow and unsatisfactory."[49]

The employers might have overcome these hurdles, but maintaining their unity proved too difficult. The diversity of commodities shipped through the port meant that no single employer dominated the scene. Describing Baltimore, the words of Eric Arnesen also apply to Philadelphia: "The multiplicity of employers and contractors rendered the port susceptible to unionization." At the beginning of the strike, employers (shipping lines and stevedores) created a committee that quickly lined up support from the police and local press. Nevertheless, some shippers and stevedores grew anxious. Those in the grain industry particularly wanted to settle the strike as their business had boomed in the first part of 1913 and suffered the most drastically during the strike. When Taylor, not coincidentally a grain shipper, brokered the settlement, he had not consulted with other employers. Certain bosses, notably Young, who headed the employers' committee, opposed the agreement. Although Taylor's compromise ended the impasse, employer solidarity crumbled at their first poststrike gathering, where it was agreed that "instead of such concerted action . . . a resolution was passed allowing each Line to make its own independent arrangement." It would take years for Philadelphia's waterfront employers to reunite. The breakdown of employer unity boded well for the nascent union.[50]

In stark contrast, there was one other essential ingredient for the strike's success—worker solidarity. The shipping interests blamed the strike on a tiny group of strikers and the IWW (typically labeled "outside agitators"), but frequent attempts to divide the strikers clearly failed. If the striking longshoremen did not have confidence in each other (engendered through gang labor) and the IWW (whose leaders and tactics proved effective), enough of them would have drifted back to work. The strikers stood firm, however, in the face of intense opposition from the employers, local media, police, and city government.

Perhaps the most notable aspect of the longshoremen's unity was its racial and ethnic component. The workforce was diverse: more than a third were African American; another third immigrants, mostly Slavs; and the rest were native-born white Americans, especially Irish Americans. Competition for jobs on the waterfront, one of the few places in Philadelphia where European immigrants and African Americans could find work, was fierce. The casual nature of hiring longshoremen was yet another obstacle to worker solidarity, as the men competed for positions three times a day under a corrupt system in which there was, inevitably, a labor surplus. Further, the strikers held firm in the face of black replacements that threatened to divide the strikers along racial lines. As the IWW reported, "the Polish, Jewish, Negro and English speaking fellow workers were solidly lined up."[51]

Thus ended the IWW's largest-to-date longshore strike, which ushered in a decade of Wobbly power on the Philadelphia waterfront. Local 8 would be a union like no other. The diverse membership continued building on the solidarity forged during the historic strike in May 1913. They soon deployed direct-action tactics and other ideals taught them by Wobbly organizers. Always most important was maintaining their racial and ethnic unity, a prerequisite for attaining immediate "bread and butter" gains (wages, conditions) and longer term goals (a more open and democratic society where workers earned the full fruits of what they produced).

3   There Is Power in a Union

On Saturday, May 16, 1914, the members of Local 8 "decided to celebrate their first anniversary and to make this a L-e-g-a-l holiday under our jurisdiction." Close to twenty-five hundred deep-sea longshoremen, virtually the entire workforce, struck, paraded, and picnicked to commemorate their union's birth. Notably, the men "marched as they worked. . . . There was no race question here, true to the tradition of the I.W.W." The years following their entry into the IWW were ones of tremendous activity, as the men tried expanding the power that grew from their shared work experience and union. First, this chapter will examine the myriad reasons, pragmatic and ideological, why the longshoremen joined the IWW; as with many aspects of this story, the workers' own diversity made the IWW attractive, for it eagerly accepted blacks and immigrants. Then, this chapter will describe how the longshoremen incorporated Wobbly tactics and ideals—especially direct action—which resulted in improved conditions on the docks, greater racial equality, and more members. Scholar Larry Peterson reminds us that "industrial unionism after 1900 was a truly international phenomenon," of which the Philadelphia story told here is but one part. Indeed, as elsewhere, the economic impact of World War I first hurt and then greatly aided the union. On the eve of America's entry into war, Local 8 was strong, inclusive, and well positioned to capitalize on the dramatic expansion in maritime commerce.[1]

It is essential to understand why these longshoremen joined the IWW, a radical union with no prior history on the Philadelphia waterfront and an awful reputation in mainstream culture, instead of the AFL longshoremen's union, the ILA, which had experience organizing diverse workforces. There are multiple factors but issues of ethnicity and race are central. Ben Fletcher later contended that "the Negroes who join the I.W.W. are no different in their motives for doing so than the whites," but his contention, which demands consideration, oversimplifies the matter.[2]

Arguably the most important reason Philadelphia longshoremen joined the IWW was their own racial and ethnic diversity. In the late nineteenth and early twentieth centuries, the river labor force was dominated by blacks and new immigrants, largely due to the racism and xenophobia of the city and country as well as the skills that Philadelphia's migrants and immigrants possessed. African Americans toiled in the least skilled, worst paying, most dangerous, and least secure lines of work, like longshoring. Thus, despite Irish and Irish American dominance for much of the nineteenth century, the sheer number of blacks resulted in more of them being hired on the waterfront. To a lesser extent, the same situation held true for new immigrants. With the important exception of Italians and Jews in the needle trades, immigrants did not possess the skills needed in Philadelphia's specialized industries. Thus, Poles and Lithuanians found their way to the riverfront. By 1910 Philadelphia's more than three thousand longshoremen were 45% African American and over 40% immigrant or first-generation American-born. By 1910 close to 60% of the city's longshoremen were African Americans and almost 30% immigrants or children of immigrants. Melvyn Dubofsky has pointed out that African Americans and urban immigrants were two of the "dispossessed" groups that gravitated to the IWW; given the dockworkers' diversity, they needed a union willing to embrace them.[3]

The AFL was not their answer. Both African Americans and the white-dominated IWW regularly lambasted the "American Separation of Labor" for its exclusive craft and racial practices. The AFL consciously forsook integration as far back as 1891, with the admission of the openly racist International Association of Machinists. In the years that followed, the AFL expanded but almost entirely among white, native-born, male skilled workers. When the AFL organized black workers, it did so halfheartedly and often in separate "Jim Crow" locals. African Americans understood the AFL's racial policy perfectly well. The influential Booker T. Washington attacked the AFL for its blatant racism. Instead, Washington encouraged blacks to ally with white employers and even break strikes as the only way to gain entry in many industries. W. E. B. Du Bois commented in 1913 that "race prejudice is a two-edged sword, and it is not to the advantage of organized labor to produce among the Negroes a prejudice and fear of union labor such as to create in this country a race of strike breakers."[4]

One of the few examples of an AFL union organizing black workers, though, was the ILA. Even Washington noted that the biracial longshore union in New Orleans belonged to the ILA. Eric Arnesen has uncovered the fascinating variations of biracial unionism among dock unions along the Gulf of Mexico; when their numbers demanded it, as in the Crescent City and Galveston, the ILA lined up blacks, for pragmatic rather than ideological reasons. However, the ILA either ignored (e.g., in New York and Baltimore) or segregated (in Hampton Roads, Virginia) black long-shoremen where their numbers were insignificant. In Norfolk, the mostly black longshoremen remained in an independent union, for despite its relatively progressive racial policy in the Gulf, on the Atlantic the ILA usually acted in a racist fashion.[5]

By contrast, the IWW preached interracial unionism, primarily due to its commitment to class struggle. Wobblies fervently believed that all workers, regardless of ethnic or racial heritage, should unite against their "true" and common enemy, the employing class. Article I, Section I of the IWW constitution declared that anyone, regardless of color or creed, could join. Thus, one of the Wobblies' major criticisms of the AFL was that it "does not represent the working class," as Big Bill Haywood put it. Yet despite this ideology, the IWW rarely organized African Americans. The first significant attempt took place in Louisiana in 1911, but the Brotherhood of Timber Workers experiment ended prematurely as a result of massive blacklistings, jailings, and violence. So it was in Philadelphia that the IWW fully tested its pledge of equality. On Philadelphia's docks, the IWW ideology strongly resonated with African Americans. As black longshoreman James Fair recalled much later, "To my knowing at that time the IWW was the only thing that was accepting negro or black work-ers . . . I mean freely. They would accept them and they did advocate just this thing, solidarity." Of course, for the thousands of black longshoremen to see one of "their own," Ben Fletcher, on the stump championing the IWW confirmed its claims. Du Bois wrote in 1919, "We respect it [the IWW] as one of the social and political movements in modern times that draws no color line."[6]

The other large group in Local 8, new immigrants, especially Poles and Lithuanians, also toiled on the margins of society and found the IWW appealing. Their allegiance to Local 8 was confirmed in a September 1913 report of the ILA's Atlantic Coast Secretary-Treasurer William Dempsey, who complained that the fundamental "obstacle [to the ILA] is the poisoned minds of both the Polish and Lithuanians." Moreover, recent scholarship demonstrates that new immigrants still were learning in America that they were "white" and did not view "black" longshoremen in the same terms that native-born whites did—at least before and during World War I. Bruce Nelson cites one New York waterfront employer who, when hiring, distinguished between Poles or Italians versus "white men." A tantalizing article by Thaddeus Radzialowski convincingly argues that Chicago's blacks did not identify Poles as "white" *and* that Poles did not learn antiblack racism until they were more thoroughly Americanized, which did not more fully occur until the 1910s; for example, James Barrett notes that during the horrific Chicago Race Riot of 1919 very little fighting between Poles or Lithuanians and African Americans happened. The alliance of black native-born and "white" immigrant workers on Philadelphia's docks supports this notion, too.[7]

Another factor in the Philadelphians' joining of the IWW was English fluency or lack thereof. Newly arrived immigrants, with no-to-limited English language skills, likely would have deferred to the native English speakers, African Americans. The Dillingham Commission reported on the heavily Lithuanian and Polish Philadelphia sugar-refinery workforce in 1910, noting that less than half spoke English. Polish and Lithuanian longshoremen possessed identical backgrounds to sugar-refinery workers. And it was in this intertwined waterfront world that the initial contact with the IWW had been made, when organizer Simon Knebel, who spoke Lithuanian and Polish, visited the docks. The ILA's Dempsey unsuccessfully had requested someone who spoke these Slavic tongues to challenge Knebel.[8]

As for the Irish and Irish Americans, they followed the able leadership of IWW organizer John J. McKelvey and local dockworker George McKenna, who had participated in the 1898 strike. As far back as 1835 Irish immigrants and Irish Americans had proved their mettle as union men in Philly. It is undeniable that Irish and Irish American workers often "proved" their whiteness through their intense hostility toward African Americans; however, it is equally true that they allied with new immigrants and African Americans in the Knights of Labor and IWW. Further, Irish Americans were in no position to disagree with the majority.[9]

The IWW's militant ideology, anarcho-syndicalism, also appealed to Philadelphia's longshoremen. Wobblies eschewed politics and never signed contracts with employers. Instead, the IWW advocated that workers act where they had power, on the job. Late in life, dockworker Abraham Moses marveled at his colleagues in Local 8: "If you told one of them something, and they didn't like it, you know what they'd do? They'd run the load about half way up, cut the steve hold [rope] and walk off the ship. That's right. That's what they would do." The bravura of Wobbly talk, song, and action also commanded respect from men who lived in a society based upon naked power. Even if they could not always articulate such beliefs, blacks and immigrants understood all too well that America was based upon class, ethnic, gender, racial, and religious inequality. Hence, IWW disparagement of politics and the ruling class resonated with blacks and immigrants, neither of whom had a stake in a society dominated by rich, native-born whites.[10]

In at least one way these workers were part of the dominant group— they were men in a patriarchal society—which made it easier to ally across ethnic or racial lines. IWW organizers in Louisiana united black and white timber workers by appealing to their masculinity. When confronted by racist whites, Wobbly Ed Lehman replied: "Yes, he is black as the ace of spades, but he isn't a nigger. . . . He is a man, a union man, an IWW—a MAN! and he has proven it by his action." George Speed organized in Louisiana just one year prior to helping found Local 8. Later E. F. Doree, another Wobbly veteran of the campaign in Louisiana, joined Local 8. Historian Dan Letwin contends that all-male workplaces were easier to organize because the problematic issue of white women was absent. The docks and seafaring culture were highly masculine. Longshore work was "manly," in that it was highly dangerous, sex segregated, and required brute, manual labor. Moreover, Wobblies frequently appealed to masculinity to recruit and retain male members. Fran Shor coined the term *virile syndicalism*, which most definitely applied to the waterfront world.[11]

IWW leadership and local history helped convince the longshoremen to join the IWW. The activists that the IWW committed to the waterfront were dynamic. Ed Lewis was hailed in the mainstream Philadelphia press and by radicals like William Z. Foster as a rousing "soapboxer." During the strike Lewis convinced the longshoremen that "we are strong enough to do anything. . . . If the bosses will not listen to us we will make them do so by tying up the entire shipping industry." George Speed was a savvy Wobbly veteran with experience organizing diverse workers across America. And, of course, the presence of Ben Fletcher, a native Philadelphian, Wobbly organizer, and African American longshoreman, cannot be overestimated. Too, the historical memory of some of Philadelphia's longshoremen proved important. Some old-timers had participated in the 1898 strike, and Fletcher (and others) had heard of that failed effort. In June 1913 the ILA's Dempsey "found the city in absolute control of the I.W.W., and though Organizer Holt and myself tried in every way to do business with the men, we were unsuccessful, owing to the fact that in 1898 . . . when this organization had a foothold in Philadelphia and the members went out on strike, they were grossly neglected by the I.L.A., so they claim."[12]

A final component of the IWW's success was that no union existed prior to Local 8. Lorenzo Greene and Carter G. Woodson persuasively argue that the *lack* of a union often resulted in more blacks working on the waterfront, just as in Philadelphia. Moreover, the Wobblies did not have to convince workers to drop the ILA for the IWW because the ILA had not established itself. In an open contest between the IWW and ILA, the black and immigrant longshoremen supported the IWW.[13]

Thus, for pragmatic and ideological reasons, Philadelphia's longshoremen chose the IWW. Simply put, the workforce was highly diverse and the IWW was the only group willing to organize them in an integrated local. Given this reality, the IWW was the obvious choice, but other factors (language, notions of whiteness, lack of unionization, the waterfront's labor history, IWW tactics and leadership) also played roles.

Local 8 wasted no time translating its newfound strength into greater worker control using direct-action tactics instead of signing contracts. Given the oppressive hiring conditions on the docks, the first goal of Local 8 was to curtail the labor surplus that traditionally reduced workers' power. Philadelphia's longshoremen were hardly unique in this desire. David Montgomery notes that all unions of unskilled and casual laborers understood that they must control the hiring process to be effective. The local passed out dues buttons with the letters "I.W.W." and the month and year emblazoned on them. Once a member paid his monthly dues, he would be given a new button, which entitled him to work on any IWW-controlled dock—no button, no work. Hence, one stevedore reported to his boss of "a great increase since that time [the May strike] in the number of longshoremen wearing the I.W.W. buttons." Grain shipper Taylor reported that "two or three incipient efforts were made through the I.W.W. influences to threaten strikes on our boats unless certain men working on them without an I.W.W. button were knocked off." Taylor's stevedore refused the IWW's demands, so a number of longshoremen quit, demonstrating their confidence in the new union.[14]

In contrast, and crucially to the union's success, the city's riverfront employers remained divided. At their first poststrike meeting, any solidarity that remained disintegrated. P. F. Young, the Philadelphia representative of the International Mercantile Marine Company (IMM), refused to pay his workers anything more than thirty cents per hour, with no overtime. He also refused to hire any union longshoremen—the IMM proved to be the union's staunchest opponent for years. Economic competition further heightened employer disunity; in December 1913 the *Public Ledger* reported that the Commercial Exchange was being investigated for colluding with a few stevedores to control the grain trade. Employers agreed to disagree and dealt with workers separately until after World War I, much to the benefit of Local 8.[15]

A month after the strike had ended, Fred Taylor still hoped to convince his fellow employers to compromise with workers on the ten-hour day, time and a half for any work over ten hours, and especially double time for Sunday work. However, many employers adamantly refused to abide by the May 18 agreement made between Taylor and the union. Local 8's demand of double time for Sunday work was intended, essentially, to force employers to stop work on Sundays and was part of a long working-class effort to do so. Local 8's efforts achieved some results. For example, Taylor announced his intent "to avoid Sunday work, excepting under extreme urgency, when double rates will be paid." Taylor acknowledged that the presence of the IWW had changed labor relations: "If we do not take such united action and finally have to grant the demands for over-time and Sunday work, it gives the I.W.W. the status of having forced it."[16]

Later that summer the much overworked and underpaid men who labored on tugboats and other river crafts organized into a separate branch of Local 8 and struck. Average salaries were well under $1 a day, which made for bare subsistence living. Organizer McKelvey called them "virtual slaves of the boat owners. They were subject to call at any time, either to load or to tow." Like the dockside longshoremen and sugar workers, the boatmen were quite a diverse bunch—native-born whites, new immigrants, and African Americans. The boatmen called for a raise to $15 per week for all harbor workers, a ten-hour day, and a six-day workweek (i.e., they aspired to a sixty-hour week). In addition, they wanted double wages for Sunday work, one half day's wages for any time worked in the evenings, and a full day's wages for any time worked between midnight and 6 A.M. Most firms quickly agreed to the wage and hour demands but the strike dragged on for several months against holdout employers, who responded with strikebreakers and armed private guards. The police and criminal justice system again actively worked to defeat the IWW. Tensions quickly erupted into violence, and three strike leaders were arrested, jailed for more than a month, and convicted upon limited evidence. With their leaders jailed and pickets defeated, the strike soon ended, but not without earning raises of $10 per month.[17]

In the midst of the boatmen's struggle, longshoremen of the IMM briefly struck in a great display of solidarity and bravado. More than five hundred men walked off the job for the sole reason that the IMM was antiunion. The *Philadelphia Inquirer*, citing IMM sources, wrote that hundreds of longshoremen put down their hooks "in sympathy with five men who were discharged . . . because they declined to take off union buttons which they were wearing." The strike quickly spread to other parts of the port and tied up three ships. Again, "armed detectives and several squads of uniformed policemen" along with "scores of private detectives" protected strikebreakers. The longshoremen walked off the job, as the *Public Ledger* commented, "at an inopportune moment, as two vessels . . . just arrived with large general cargoes." Sailors from one of the ships "threw garbage and bottles at non-union longshoremen." The result of the strike is unknown, although Local 8 members continued to work these docks, so it can be assumed that the strike likely was a standoff. Afterward, the IMM established a "Benevolent Society" (i.e., a company union), indicating that it had no intention of giving in to the IWW.[18]

Quite likely, Local 8 instituted one other policy of the utmost importance: the integration of work gangs. It is clear that, prior to the rise of Local 8, longshoremen worked in segregated gangs. It also is documented that gangs were resegregated after Local 8's fall. Given Local 8's (and the IWW's) commitment to racial equality, the large number of black longshoremen, and the fact that employers had maintained segregated gangs, it seems undeniable that it was the union that forced the integration of work gangs. However, there is no mention of when this action occurred, nor of any backlash. Admittedly, the evidence is circumstantial, yet the issue must be raised. Yet, based upon their many bold actions that summer, the longshoremen clearly felt empowered by their IWW membership and could have instituted this key change then and there.[19]

As of the fall of 1913 Local 8 had four branches, two of longshoremen in different parts of the port, one of firemen and sailors, and one of boatmen, each with representatives on a central committee. Local 8 rented a hall that served as headquarters to the organization for the next decade, the second floor of a building at 121 Catherine Street; the headquarters was two blocks from the Delaware River and in the heart of South Philadelphia, where working-class African Americans, Irish Americans, Poles, Italians, Lithuanians, and East European Jews all lived.[20]

Throughout its tenure, Local 8 periodically battled the AFL, and they vehemently hated each other. Wobbly leader John J. McKelvey was told by the editor of the *Trades Union News*, the AFL's Central Labor Union newspaper in town, "that Philadelphia was not large enough for the I.W.W. [and the AFL] and that we were to be driven from the city." The AFL editor belonged to the federation's Labor Forward Movement, a Christian labor group that collaborated with employers on the waterfront to displace Local 8; one organizer for the left-wing Amalgamated Clothing Workers, which had split from the AFL, condemned the domination of Philadelphia's AFL by the "Bible-house gang."[21]

In the summer of 1913 the ILA returned to Philadelphia. Seeing the AFL as a moderate alternative to the radical IWW, shipping interests and the press supported the ILA. Sensing the threat, the IWW dispatched national organizers Joseph Ettor and Elizabeth Gurley Flynn, but the ILA still achieved modest success. The smaller of Local 8's longshoremen branches declared itself independent; notably, these longshoremen worked on piers run by the fiercely anti-IWW IMM. This branch held a meeting in which both ILA officials and Ettor addressed the membership. The Wobbly McKelvey claimed that "there was also lots of good A. F. of L. booze on hand which was used freely before the meeting was opened" and that the ILA offered the officers of the renegade branch salaries of $11 per week plus expenses—double the average weekly salary of a Philadelphia longshoreman (local IWW officers worked on a volunteer basis). In response, Local 8 offered to lower initiation fees from $2 to $1.50 if the members rejoined. The following day a majority of the 130 voted to join the ILA. The ILA immediately divided its new members into Locals 843 and 844, one in Port Richmond, the other in South Philadelphia.[22]

Yet the ILA could not expand this wedge. The branch, as a part of Local 8, had controlled two docks. After changing affiliations, the branch signed a contract with the stevedore, a practice never performed by Local 8 or any IWW local in order always to possess the option to strike. In the fall the ILA branch organized several meetings, including at a Catholic social club, but few attended. The location suggests that what support the ILA had came from either Irish Americans or East European immigrants, that is, Catholics, rather than African Americans, who mostly were Protestant. As McKelvey wrote, the ILA "could accomplish only one thing—disrupt the [IWW's] organized movement on the [water]front." The ILA branch crumbled by the fall, the ILA leader Dempsey lamenting, "The situation here in Philadelphia is very slow in maturing to our favor."[23]

The ILA's return to Philadelphia was just one issue confronting Local 8 at the IWW annual national convention in September 1913—there also was a floor fight over the seating of Local 8's delegate. Representing Local 8 was James H. Murphy, continuing the tradition of a strong Irish American presence among longshoremen. Curiously, Ben Fletcher still represented

Philadelphia's mixed branch, Local 57, perhaps so the longshoremen could double their representation. A debate ensued over the seating of Murphy that shed some light on an otherwise invisible aspect of the IWW, the National Industrial Union of Marine Transport Workers (NIUMTW), which foreshadowed years of disagreement over the relationship between the local and national union. The Credentials Committee asked why Local 8 sent a delegate when the NIUMTW did not. NIUMTW President C. L. Filigno steadfastly defended Murphy's presence at the convention. Filigno recently had attended a Local 8 meeting and gave quite a favorable report: "In Philadelphia I had to do business nearly every day with them getting supplies and dues stamps and that is the only local in the organization that is practically in good standing." The local purchased more than two thousand dues stamps each month, more than the rest of the entire NIUMTW combined, so Filigno turned over one of his two convention credentials to ensure Local 8's representation.[24]

IWW concern over the ILA guaranteed that Murphy was seated. Ettor reminded the convention of the continued threat the ILA posed. If Murphy was not seated, Ettor contended that the IWW risked alienating thousands of longshoremen. "I was sent here by Local No. 8 of Philadelphia," Murphy testified. "There is in the neighborhood of thirty-five hundred members in that one local. With reference to the local turned over to the American Federation of Labor the Fellow Workers there did make a bit of friction, the same as Fellow Worker [Ettor] said. There are a whole lot of fellows just waiting for a chance so that we are not represented in the I.W.W., so it is up to you fellows to say that we are." Shortly thereafter, the convention seated Murphy, but this dispute revealed a profound disagreement over the relationship between the local and national organization that, after the war, proved fundamental to Local 8's and the IWW's undoing.[25]

As spring arrived in 1914, after one of the coldest winters in memory, Local 8 members decided to commemorate their union's first anniversary. Without consulting employers, they chose Saturday, May 16, approximately one year from the launch of their initial strike. When the longshoremen left work on Friday, their bosses informed them that if they did not report the next day, they would be fired. Using the gallows humor they were famous for, *Solidarity* described the threat as "not only to prevent the demonstration but if successful to break up the union when they could take the coffin out of storage and in thanksgiving orate on their success in killing the monster [Local 8]." In this instance, however, employers miscalculated, as approximately twenty-five hundred paraded, most waving pennants emblazoned with "M.T.W., Local 8." The participants marched through South Philadelphia and downtown with three bands in tow. The IWW paper proclaimed, "Workers representing most European countries, many who could not speak the English language, together with natives, both colored and white, marched as they worked." To the men's delight and in "quite a difference from the night before, when they threatened our men with discharge if they failed to show up . . . [bosses were] begging for permission to have some of our members work after the parade."[26]

After the parade, the marchers adjourned to Central Park for a picnic and mass meeting. There, "the same condition prevailed," according to *Solidarity:* "There was no race condition here, true to the tradition of the I.W.W." The speakers included national figures Ettor, Filigno, and McKelvey. Representing Local 8, Charles Danberg spoke in Polish, and Glenn Perrymore, who became one of a cadre of black leaders in Local 8, spoke in English. Ben Fletcher, recently elected secretary of the IWW District Council in Philadelphia, encouraged "having his friends [black men like the Georgia-born Perrymore] write 'down home' about the I.W.W." in order to increase the union's visibility among African Americans in the South. After the speeches, the members danced, played baseball, and listened to music. Interestingly, the only newspaper other than the IWW's own that reported on the events was the Baltimore *Afro-American.*[27]

When they returned to work on Monday morning, the membership could reflect on the power they had gained during the last year. Perhaps nothing better demonstrates their strength than this annual act, which employers grudgingly accepted because the IWW controlled the workforce. McKelvey pointed the way: "Job control is the thing. While we have partial control, the parade means that no letup will be countenanced." Local 8 remained active, championed among "the live ones" by the national paper for being one of a handful of locals nationwide that received one hundred copies of the weekly *Solidarity.*[28]

In response, the city's shipping interests made concerted, albeit unsuccessful, attempts to destroy Local 8. The Independent Pier and Lighterage Company, one of the city's largest dock employers, did not want to hire any IWW longshoremen. However, in late July, when the *Rivulet* arrived in Philadelphia with a hold full of copper ore, the stevedore could hire only enough nonunion men for two hatches, so Wobblies were hired to work another hatch (on deck and in the hold) and as the entire dock gang. The Wobblies then suddenly refused to handle any cargo not worked by IWW men. Seeing an opportunity, the following morning every Wobbly who did not currently have a job, possibly as many as five hundred, appeared for picket duty at the pier. The company attempted to work the *Rivulet* shorthanded, but that day another ship arrived. To the stevedore's chagrin, not a single man appeared at the afternoon shape-up, so the ship remained fully loaded. In solidarity with the strikers, Wobbly longshoremen in Port Richmond stopped working. The end result of the eighteen-hour clash was union victory: all nonunion longshoremen on the Independent's piers were fired and all Wobblies rehired. As McKelvey wrote, "For IN ONE UNION ONLY WILL WE BE ABLE TO ACQUIRE THE RIGHT TO RUN THE JOB."[29]

Due to such events, the shipping interests, Philadelphia business community, and city government all perceived Local 8 as a threat. A series of public-private partnerships actively worked to expand and modernize the port's facilities, increase commerce, and create more stability in the shipping industry. The Port of Philadelphia Ocean Traffic Bureau advertised the port in shipping and industrial centers throughout the world. The city government, with much support from the local shipping industry as well as the state and federal governments, dramatically deepened the Delaware and removed islands from the river. The city government created the Department of Wharves, Docks, and Ferries to govern more efficiently and increase the city's riverfront holdings so that it could build larger, more modern wharves. Alas, in his memoir port director George Norris never mentioned the men who performed the labor on the waterfront while he actively worked with local employers to break Local 8.[30]

Just as the city's shipping interests and government promoted their interests, so did Local 8. Enforced by Local 8's thousands of members, the deep-sea longshoremen's wage scale in August 1914—more than a year after their initial strike—remained at thirty cents per hour for day work, forty-five cents for night work, and sixty cents for Sundays and holidays. In contrast, nonunion longshoremen received significantly lower wages: twenty cents per hour at the Merchants and Miners' Line, twenty-two-and-a-half cents per hour on the Clyde Line, and thirty cents per hour (with forty cents for overtime and fifty cents on Sundays) from stevedore Steve Schell of the Southern Steamship Line and IMM. Additional good news came when the renegade longshoremen who had left for the ILA rejoined Local 8; the start of World War I initially caused a decline in shipping, forcing the stevedore who hired ILA longshoremen to fire them. Subsequently, these longshoremen rejoined the IWW, but this time they were forced to pay the much higher initiation fee of $5. As McKelvey wrote, "The I.L.A. has since passed to the great beyond. . . . They are the champion American Federated Labor Suckers. . . . The Marine Transport Workers, I.W.W. are still very much alive and maintaining job control."

The ILA's Dempsey confirmed McKelvey's boast at its annual convention: "I spent considerable time in an endeavor to undermine the I.W.W. there and although successful in securing a local, I found the men so enthused with the spirit of I.W.W.ism that it will take considerable time and money to educate them to the knowledge of real organization and the benefits to be derived there from." Although the port experienced less commercial activity in the winter of the 1914–15, the Wobblies still sought to extend their "control [of] the port of Philadelphia, regardless of whether a transport worker works aboard ship, truck, railroad, or street car."[31]

The union worked hard to keep all of its members active through various educational programs. To that end, the union hall opened every day, including Sundays, when the union held its regular business meeting. The local also scheduled educational and propaganda meetings, open to all workers, throughout the week, especially nice given the irregularity of employment. English-speaking workers had two sessions, always integrated, on Sundays. Poles and Lithuanians held meetings in their native tongues on Wednesday nights. The local still received one hundred copies of *Solidarity* weekly as well as one hundred copies of the IWW's Polish paper *Solidannose* and fifty copies of *Voice of the People,* a Wobbly sheet published in New Orleans by the organizer-bard Covington Hall. The local also scheduled special speakers; for instance, in November national organizer Walter Nef talked about how to sign up members and spread the industrial union gospel. At the end of the month the acclaimed leader of English dockworkers, Tom Mann, spoke in Philadelphia as part of his IWW-sponsored, four-month lecture tour. As historian Larry Peterson writes, "Industrial unionist ideas [were] being spread from one country to another, often through seamen and labour unionists in port cities, through the international contacts of labour leaders, or through Europeans who carried such ideas back to Europe after a period of activity in North America."[32]

Local 8 and all of Philadelphia's Wobblies agitated in support of other working-class causes. Philadelphians organized a meeting to protest the life imprisonment of Richard "Blackie" Ford and Herman Suhr and raise money on their behalf in the highly publicized Wheatland (California) Hops Riot. Ettor, McKelvey, and Local 8 member Edmond Rossoni, who also served as associate editor to the IWW Italian-language paper *Il Proletario,* spoke at one meeting. The local also passed a resolution condemning the U.S. military presence in Mexico and urged both U.S. and Mexican workers not to participate in the battle as "all Governments are mainly the slugging committees of the ruling class . . . [and] no matter which side should win in that war, the working class would not win."[33]

Foreshadowing future conflicts between Local 8 and the national organization, Local 8's delegate Paul "Polly" Baker submitted a resolution at the 1914 annual convention regarding dues remission. Baker advocated keeping more money at the local level. General Executive Board (GEB) member Frank Little, later brutally murdered in Montana, responded that many places needed financial support. General Secretary Vincent "The Saint" St. John seconded Little and noted that the national already was strapped financially. The resolution failed, and the debate bode ill for future relations between Local 8 and the national.[34]

The IWW was not the only institution in financial distress, for after World War I broke out in August 1914, exports to Europe fell off dramatically, causing a deep nationwide recession. In its January 1915 issue, the *Journal of the Philadelphia Chamber of Commerce* reported that "the last five months of the year just closed was a very unsatisfactory period for the foreign trade because of the European War and interruption of shipping." The economic slowdown continued, and in July the city's Chamber of Commerce announced that shipping in the first half of 1915 was well below the comparable period in 1914. Yet Philadelphia boosters were united in their efforts "to merit more truly the [self-named] title of 'The World's Greatest Workshop.'"[35]

The end of 1914 also witnessed the arrival in Philadelphia of a man who became one of the finest organizers in the local, John J. "Jack" Walsh. Walsh had a long, active career prior to his involvement with Local 8. Born around 1880 in New York City, he had worked as a longshoreman in New York for a decade. He was one of the leaders of the 1907 strike led by the Longshoremen's Union Protective Association (LUPA), in which more than fifty thousand participated. Walsh joined the IWW in 1905 because he did not believe that craft unions could adapt to changing industrial conditions. He cited the LUPA strike as proof of the failings of craft unionism because teamsters, sailors, marine cooks and stewards, firemen, water tenders, and oilers all worked during the strike with "scab longshoremen." Walsh proudly claimed that there "never have [sic] been a scab in my family. I would drown them if there were."[36]

As a Wobbly Walsh had organized all over the nation. In 1911 he traveled more than one thousand miles to participate in a strike against the Hearst newspaper in Chicago. As he said at his 1918 trial, it "tickled me to death to be in a strike . . . you know what the bull-headed capitalists are. They hate like the deuce to come across with the dinero, so you have to choke it on them." Walsh's tactic, used by many organizers, was to secure work and then organize on the job. For example, Walsh stayed in the City of Big Shoulders after the Hearst strike to work as a lumber handler along Lake Michigan (taking out an ILA card) and in the building trades as a member of the Hod Carriers and Building Laborers Union. He also participated in the Lawrence textile strike of 1911, the Paterson silk strike of 1913, and the organizing campaign among Detroit's Ford automobile workers in 1913 (which contributed to Henry Ford's decision to lower the workday to eight hours and raise the salary to $5 a day), before heading to Philadelphia in 1914. He was one of the most active and radical members in Local 8 prior to his arrest in late 1917. His steadfast commitment to the multiracial Local 8 also indicates how Irish Americans could ally with African Americans.[37]

Despite the recession, grain trimmers struck in late January 1915, demanding a spectacular raise from thirty cents to sixty cents per hour, with equivalent increases in overtime, Sunday, and holiday rates. The longshoremen claimed they deserved such a raise because of the high rates that shipping companies charged their customers due to the war. The strike began on the Charles M. Taylor's Sons' and Murphy-Cook Company's piers, but quickly spread beyond the grain docks. The unionists, led by Ben Fletcher, even succeeded in getting the nonunion workers of the Independent Piers Company and Southern Steamship Company to strike. The *Public Ledger* reported that the thirty-four hundred strikers immediately tied up ten ships. That same night Local 8 Secretary Joseph Green, a black man, announced the strike's settlement, with the grain trimmers achieving a pay scale of forty cents per hour based on a ten-hour day, sixty cents for overtime, and eighty cents for Sundays and holidays. Quite possibly, the strikers' demand to double wage rates was a clever tactic that resulted in a still impressive 15% wage increase.[38]

Only one boss, Charles Taylor, refused these new rates, precipitating a multiweek showdown. Taylor's firm had brokered the original agreement between the bosses and union in 1913, but now he locked out all Wobblies. Joining with Steve Schell, the antiunion stevedore of the Hamburg-American and Southern Lines, Taylor attempted to work his vessels with scabs. Taylor hired upward of four hundred new men at the old rate of thirty cents per hour. Local 8 responded by throwing up a picket line around Taylor's piers. General Organizer Ettor returned to help. James Larkin, the general secretary-treasurer of the Irish Transport Workers' Union, a group similar to the IWW, also rallied the strikers. Larkin spoke of the hard conditions among Irish longshoremen and necessity of industrial unionism. He highlighted a victorious Dublin strike that instituted "ca canny," an on-the-job work slowdown, for five months. Larkin promised that Irish dockers would refuse to handle any "hot cargo."[39]

Despite these efforts and prominent allies, the union called off its strike. The longshoremen returned to work at the original rate. The strikers could not afford to stay out any longer: winter always whipsawed longshore families with the twin challenges of increased household expenses (coal for heating) and a decline in shipping activity—on top of the recession. Moreover, the IWW never gave strike benefits. Perhaps the deciding factor was that Taylor agreed to take back all striking unionists and discharge their replacements. In the May 1913 strike his brother, Fred Taylor, repeatedly noted the exorbitant costs involved in hiring strikebreakers as well as the substandard work of the replacements.[40]

The rest of 1915 marked one of Local 8's lower points. Most significantly, the war-induced economic downturn in 1914–15 crippled the marine transport industry and left longshoremen scrambling for jobs. Citywide, job competition became ferocious; for instance, in December 1914 five thousand men showed up for three hundred openings at the Philadelphia Ship Repair Company. There are no reports about Local 8 in IWW newspapers or any other for the remainder of the year. Further, local employers initiated a major open-shop campaign, proudly labeling their city the premier "scab recruiting station" in the land. ILA President T. V. O'Connor reported similar problems in his union: "Last August when the great European war broke out, the members of the I.L.A. were undoubtedly among the very first workers to feel the effects of that struggle for the reason that many large steamships plying between the United States and Europe were interned. This resulted in the curtailment of longshore work to such an extent that the membership of some of our locals were almost, if not entirely, deprived of employment." Thus, the recession combined with fierce employer resistance greatly weakened Local 8, as occurred in many IWW outposts across the land.[41]

Similarly, the 1916 revival of Local 8, overwhelmingly a union of deep-sea longshoremen, was greatly aided by World War I, which—after the initial downturn—caused an explosion in exports. The value of exports from Philadelphia almost tripled, to over $310 million, from 1915 to 1916 and represented an increase of close to 500% from 1914 to 1916. Grain exports, one of the port's main commodities, experienced a huge increase, as did coal, munitions, and sugar. In April there were more grain vessels in port than ever in the port's history (and the grain docks were a stronghold for Local 8). The boom caused a labor scarcity that spread beyond the waterfront and resulted in higher earnings across the city's and nation's economies.[42]

With the economy's resurgence, Philadelphia longshoremen rebuilt their weakened organization. The first conflict erupted over divergent interpretations of the state's first Workmen's Compensation Act. The

Southern Steamship Company, long one of the fiercest antiunion employers, refused to accept the new law, contending that in the event of an on-the-job injury, the onus of compensation rested on the stevedore who subcontracted the work. To protest, fifty Wobblies struck. In a particularly elitist statement, one Southern representative claimed that the new law was "a little too technical" for the understanding of the blacks and immigrants who worked on (and walked off) the docks. After a few days the company accepted the law, and the men returned to work, but as the committed anarcho-syndicalist Jack Walsh said, "We found out afterwards, anyhow, the law was only a good piece of bunk . . . not worth the paper it was written on." Longshoremen in Philadelphia and elsewhere continued to suffer from a high rate of injuries and deaths without much protection or compensation.[43]

Using these actions as a lever, Local 8 organizers reenergized waterfront workers. By April more than three thousand were paid-up unionists. In addition to the deep-sea longshoremen, Local 8 lined up coal heavers, who loaded coal onto steamships, for the city's coal exports also boomed. The boatmen rejoined Local 8, and the union even signed up the captains of the lighters. Invoking the creed of industrial unionism, the longshoremen promised not to unload lighters until the boatmen received a raise. The local also maintained a propaganda committee, which held street meetings regularly. With the exception of two companies' docks, Local 8 maintained job control on all of the city's deep-sea piers; no one without the proper month's IWW button worked those docks. For instance, on February 11 a Wobbly gang was hired, but one longshoreman had not kept up his dues, clearly indicated by the fact he was not wearing the appropriate button. In one of an untold number of such quick and direct actions, the rest of the gang refused to work—and would not let him work—until he went to the hall and paid his dues, which he promptly did. Of course, the longshoremen's militancy mirrored many Americans, who struck with increasing frequency as the economy prospered from growing Allied war orders. David Montgomery notes that the annual rate of strikes in the United States reached unprecedented levels during the war.[44]

With the docks again organized, the IWW fixed their gaze on sailors, so the union hired Manuel Rey, a Spaniard. Rey left his village in Galicia as a teenager and sailed throughout the Atlantic world, picking up several languages, before settling in the United States in the 1910s. Like many of his countrymen, Rey was an anarchist, leading an anarchist group in Philadelphia called the Pro Prenza Society. Rey organized Spanish sailors who made Philadelphia their home port, or regularly passed through it, into a foreign-language branch of Local 8. The seamen often held their

own meetings and established a Spanish-language library of IWW literature, songbooks, and fiction. Wobbly newspapers like *Cultura Obrera*
(Worker Culture) and *El Rebelde* (The Rebel) were read by sailors, well
known for voracious reading habits.[45]

The union had lined up two hundred Spanish sailors by May 1916.
An overwhelming majority of sailors, even on U.S. registered ships, were
foreigners. A good number of these were Spaniards, especially in the
"black gang," firemen and coal passers who toiled in the engine room
below decks. Eduardo Paredes, a twenty-three-year-old Spanish fireman
and coal passer, claimed that fully 97% of the men who worked below
decks were Spaniards, 1% were Portuguese, and 1% "English." While
not being as specific, Elias Castellano and Jose Cuevas agreed that the
majority of the "black gang" and IWW sailors were Spaniards.[46]

The IWW's MTW competed with the AFL's ISU for the sailors' hearts,
minds, and membership. John Walsh and Manuel Rey held an impromptu
debate aboard one ship anchored in the harbor. Targeting the deck hands,
one ISU representative said he would not sign up any "niggers" and
branded the IWW a collection of "foreigners." The ISU organizer's statement indicates several key differences between the two unions. First, the
ISU openly discriminated against African Americans and non-Americans.
Moreover, the ISU was a craft union; in fact, its longtime president Andrew Furuseth was one of the staunchest advocates of craft-based unions.
The ISU representative apparently had no qualms about alienating the
firemen and other seamen who worked below decks, most of them Spanish, so long as the "white" deck sailors joined the ISU. Walsh quickly
pointed out his adversary's racism and argued that the Seamen's Act,
championed by Furuseth, established a two-tier wage system for sailors
and was another example of ISU divisiveness.[47]

The Spanish contingent within Local 8 was active and quite radical.
Leonard Guillel had traveled the world countless times since he first
shipped out around 1900. He took out an IWW card in September 1915,
while "on the beach" in Philadelphia. Guillel explained why he joined
the MTW when he testified at the IWW federal trial in 1918. Through an
interpreter, Guillel stated, "I and my fellow-members have got together
for the only end of bettering our position as workers." Eduardo Paredes
voiced the socialistic message: "I was born there [Spain]; [but] my country is the whole world of workers." Another Spaniard, Francisco Alonso,
also signed up in Philadelphia in 1915 after arriving on a vessel that had
made port from Cuba and then plied the coastwise trade between Philadelphia and New York. The heavily Spanish composition of Local 8's
seamen's branch is notable precisely because American seamen's unions

were notoriously racist. ISU sailors, U.S. citizens or not, were generally whites of North European descent. Not surprisingly, the five thousand Spanish sailors who briefly left the AFL for the IWW in 1913 had felt discriminated against in the AFL.[48]

In addition to expanding their organization, Local 8 members won their first pay raise in more than a year. Wobbly P. C. Wetter credited the efforts of Delegate Paul "Polly" Baker and Financial Secretary George McKenna for the unprecedented strike-free five-cent-per-hour raise. McKenna and Baker were the sorts of men the IWW loved in its ranks. Born in Philadelphia to Irish immigrant parents, George McKenna, aged thirty-two, had worked various jobs on the Delaware since the age of twelve, before finding work as a deep-sea longshoreman. Joining the IWW during its first strike, McKenna had come to believe fervently in IWW principles. As a witness at the 1918 trial of IWW leadership, McKenna claimed, "Well, anything that would benefit the working class I cannot see where it would benefit the capitalist class." Baker, aged thirty, was an immigrant from Russian-controlled Lithuania who came to the United States with his family in 1888. He lived with his father, sister, and her family in South Philadelphia until Baker married a native-born woman, had a child, and rented a place nearby, also not far from the river. Thanks to men like Baker and McKenna, deep-sea longshoremen saw their wages rise to thirty-five cents an hour.[49]

Coastwise longshoremen, however, toiled for far less, earning twenty-five cents per hour, with five cents more on Sundays, and had to strike for a five-cent wage increase. On Saturday, May 10, 110 longshoremen walked off the Race Street piers. That same day Local 8 celebrated its third anniversary. Three thousand longshoremen withheld their labor to honor themselves. Escorted by five bands, the proud members of Local 8 marched along Delaware Avenue and convinced more coastwise longshoremen to strike.[50]

Still riding the economic boom, Local 8 sought to claim a larger share of the port's newfound riches. The longshoremen had gained a wage increase from thirty cents to thirty-five cents per hour two months earlier. Now, in June, the longshoremen demanded another five-cent raise. Though first refusing, the stevedores soon agreed—except the Southern Line, Local 8's fiercest opponent. Notably, Walsh attributed the strike's quick success to "class solidarity. Whites and blacks struck together." The strike against Southern continued.[51]

Walsh justifiably could boast about the longshoremen's success. The branch included 3,500 longshoremen, 160 sailors, mostly firemen, as well as the harbor boatmen. Since 1913 wages for deep-sea longshoremen had risen from twenty-five to forty cents per hour. Where there had been no extra pay for overtime, night, Sunday, and holiday work, now they earned sixty cents per hour for night work and eighty cents per hour on Sundays, holidays, mealtimes, and Saturday afternoons.[52]

Local 8's success and the war-induced economic growth encouraged other waterfront workers. For example, the lumber handlers on the Philadelphia & Reading Railroad's piers at Port Richmond, a huge facility covering over two hundred acres and one mile of improved waterfront, struck. The terminal could hold up to six thousand railcars, and its dozen piers could handle over one million tons of cargo in a year. Despite soaring company profits, the nonunion lumber handlers received different wages at different piers of the same company; some earned thirty cents per hour while others recently had received a raise to thirty-five cents. On June 15 110 lumber handlers, mostly black, struck for a raise to forty cents per hour, specifically citing Local 8's new wage scale. That they struck, albeit unsuccessfully, that day was no coincidence, the *Public Ledger* reporting that June 15 was the port's busiest day in a record-breaking year.[53]

Meanwhile, Local 8 again set its sights on the front's four sugar refineries. Local 8 spawned the Sugar Refinery Workers' Industrial Union #496. Quickly, workers at the Spreckles sugar-refinery struck, demanding time and a half for night work and double time on Sundays. Jack Walsh envisioned spreading the strike to San Francisco, Boston, and New York, where the MTW had locals at Spreckles refineries. When the strike spread to the Atlantic Refining Company, the state's Bureau of Mediation and Arbitration arrived on the scene.[54]

Of more immediate import was a Local 8–led strike of coastwise dockers. In June coastwise longshoremen had managed to convince the stevedores and shipping companies to raise wages, with the exception of the Southern Steamship Company. M. H. Pressley, the Southern's local agent, contended that his company could not afford the higher wages paid by companies benefiting from the export boom. In response, the union struck and threw up an integrated picket line of four hundred Wobblies. The picketers often were joined by hundreds, even thousands, of sympathizers.[55]

The Southern sought to break the strike by hiring strikebreakers. By early July the company had replaced about half its workforce, despite high turnover. The company had "converted [pier 46] into an emergency camp, with accommodations for 100 . . . furnished with food of excellent quality, soft, springy cots to sleep on and clean sheets three times a week." The Southern Line and Pennsylvania Railroad had, according to the *Public*

Ledger, many "special officers" guarding piers "augmented by policemen." The police again used the tactic of arresting picketers for vagrancy. About fifty strikers were sentenced to ten days each in the county prison. These actions did nothing, however, to unload Southern ships.[56]

The racial equality among the strikers stood in stark contrast to race relations elsewhere in Philadelphia. Numerous clashes pitted picketers against replacements, with charges made that the strikers beat up strikebreakers and stole their earnings. Some of these clashes involved black and white unionists battling black strikebreakers; crucially, the union longshoremen allied across race lines to combat a common enemy and never made the race of the replacements an issue. While Local 8 forged interracial bonds, historian Robert Gregg contends that blacks were starting to experience greater segregation in education, housing, and public spaces citywide. The same month white residents in West Philadelphia attacked a house occupied by a black family, and the city transferred all of its black policemen from South Philadelphia to other assignments, at the request of local merchants. Black Philadelphians, of course, liked having black police, especially after black protestors suffered from white police brutality while demonstrating against the racist film *The Birth of a Nation* the year prior.[57]

Strikers, strikebreakers, and strike sympathizers, numbering in the thousands according to the local press, clashed, resulting in many injuries and one death. One attack occurred the night of July 5 when seven black cooks, including Warner Maddox, left work after feeding replacements. Possibly mistaking the cooks for strikebreakers, an argument between the cooks and strikers ensued. The shouting match soon turned into a brawl, with Maddox suffering the worst of it. Maddox and another cook fled north on Delaware Avenue, with many in hot pursuit. After five blocks, at South Street, Maddox, several ribs broken, backed up against a warehouse and began firing his revolver. Thomas "Half Shirt" Kenny, either a striker or sympathizer, was shot dead. Maddox continued firing, shooting several innocent bystanders and one of his fellow cooks, as people scattered in every direction. Maddox then barricaded himself in the Gloucester ferry house to protect himself from the crowd enraged by the killing of "Half Shirt." Police surrounded Maddox, who fired until out of ammunition and then succumbed.[58]

The situation deteriorated further the next day, with more fighting, beatings, and arrests. Neighborhood residents, generally sympathetic to the union, were warned that the police had orders to shoot first in the event of any problems. Southern Line officials requested more police and threatened to pull its eight ships out of the city if the strike did not end

quickly. Yet, fighting continued, with the longshoremen again suffering
the worst of it. A black detective named Barnes, disguised as a replacement, was stopped by picketers along Delaware Avenue. What happened
next is disputed. According to IWW sources, one picket, Local 8 leader
Glenn Perrymore, confronted Barnes. Rather than identify himself as
a policeman, Barnes pulled his pistol. Barnes and Perrymore wrestled,
and Barnes fired five shots. Perrymore somehow was not hit, but another black Wobbly, Joseph Chambers, narrowly avoided being killed
by Barnes. The mainstream press reported that Barnes was mistaken for
a strikebreaker and attacked so, in self-defense, opened fire. All agreed
that, after the scuffle, a troop of fifty mounted police "charged down the
avenue at full gallop" and proceeded to severely beat Perrymore. Another
black striker was shot by a detective, while Perrymore and Chambers
were arrested. The following day the district looked as if martial law
had been imposed. Mounted police and detectives patrolled Delaware
Avenue, dispersed all pickets for "loitering," arrested "vagrants" (now
defined as anyone who could not explain why they were walking), and
badly beat up at least one innocent black man incorrectly assumed to
be a striker.[59]

The union held a funeral for Thomas Kenny, the dead man, with
Local 8 declaring a brief strike during the funeral that shut down the
entire waterfront. In the procession "a guard of big husky longshoremen
paraded with it, despite the hints of interference by the police from the
capitalist press." Local 8's deep-sea members resumed work, while the
strike against Southern languished.[60]

Amid the coastwise strike, the port continued breaking export records, and other waterfront workers, with IWW encouragement, became
increasingly militant. When teamsters struck for higher wages, their leaders cut a deal with the employers for less than the members wanted. A
wildcat strike ensued, with the renegade teamsters holding a meeting at
the IWW hall. Polly Baker, George McKenna, and Jack Walsh addressed
the radicalized teamsters. The following day the teamsters received the
wages they originally demanded. Walsh imagined lining up a teamsters'
branch of Local 8, but that never occurred.[61]

The local remained strong through the summer. Due to record exports, the longshoremen's branch had increased to over three thousand
members and the seamen's to four hundred. Apparently, there had been
a small ILA local, #160, of lumber handlers until the members voted
overwhelmingly to join the IWW. Wobbly George McKenna had a public
debate with the ILA's Dempsey and "wiped the floor with him," according to a biased Walsh. Still, Dempsey demonstrated his view that the ILA

could not capture Philadelphia when he took Local 160's minute book and treasury when he left town.[62]

By the end of 1916 Local 8 had been in power for two-and-a-half years. The longshoremen, grain trimmers, coal passers, firemen, tugboaters, sugar-refinery workers, and iron-ore workers who made up Local 8 had withstood fierce attacks and weathered economic downturns. Philadelphia's stevedores and shipping companies were assisted actively by the city government, most notably the police. Business organizations, including the Chamber of Commerce and Bourse (a shipping association), had fought vigorously for a return to the open shop. Wobblies also contended with periodic challenges from AFL rivals.

Despite these opponents, Local 8 had increased its membership, improved wages, and promoted racial equality. More than three thousand men, over twenty-five hundred in the deep-sea trade, belonged to Local 8, and about half of these were African American. The case of Local 8 member Charles Carter is instructive. Born a slave in Prince Anne, Maryland, in the early 1860s, Carter moved to Philadelphia in 1879 and had been "loading chutes" ever since. In 1913, around the age of fifty, Carter joined Local 8 as soon as it was chartered. Five years later Carter remained true to his union, despite government repression: "I am [proud] and expect to stay [in Local 8] as long as there is only two men in it—I expect to be one." Why was Carter so committed to his union? "Before the I.W.W. came there, you knowed when you start to work but you never knowed when you was going to stop. You could go in from one hour to fifty and over. . . . No over time. Sunday was the same as any other day. Night was the same as day. We got 10 cents an hour in many instances." In contrast, at the end of 1916 deep-sea longshoremen earned forty cents per hour for day work, sixty cents for night work, and eighty cents for Saturday afternoons, Sundays, holidays, and meal hours. Where previously, the hours worked depended entirely on the employer, now longshoremen worked full days Monday through Friday, 8 A.M. until 6 P.M., with an hour for lunch, and Saturday morning from 8 A.M. to 1 P.M. Only the strength of the union allowed workers to gain these raises and limit their hours. Refusing to sign contracts, acting at the point of production, extending their power along the waterfront, trying to bring all maritime workers into the One Big Union—the longshoremen of Local 8 were squarely within the era's wave of new unionism.[63]

Local 8's power came from its commitment to solidarity, especially racial and ethnic equality, which always proved a challenge to maintain. Without such an ideology, a waterfront union was inconceivable, and only the IWW willingly pushed such an agenda. As African American numbers on the riverfront continued rising, they readily joined Local 8—no surprise given the union's power and commitment to equality (as evidenced by the integration of work gangs and presence of numerous black leaders). The inclusion of other river workers and Spanish seamen also demonstrates the union's commitment to industrial unionism and equality. Before Local 8, employers used craft, ethnic, and racial differences to foster disunity. Now employers squared off against the IWW, which maintained its steadfast commitment to solidarity as the base upon which Local 8 built its house. However, though World War I had aided its organizing efforts, when the United States formally entered the war Local 8 suffered the devastating consequences of repression.

4 War on the Waterfront

The year 1917 was one of profound changes. The United States officially entered the war in Europe in April. Three months later, on September 5, 1917, Local 8's headquarters at 121 Catherine Street and the MTW offices near City Hall were stormed by federal agents of the U.S. Department of Justice. The six most important Wobblies were arrested, and all of the union's records confiscated. The raids in Philadelphia were part of a well-coordinated federal plan to destroy the entire IWW, perceived as a threat to the Allied war effort. Two months after the raids the Bolsheviks overthrew the new, already tottering, parliamentary government in Russia and declared the world's first Communist nation. The United States and entire world were forever changed by these events.

The war years presented dramatic challenges to the members of Local 8, who served the war effort loyally but also sought to protect themselves and expand their power. As other workers did, Philly longshoremen worked very hard to serve the nation, but also used the war as leverage to improve their wages. They also sought to expand their influence by working toward the One Big Union, specifically targeting the large riverside sugar refineries. Concurrently, the federal repression suffered by Local 8 and the IWW nationwide was the greatest threat the union had yet experienced. Although profoundly hurt by the loss of their dynamic leaders, Philadelphia's longshoremen emerged from this battle still holding on to job control. After the war they joined millions of other American workers in an unprecedented surge of militant strikes.

The year 1917 also saw tremendous growth for the city's many industries and its port, in both trade and shipbuilding. The Philadelphia

Chamber of Commerce boldly declared, "When Uncle Sam calls the roll
of those who are furnishing most to wage this mighty war, he finds that
th[is] district . . . leads all the rest. . . . Philadelphia counts in this war
with the weight of a belligerent nation." In his celebratory book *Philadelphia: A Story of Progress,* Herman LeRoy Collins declared, "In one
war year 7000 vessels came to Philadelphia wharves and docks to sail
away fully laden." More than $600 million in exports and imports in
1917 shattered the record set the year prior. For example, grain exports
doubled from 1914 to 1915 and remained at these record levels through
1918. Sugar refining also benefited from the economic upswing; production in this waterfront industry surged, making it the city's fourth largest
manufacturing industry.[1]

Local 8 quickly capitalized on the economic upswing, in part thanks
to a new leader, Walter T. Nef. Nef's presence signaled a renewed IWW
commitment to organizing in the East, which, with the notable exception of Local 8, had lagged after the failed Paterson strike in 1913. Arriving from Switzerland in 1901 at the age of nineteen, "Big Nef" quickly
found his way to northern California, working jobs as varied as logger
and milk driver. He took out union cards in whatever field he worked,
most notably in an industrial union that subsequently was split into craft
unions upon affiliating with the AFL. In 1908 Nef heard IWW organizer
George Speed, who later helped charter Local 8, speak on the San Francisco waterfront about the futility of craft unions. Speed's talk resonated
with Nef, who shortly thereafter joined the IWW in Portland. During
the winter of 1909–10 Nef helped lead the first major IWW free-speech
fight in Spokane, Washington, and served time, along with hundreds of
Wobblies, in that city's jail. Nef remained in the Pacific Northwest until
the spring of 1915, when he was elected secretary-treasurer of the IWW's
new Agricultural Workers Organization (AWO). Nef spent the next two
years building up the AWO. In the process, he led the entire IWW (Local
8 included) out of the doldrums it had experienced at the war's start.
Differences with IWW General Secretary-Treasurer Haywood over the
role of the AWO led to Nef's resignation in November 1916. Still, Nef
remained a darling in the IWW.[2]

Nef had big plans for the MTW 100, intending to apply the same
methods that had worked so successfully among "bindle stiffs." As with
the AWO, Nef hoped to establish a delegate system for the MTW. By
increasing the number of delegates (organizers) on the job, rather than
on the streets or by the docks, the union could agitate more effectively.
In Philadelphia Nef was assisted by two port delegates, one Spanish and
one English speaking, at the meager wage of $18 a week (still, most ports

maintained only one delegate). Then, Nef promptly raised the initiation fee to $2 for taking out a "red card" in any industry, a high amount in the IWW, and $5 in any industry where the IWW maintained job control, namely Philadelphia's deep-sea piers. Nef argued that the increase was needed to create a powerful and stable organization that could improve conditions and wages on the job and increase delegates. Nef concluded, "Now all together for the one Big, Powerful Union of all workers in all industries."[3]

A second seasoned and equally well-traveled IWW organizer, Edwin Frederick Doree, arrived to help Nef. Born to Swedish immigrants in Philadelphia in 1889, Doree first experienced the migratory existence of the American working class while just a child, when his family moved to Skagway, Alaska. At the age of thirteen Doree started apprenticing in a railroad car factory until, eighteen months later, he lost several fingers in a workplace accident. He drifted down to Washington State, where he first joined the IWW in 1906, becoming an accomplished organizer but only after a stint as a professional baseball player. In 1912 Doree accompanied George Speed to Louisiana to assist the Brotherhood of Timber Workers. In those nine months he witnessed some of the most oppressive conditions in the nation, agitated to keep an interracial union alive despite massive resistance, and spent time in jail. Doree also received a nasty head wound that laid him up for several months. Afterward, Doree organized textile workers in Rochester, New York—where he met his wife, Chika, a Jewish immigrant, at a strike meeting—and migratory farm workers throughout the Midwest, following the workers north as they followed the harvests. Possibly, Doree met Nef when the latter took the reigns of the AWO, although they likely met in the Spokane free-speech fight. In 1916 Doree again organized textile workers, this time in Baltimore. When Nef moved to Philly, so did Doree. Nef then met Doree's sister-in-law, Feige, who soon married Walter. As its textile industry employed more than one hundred thousand workers, Philadelphia was a logical place to base a newly created Textile Workers Industrial Union (TWIU), #1000, with Doree's TWIU office next to Nef's reborn MTW. Doree also organized for Local 8 and, at times, found work as a longshoreman.[4]

With Nef and Doree's arrival, two of Local 8's most able organizers were dispatched to other ports. Ben Fletcher, a national organizer as of the previous fall, went to Providence, Rhode Island, to organize longshoremen, many of whom were Cape Verdean (i.e., of African ancestry). Jack Walsh spent the end of 1916 and start of 1917 in Baltimore helping Jack Lever, the main IWW organizer. Emil John (Jack) Lever, a Russian immigrant, joined the IWW in 1914 while in Salt Lake City and later that same year worked as a machinist in Toledo, where he witnessed organized labor's racism firsthand as a member of the AFL's International Association of Machinists. Lever later met Walsh and Fletcher in Philadelphia, where, according to Lever, "we found out we were in agreement" on issues like industrial unionism and racial equality. As in Philadelphia before Local 8, longshoremen in Baltimore were a mixture of African Americans, Irish Americans, and Poles, none of whom got along. The ILA had established an all-white local in 1912; as Lever put it years later, "The ILA came in and organized whites and left the Negroes out. And we said, a union is a union. And we proceeded to organize the Negroes." Lever and Walsh signed up nearly fifteen hundred black longshoremen before Walsh requested Fletcher's presence. Walsh hoped to convince white longshoremen to switch to the IWW when the ILA's contract expired, but most whites, immigrant and native-born, stuck with the ILA.[5]

As Fletcher, Lever, and Walsh organized along the Atlantic seaboard, Local 8 again targeted Philadelphia's sugar workers after they spontaneously struck. Unlike longshoremen, the men *and* women who toiled in the sugar refineries remained weak and completely subject to their employers' will. Most received a wage of twenty-five cents per hour (some less) for twelve-hour days (or nights, the factories ran twenty-four hours a day, seven days a week), fourteen hours a shift during busy times, without higher overtime or night rates. The sugar-refining boom during the war forced employees to work even harder, until they walked out of the Spreckles Sugar Refinery on February 1, demanding a raise of five cents per hour, time and a half for any work over ten hours a day, and Sundays off. Most of the workers were immigrants, especially Lithuanians, Poles, and Russians, though some were recent Southern black migrants. At the walkout's start, the workers were overwhelmingly nonunion, but hundreds quickly joined the IWW. Within two days the strike spread to the McCahan and Pennsylvania refineries, and picket lines emerged around all three plants.[6]

The Philadelphia sugar strike was part of a national wave of worker militancy. In fact, the number of strikes in 1917 surpassed that of any previous year in U.S. history. Sparked by the wartime labor shortage and inflation, unprecedented numbers of workers, often nonunion, struck for better wages and fewer hours. As in Philadelphia, strikes occurred in other sugar-refinery centers; in Brooklyn workers went out in late January, soon spreading to Long Island, Jersey City, and Yonkers.[7]

With no settlement in sight, the IWW, led by Doree, Nef, and Joseph

Weitzen (the secretary of Local 8 and an African American), determined that the strike could be won only by expanding it. In an uncommon instance of skilled-unskilled worker solidarity, IWW engineers, coopers, machinists, oilers, foremen, and sack sewers joined the strike, which soon spread to the city's molasses refinery, the "Smear works." The city's newspapers reported between two thousand and three thousand sugar workers out, the IWW claimed over four thousand. The IWW signed up more than one thousand strikers to the Sugar Workers' Industrial Union 497. A week into the strike a thousand Wobbly longshoremen who worked the refineries' piers also struck. IWW seamen refused to divert ships to alternate ports.[8]

From its start the strike proved quite effective, despite daily beatings and arrests from local police, assisted by private detectives hired by employers. With over three-quarters of their employees out, refinery officials admitted that production had slowed to a fraction of normal. Six large steamships and several lighters loaded with sugar were dead "in the stream." A million pounds of unrefined sugar was diverted to other ports.[9]

As Philadelphia refined one-sixth of the nation's sugar, sugar prices quickly rose, which sparked female-led protests. Several thousand women, mostly immigrants, clashed with the police in what the *Public Ledger* called "food riots." One wholesale grocer gave voice, no doubt, to others' fears: "The consumer . . . is also tending to force the hands of the refiners to do something which the refiners may consider unwise or unjust in composing labor difficulties." Women, some of them refinery workers, many with babies in their arms and others leading toddlers, repeatedly attacked strikebreakers despite police protection. Historian Temma Kaplan contextualizes such actions: "When women left their households to protest against certain indignities or demand changes in their own and their families' lives, they presented themselves not as political actors, but as the very conscience of the community."[10]

Such protests incited thousands of strikers and sympathizers, who clashed with hundreds of police, leaving one dead, many injured, and scores arrested. After two hours of fighting one night, Martynas Petkus, a Lithuanian Wobbly and rank-and-file activist, lay dead. In an interview with the *Public Ledger*, Florence Sholde—the wife of a Polish striker, a mother of four, and of late a convicted criminal—spoke passionately of the strike. Revealing the close bonds in her working-class neighborhood, she claimed, "We would be starving down here now if the butcher and the grocer did not trust us until my husband goes to work. If they stop charging it on the book, we will all go hungry. All the women and their families are just the same."[11]

The strikers held several large events for the fallen striker. Thousands viewed his body in an open casket at the Lithuanian Hall, despite police opposition in the name of "public safety." The large room was full of flowers, many donated by the IWW and the Lithuanian Socialist Federation, to which Petkus also belonged. The following day many thousands, red carnations in their lapels, marched, again defying the police, which had refused a permit. After the funeral, Wobblies Joseph Schmidt, Joseph Graber, A. Mariella, and Doree spoke in Lithuanian, Polish, Italian, and English, respectively. Kaplan explains that "collective mourning at political funerals is a civic ritual that unites a community, enables it to reclaim sacred spaces, and permits it to cleanse itself of death."[12]

The death hardened both sides. Clashes, injuries, and arrests continued unabated. Members of the state and federal governments' arbitration services shuttled between employers and strikers, yet neither side relented. Earl D. Babst, president of the American Sugar Refining Company, the parent of Spreckles, announced that his company "would not yield an inch. . . . [I] would not propose to hand over the control of this industry to any outside organization [IWW]." Just as firmly, the strikers claimed, "There is no vindication of the dead unless we have a victory for the living."[13]

After dragging into an eighth week, the strike fizzled. The strikers had succeeded in significantly curtailing sugar refining in Philadelphia. The strike lasted for as long as it did because the union maintained the solidarity of the strikers across craft, ethnicity, gender, and race lines with tremendous support in the diverse, working-class waterfront neighborhoods. Nevertheless, the employers' strength outmatched strikers' solidarity. Still, as often happens in strikes, employers did raise wages almost to the level demanded by the strikers (from 25 to 29.7 cents an hour). For many strikers, though, the outcome has to be seen as a failure—thousands lost two months' wages, hundreds lost jobs and were arrested, and the refineries remained nonunion.[14]

Perhaps more alarming, workers inside the sugar refineries found themselves more racially divided. This splintering of workers, orchestrated by employers, had profound ramifications. The Spreckles superintendent acknowledged that "Negroes had been employed to replace and 'equalize' the foreign laborers." As a result, the governmental report *Negro Migration in 1916–17* concluded that "there has been developing [since the strike] a strong undercurrent of [racial] prejudice among foreign workers, particularly the Slavs." One "Negro dock foreman" complained that Poles "dislike to work beside the colored men, and are going to make trouble for us." This strike, then, contributed to rising antiblack sentiment among recent immigrants—which contributed to the ultimate decline of Local 8. Notably, this same report concluded that "there had been no race trouble on the docks where whites and blacks [who were Local 8 members] had worked side by side." Of course, unity never was a given and played a major role in Local 8's postwar unraveling.[15]

Local 8 and the IWW strove to keep its heterogeneous members, in particular the African Americans, committed to the union. Big Bill Haywood, the IWW's general secretary-treasurer, addressed this issue in his petition "To Colored Working Men and Women." Haywood contended that black and white workers had the same goals—to improve their conditions in work and life. Haywood argued, however, that under the present system, black (and white) people had yet to achieve true freedom. Haywood noted that African Americans were virulently discriminated against, that "as [black] wage workers, the boss may work us to death, at the hardest and most hazardous labor, the longest hours, at the lowest pay." Then Haywood argued that white workers did not fare much better, "regarded by the boss only as a means of making profits." Thus, the crux of Haywood's argument (echoed by other socialists like Fletcher) was that all workers shared common interests. Haywood also noted how employers sought to divide white and black workers to keep them weak. To build a strong union, Haywood contended that "race prejudice has no place in a labor organization." The challenge of organizing across racial lines soon was compounded by the war-induced Great Migration and—perhaps an even greater threat to the IWW's viability—the wrath of the federal government.[16]

In April 1917, the United States entered World War I, and most Americans quickly rallied around the flag. The immediate cause was Germany's decision to resume unrestricted submarine warfare against all vessels sailing toward Britain. After the German announcement, American ships remained in their safe harbors, unwilling to challenge German U-boats, so wheat, cotton, and other goods piled up on piers all along the Atlantic seaboard. When President Wilson asked Congress to declare war, the citizens of Philadelphia immediately responded. To mobilize food, fuel, and workers, recruit troops, and sell war bonds, the Pennsylvania Council for National Defense was created. In Philadelphia so-called Four Minute Men marshaled an army of speakers to rally the city's populace. Philadelphians purchased a billion dollars in Liberty Bonds to help the war effort.[17]

While the port of Philadelphia experienced major growth in 1915 and

1916, the true economic boom was in 1917. In the years 1910 to 1914, foreign trade hovered around $165 million. In 1917 foreign trade rose to more than $600 million. During February 1917, despite the sugar strike and though the winter traditionally was a slack time, exports from Philadelphia totaled $57 million, a stunning $48 million increase over February 1916. According to one source, fully 40% of all war-related commodities shipped to Europe left from Philadelphia. The city government worked actively to promote the port, making "liberal appropriations" to harbor development and public relations.[18]

In the short term, America's entry into the war materially benefited all Philadelphia waterfront workers. One MTW circular advised workers to organize to improve their wages and conditions during the war as, "on account [of] the European War, prosperity reigns on the seas. The Ship-owners are making millions of dollars." In Philadelphia, as in other ports, the wages of waterfront workers rose during the war. Local 8 won its demand for a raise to sixty cents per hour for loading gunpowder and munitions. As for Philadelphia sailors, they also agitated for raises, knowing that ships could not get enough able-bodied seamen. Just prior to the U.S. declaration of war MTW 100 struck for a $10 raise in monthly wages across-the-board instead of striking individual ships. World War I, which simultaneously led to a tremendous increase in production and a shortage of labor, drove wages up for American workers. In other ways, the war was far more disadvantageous, especially for Wobblies.[19]

The IWW's stance on the war confirmed its ideology and revealed its view of American society. Like other socialist organizations, from 1914 onward the IWW labeled the European war a capitalist enterprise, caused by and solely benefiting the rich and powerful at the cost of the overwhelming majority of people, who fought and died on Europe's battlefields. In 1916 the IWW GEB declared, "We reaffirm with unfaltering determination the unalterable opposition to all wars." Throughout 1916 and 1917 the IWW made its stance on the war clear, declaring once, "Capitalists of America, we will fight against you, not for you." The IWW also contrasted its stand on war with the AFL, whose superpatriotism appalled many socialists. However, many in the IWW, including its leadership, took the fatalist stance that America inevitably would enter the fray.[20]

Yet, despite its doctrinal opposition to the war, the IWW did not tell its members to refuse registering for military service, nor did it participate as an organization in antiwar activities. IWW leaders were fully aware that, by 1917, most Americans supported the war, which was a perfect excuse for the government and employers to suppress leftist organizations, especially the IWW. Thus, the union (also demonstrating its

anarchist tendencies) let individual members decide whether to register.
IWW publications noted on more than one occasion that failure to register
would bring only more hostility down upon the IWW. So, although no
official position was taken, it was clear that the IWW leadership believed
its members should, in fact, register for military conscription, which
most Wobblies did.[21]

In Philadelphia fully 100% of Local 8's members registered for the
draft. MTW 100 Secretary-Treasurer Nef did not register because he was
too old, but he advised Jack Lever and James Phillips, secretaries of the
Baltimore and Boston MTW respectively, to inform their members of
the Selective Service Act (Lever himself volunteered). Doree also encouraged many Socialists (some of whom were Wobblies, too), who opposed conscription, to register. Still, Doree was critical of the draft; in a
letter to IWW Secretary-Treasurer Haywood, Doree wrote of "physical
discrimination" practiced by the Philadelphia draft board, believing a
higher percentage of working-class residents was called up than upper-
class ones.[22]

Beyond advising members to register, both Local 8 and the national
IWW left decisions about the war up to individual members. Doree and
others did not believe in speaking publicly against the war; instead, during the war he resolved to "keep his mouth shut." At his trial in 1918,
Doree made it clear he opposed wars as "trouble" and that he had enough
of that already. Doree registered because he saw the Allies as the lesser of
two evils, citing German Socialists as useless after they failed, in 1914,
to call a general strike to prevent their nation's militarism. Nef, himself
a German Swiss, had supported the Allies since 1914, opposing Prussian
militarism from his youth.[23]

The rank and file of Local 8 actively supported the war effort. At its
hall, the local maintained an honor roll of members serving in the military. Several local hiring bosses estimated that more than seven hundred
members of Local 8 performed military service during the war. At one
wartime meeting, the members agreed "that any Member of our Local
Union who has been in the United States Army or Navy service and
shows an Honorable discharge when he returns, his book be straightened
up," meaning a veteran could rejoin the union without paying another
initiation fee or back dues. Nor was Local 8 the only IWW branch that
acted so strongly on behalf of the Allies.[24]

Perhaps the most extraordinary example of Local 8's support of the
war was a meeting organized by Ben Fletcher, Polly Baker, and Jack
Lever in early 1917. At the behest of Colonel Freely, commander of the
Schuylkill Arsenal, an Army supply depot in Philadelphia, the three

Wobblies set up a meeting at Local 8's hall. The building was filled to capacity, six hundred strong, to hear Fletcher, Nef, and Walsh address the membership on the need to support the war effort by working efficiently. Lever later wrote that Fletcher's "high standing with his race [African Americans], who formed about 60% of the port workers, was invaluable" at that meeting. The members of Local 8 later voted not to strike for the duration of the war.[25]

In addition to those already discussed, Local 8 supported the war for numerous reasons. Most obviously, the men needed work and the union needed to operate. As most work on the river was war-related, an antiwar stance was not only potentially dangerous, but it was not viable. Second, though a great many Germans and Italians resided in Philadelphia, few, if any, were longshoremen, and Nef was a vocal critic of Germany. Third, the large number of Local 8 members who served in the military, the Liberty Bonds purchased by the union, and the no-strike pledge suggest some patriotic tendencies. As for the African Americans, who made up roughly half the union, generally the black community supported this war. Most famously W. E. B. Du Bois, the influential editor of the NAACP's *Crisis*, encouraged blacks to rally around the flag and support the push for democracy (falsely assuming that black loyalty abroad would be rewarded at home after the war).[26]

The IWW, including Local 8, also saw World War I as an opportunity to organize, understanding that the war could create the sort of crisis in which revolutions happen. The IWW argued that workers should continue to prepare for the *true* fight, the class war. Indeed, the actions and attitudes of Local 8 members echo those of syndicalist (and later Communist) William Z. Foster. By this time Foster had broken from the IWW and focused on "boring from within" the mainstream AFL. Foster publicly supported the war and bought war bonds, but also took advantage of the war to organize a brilliant campaign in the Chicago stockyard and later the national steel strike in 1919. Whether Local 8's stance is considered patriotic, opportunistic, or syndicalist (i.e., ignoring the politics of war in favor of sticking with organizing on the job), it was not alone among Leftists.[27]

Philadelphia was one of the most important U.S. ports in the war effort. Out of Philadelphia went many of the men as well as much of the food, munitions, oil, and steel on its way to Europe. In 1917 more than 75% of the cargo that left Philadelphia went to help fight the war. A report in 1919 by the recently created United States Shipping Board (USSB) stated that the longshoremen of Local 8 "loaded a large part of the munitions sent to Europe."[28]

The only work stoppage that Local 8 conducted during the war was its anniversary strike. In May 1917 the union celebrated its birth just as it had in previous years, by shutting down the docks and celebrating. The membership notified employers that despite the recent American declaration of war, longshoremen would not work on May 15. As the Wobblies marched down Delaware Avenue led by three bands, IWW organizer C. L. Lambert commented, "You could see in the lines of men walking five abreast, American, Polish, Lithuanian, Belgian and colored in the same line" chanting, "No creed, no color can bar you from membership" and the official IWW motto, "An injury to one is an injury to all." Local 8's annual strike reaffirmed its commitment to solidarity and disproved the notion that the IWW could not organize a radical yet stable union. As Nef wrote, "I have always urged the men to do their work well and if they had any complaints to bring them up at the union meetings so that they could be acted upon in an orderly fashion."[29]

That the members of Local 8 stopped work during the war to celebrate their anniversary reveals a great deal about their power and how they perceived themselves. Local 8 wielded job control all along the Philadelphia waterfront and beyond. In 1917 Local 8 claimed close to four thousand paid-up members in Philadelphia, Camden, New Jersey, and down river in Wilmington, Delaware. Francis Fisher Kane, the U.S. Attorney for the Eastern District of Pennsylvania during the war, later testified that every longshoreman in Philadelphia was a Wobbly. Local 8's power was so complete that its members handled all of the munitions as well as the oil for the Army and Navy. William Anderson, a Local 8 member (along with his father), worked as a foreman at Murphy-Cook, which held an Army contract. Anderson said that if a ship loaded, say iron, at an unorganized dock but was slated to carry a load of gunpowder as well, activity stopped until a gang of Wobblies arrived to work the ammunition. Among the Dupont Company powder workers at both Carney's Point, New Jersey, and Wilmington, which Local 8 dominated during the war, vessels simply were not allowed to load gunpowder at a non-IWW pier. Thus, Wobblies contributed mightily to the Allied war effort, and workers, employers, and government all knew it. Local 8's power paralleled that of other IWW strongholds in important war industries, including the copper mines of Montana and Arizona and the Pacific Northwest's woods.[30]

Every deep-sea stevedore and shipping firm dealt exclusively with Local 8, with the exception of two companies. The Hamburg-American Line and Furness-Withy, both of whom contracted for their longshoremen through the Atlantic Transportation Company, refused to recognize the union. All other jobs on the waterfront either went through the IWW hall or at the "hiring corner" less than two blocks from it. As Jack Walsh proclaimed: "Any time they [bosses] ran short they telephone[d] up to the IWW hall for men." Even the Office of Naval Intelligence (ONI) acknowledged that Local 8 "is an extremely powerful organization locally."[31]

As in other war-related industries, the federal government took an active role in labor relations in maritime transport. The government dramatically increased spending on shipbuilding to develop an American merchant marine fleet, through a new body called the Emergency Fleet Corporation. Another new agency, the USSB, was created to coordinate and regulate the industry, including labor relations aboard ships and in ports. Following the lead of the president, the National War Labor Board encouraged cooperation between employers and employees and their unions, for the sake of efficiency.[32]

The federal government simultaneously supported the "bona fide" labor movement, embodied by the AFL, and worked to dismantle the renegade IWW. The AFL recognized that the government had the power to eliminate the IWW, thereby ridding the AFL of its main rival; in his autobiography, Samuel Gompers labeled the IWW "a radical fungus on the labor movement." Accordingly, in August 1917 the USSB created the National Adjustment Commission (NAC), along with a committee representing shipping interests (in particular the American Steamship Association, which represented dozens of shipping lines) and the ILA (which represented at least some longshoremen in every port excepting Philadelphia). The USSB, War Department, shipping interests, stevedores, and ILA all were represented on the NAC, which resolved disputes concerning wages, hours, and conditions. The shippers, ILA, and government formally excluded Local 8 and the MTW from these discussions, despite what the USSB labeled "the important work" performed by Local 8 members. Nor did the NAC establish a local presence in Philadelphia. Crucially, T. V. O'Connor, the ILA president, and Joseph Ryan, the ILA leader in New York, sat on the commission. O'Connor later headed the USSB; in his autobiography, Gompers praised O'Connor and the ILA for trying to drive the IWW off the docks. In 1917 the ILA journal *The Longshoreman* ran many anti-IWW stories, accusing it of "treasonable" acts and wanting "to destroy society—to overturn civilization—to stamp out individuality, and to erase the laws of private property of any sort."[33]

Local 8 continued to battle the ILA during the war. In 1916–17 the ILA chartered two locals in Philadelphia. Correspondence in June 1917 between one local president and AFL headquarters confirms that the ILA had a difficult time. Charles Goodwin, the local's president, wrote,

"We have a rival organization here about 4000 strong to fight," so he requested more money to organize. During the war an ILA local signed an agreement with the NAC to handle lumber in Philadelphia. This contract also acknowledged the power of Local 8: "The organization of Local 916 was to some extent disorganized by competitive organizations." A few months after signing the contract, ILA President O'Connor admitted in *The Longshoreman* that Philadelphia was "very much in need of attention and it will be necessary for considerable organizing work to be done before we can hope to have anything like the membership we should have when the population and amount of shipping to, and from," is considered. The ONI confirmed that the ILA "has frequently endeavored to gain a foothold in Philadelphia, but has been uniformly unsuccessful." Both ILA locals collapsed within a year.[34]

As the IWW never signed contracts with employers, Local 8 would not, on principle, have participated in the NAC. Jack Lever discussed the Wobblies' direct-action approach: "We didn't get formal bargaining, but we simply told people to stop work until they got what they wanted." Still, Local 8's exclusion from the NAC was pushed by the ILA. For instance, Patrick Quinlan, an AFL organizer, recommended to Todd Daniel, the senior Philadelphia agent of the U.S. Bureau of Investigation, that he work with Polish Catholic priests, who opposed the atheistic IWW, to subvert Local 8; still, there is no evidence of any Catholic parishes opposing Local 8. ILA efforts in Philadelphia parallel its actions in Norfolk, Virginia, where Earl Lewis has documented how the ILA used the USSB to displace the all-black, independent Transportation Workers Association. The AFL colluded with the government, hoping to subvert the IWW nationwide.[35]

Nevertheless, Local 8 maintained job control and the Wobblies performed their work admirably. Not a single work stoppage occurred after May 15, 1917. This policy even extended to their annual birthday strike. At one April 1918 meeting, the members voted "that we postpone the Celebration of the 15th of May which is our legal holiday ever since our Organization is in existence so as not to hamper the war work of the Government." Clearly, the membership supported the war effort, shocking given the IWW's politics and the government's wartime repression—or perhaps not. Local 8's action combined one part patriotism (white hot by 1918), one part fear (of further arrests and raids), and one part pragmatism (almost all work was war-related). Rationales aside, when literally millions of tons of explosives and munitions were loaded and unloaded in the port, not a single explosion, accident, or shifting of cargo occurred in Philadelphia. In contrast, there were numerous explosions, fires, and accidents at other Atlantic ports, where ILA men worked. Incredibly, given the federal government's anti-IWW stance, the Navy did not allow any explosives to be loaded aboard a vessel in Philadelphia unless done so by Wobblies. Moreover, when a fire or explosion occurred on a ship loaded in New York (as when the *Henderson* caught fire at sea), it was sent to Philadelphia to be reloaded. Gompers claimed, without evidence, that such "accidents" on New York's Chelsea piers were sabotage conducted by pro-German Wobblies. Local 8 members were proud of their unblemished record and quick to point out that less efficient longshoremen were not Wobblies.[36]

As the city's shipping industry prospered, so did the union. Local 8 initiated dozens of new members, many African American, each week. Also of interest, the ONI reported that membership was "increasing daily, owing to the influx of a large number of West Indian negroes." As Local 8's power increased, the longshoremen yet again set their sights on the Spreckles sugar docks, despite the brutal two-month winter strike. The campaign was part of a larger effort to increase IWW power by putting more delegates on docks and ships. This program also targeted Spanish-speaking workers by printing many pamphlets, including the union's constitution, in Spanish. These efforts, however, quickly were overshadowed by national events.[37]

On September 5, 1917, the U.S. Department of Justice carried out raids at sixty-four IWW halls and offices across the nation, ostensibly to prevent an IWW general strike. Federal agents confiscated more than five tons of IWW organizational minutes, official and personal correspondence, financial records, pamphlets, newspapers, circulars, books, stickers, membership lists, buttons, cards, publications, and office equipment—all as "evidence." The IWW in Philadelphia did not escape. Local 8's hall was raided, as were the headquarters of the MTW and TWIU. Walter Nef testified that "I found these officers taking everything except the framework of the desks," including membership letters, correspondence, account books, financial records, and literature. In addition, and more seriously, the Department of Justice issued arrest warrants on the charges of treason and sedition for 166 Wobblies, including six from Philadelphia—Benjamin H. Fletcher, Walter T. Nef, John J. Walsh, Edwin F. Doree, Manuel Rey, and Joseph Graeber (a Polish organizer who did not belong to Local 8 but who helped with sugar-refinery workers).[38] All of those arrested were accused of interfering with the Selective Service Act, violating the Espionage Act of 1917, conspiring to strike, violating the constitutional right of employers executing government contracts, and using the mail to conspire to defraud employers. Possibly the most well-known chapter in the history of the IWW, this federal repression forever affected the union. Local 8 suffered from these raids, though it persevered far more effectively than most other branches.[39]

Local 8's rank and file organized to exonerate its local and national leaders. Out on bond prior to their trial, Doree and Nef volunteered for the IWW General Defense Committee (GDC), formed shortly after the raids. In Doree's words, the GDC worked "to raise funds, secure legal counsel, locate witnesses, and generally assist in the defense of the various members of the I.W.W." Local 8 sold "liberty bonds" in order to raise money for the defense fund. The GDC also helped defendants' families. The ONI reported that Local 8 "has contributed liberally to the Defense Fund."[40]

The purpose of the raids and arrests was abundantly clear: to destroy the IWW. In his deposition, Doree detailed the myriad ways in which the government obstructed the work of the GDC, by denying it mailing privileges, confiscating mails, intimidating lawyers and witnesses, and preventing the IWW Publishing Bureau from printing defense literature. Historian William Preston notes that the American entry into World War I allowed the Wilson administration to equate the threat of IWW strikes with "seditious interference in war production." The Department of Justice's strategy was in keeping with the actions of Military Intelligence. According to historian Mark Ellis, Major General Ralph "Van Deman became convinced that the security of the United States and the war effort faced internal threats, not only from enemy agents, but also from the antiwar activities of American left-wing radicalism, in the form of unions such as the Industrial Workers of the World." One hundred percent Americanism and the "atmosphere of war hysteria [that] colored all decisions from the local to the national level" also help explain why federal officials saw the IWW as "a vicious, treasonable, and criminal conspiracy." At the Chicago trial the prosecution equated the IWW's anticapitalist beliefs with pro-German sentiment and, by extension, treason.[41]

The repression of Local 8 lends further credence to the idea that the government's actions were geared more toward wrecking the IWW than protecting the nation since the members of Local 8 worked so diligently during the war. Philadelphia longshoremen loyally loaded thousands of vessels for the war effort, with but one short strike and no major mishaps. Hundreds of members joined the military, and others purchased Liberty Bonds. Nevertheless, Local 8 was undeniably an IWW outfit, the men proudly wearing their buttons to work—even at the Navy Yard. Although Wobblies loaded ships for the war, it was not because the government endorsed the IWW but rather because of the union's power. Even though no problems occurred, the federal government still equated Philadelphia Wobblies with anti-Americanism, capable of subverting the war effort. Addressing this issue in a letter written to his wife while jailed at Leavenworth, Doree claimed, "I did not know then [1917], and have not since learned, of any 'general strike scheme' on the part of the Industrial Workers of the World for the purpose of crippling the war program of the United States. Nothing of this was proven at our trial." The plans for the federal raids emanated from the nation's capital, where the Departments of Justice, Labor, and War worked closely to suppress the so-called IWW threat. Since the IWW was powerful on the vital Philadelphia waterfront, it should come as no surprise that Local 8 was a main target.[42]

Further proof confirming the true purpose of the arrests—to crush the IWW—comes from whom the Department of Justice did *not* consult, namely federal officials in Philadelphia. The Philadelphia representatives of the Department of Justice were not asked in advance about the raids. Had they been, they would have told their superiors that there was no reason to suspect that the longshoremen were disloyal. Further, the Navy did not see Local 8 as a threat, despite the nature of the Department of Justice's charges. Only five months *after* the raids did Assistant Attorney General William C. Fitts contact the Secretary of Navy requesting evidence "to show that the needs of the Navy of the United States, with respect to preparation for participation in the war, were materially interfered with and retarded by the unrest fomented and low-down methods injected into the situation during the spring and summer of 1917 by the I.W.W." In short, there was no concrete evidence that the American war effort was being subverted by the IWW or that a general strike was in the works. In particular, the Navy never supplied one shred of evidence that Philadelphians ever sabotaged the war effort or planned to. In fact, the U.S. pardon attorney who later investigated the cases of Local 8's leaders wrote that he had "considerable difficulty" in "ascertaining just what" these longshoremen had done "that constitute[d] the offense of which they were convicted." Furthermore, the federal agent who conducted the raids on Local 8 in 1917 later admitted, "I personally do not know of any crime that he [Nef] has committed against the country." Rather, in 1922 this agent volunteered to the pardon attorney that "I wish to state that Walter Neff [*sic*] is a clean cut high class intelligent man and a perfect gentleman"! Finally, the U.S. Attorney for eastern Pennsylvania during the war wrote on behalf of the Local 8 leaders jailed, encouraging the president to pardon them.[43]

Nevertheless, given the antiradical sentiments of the time, 101 Wobblies quickly were indicted by a grand jury in Chicago, where IWW head-quarters were located, on five counts of conspiring to hinder eleven acts of Congress and presidential decrees concerning the war. The 1918 trial of the Wobblies was the longest in U.S. history up until that time. Nef testified to the strength of Local 8 in Philadelphia. Doree concentrated his discussion on the "brutal oppression" of timber workers in Louisiana whom he organized before moving to Philadelphia. Walsh "kept the courtroom in an undignified state of continual laughter with his references to 'Fellow Worker Nebeker' [the prosecuting attorney] and other Irish pleasantries." Fletcher, curiously, did not testify. In a letter to the editor published in *The Crisis* in 1919, F. H. M. Murray wrote of running into Fletcher during the trial and asking him what he thought; according to Murray, Fletcher "smiled broadly" and replied that Judge Landis was "a fakir. Wait until he gets a chance; then he'll plaster it on thick." After four months of testimony—in which the entire government case was based upon letters, newspaper articles, and other materials written *prior* to America's declaration of war—the jury delivered a verdict in less than an hour that every defendant on trial was guilty on all counts. The men from Local 8 were sentenced as severely as the other defendants. On August 30, 1918, Judge Kenesaw Mountain Landis sentenced Nef to twenty years in the federal penitentiary at Leavenworth and fined him $30,000 plus court costs. Doree, Fletcher, Walsh, and Graber were sentenced to ten years and $30,000 plus costs. Rey was sentenced to twenty years and $20,000. A decade later Big Bill Haywood wrote that, upon hearing the verdicts, "Ben Fletcher sidled over to me and said: 'The Judge has been using very ungrammatical language.' I looked at his smiling black face and asked: 'How's that, Ben?' He said: 'His sentences are much too long.' At one time previous to this during the great trial in a spirit of humor, Ben remarked: 'If it wasn't for me, there'd be no color in this trial at all.' I might explain that he was the only Negro in the group."[44]

To the membership of Local 8, the loss of their leaders, Fletcher in particular, was devastating. Black longshoreman James Fair recalled, "Some of us were very hurt over it, because we knew what he was doing was something for us to earn a livelihood to support ourselves and families and it was just like well, I would say it was to ones who was interested in organized labor and improving our standards of life it was something near like Martin Luther King [being sent to jail]." While waiting in the infamous Cook County Jail—the same prison where the Haymarket martyrs were hung thirty years before—to be loaded on a train for Leavenworth, Fletcher made light of the situation while simultaneously calling into question the authority of the entire proceedings. Haywood recalled

Fletcher holding a mock court. Imitating Judge Landis, "looking solemn and spitting tobacco juice," Fletcher "swore in the prisoners as a jury; calling the guards and detectives up to him he sentenced them without further ado to be hanged and shot and imprisoned for life."[45]

After the raids, the MTW continued its mission of organizing seamen. MTW headquarters moved to South Philadelphia; the headquarters also housed other radical organizations, including the Russian Socialist Society. Most Wobbly seamen, especially in Philadelphia, were Spaniards and Italians. Nef estimated that between four thousand and five thousand seamen belonged to the MTW on the Atlantic coast. On virtually every coastwise vessel, much of the crew below decks—firemen, engineers, oilers, and water tenders—were Wobblies. Although not in the Navy, the merchant marine, including Philadelphia-based Wobblies, risked their lives on a daily basis for the Allied cause. Leonard Guillel and Francisco Alonso, both Spanish-born Wobs, were aboard the Standard Oil steamship *Helton* that was torpedoed on its way to Rotterdam; twenty-two crewmen, twelve of them Wobblies, died. To curtail the MTW's power, Rey had been sent to Leavenworth for twenty years. Another Spanish anarchist, Genaro Pazos, took Rey's place as secretary-treasurer of MTW 100. Pazos had been very active in spreading IWW-MTW propaganda throughout the Atlantic and in raising money for the IWW Defense Committee. Even though the MTW had only a fraction of the ISU's members, the ONI recommended that Pazos and the union "be kept under close surveillance."[46]

Despite Local 8's record of reliable, efficient labor and having its leaders imprisoned, the federal government still did not trust Local 8. In a comprehensive report entitled *Investigation of the Marine Transport Workers and the Alleged Threatened Combination between Them and the Bolsheviki and Sinn Feiners*, the ONI, in close collaboration with the Department of Justice, Plant Protection Sections of the Military Intelligence Division, and Emergency Flect Corporation, concluded: "It is the opinion of this Office that subject [Local 8] is extremely dangerous potentially. . . . This Office recommends that . . . it [Local 8] should be kept under strict surveillance by the aid for Information of the Fourth Naval District. It is further recommended that the leaders likewise be carefully watched, and punished for each and every infraction of the law, however slight." The ONI soon placed one of its operatives inside Local 8.[47]

Yet, in spite of these enormous losses and threats, Local 8 achieved significant wage increases during the war. By the end of 1918 the wage rate for deep-sea longshoremen had jumped to sixty-five cents per hour, which can be attributed to a combination of labor scarcity and union power. Philadelphia's wages for deep-sea longshoremen paralleled those of other Atlantic ports, from thirty cents in the summer of 1917, to forty cents in July 1918, and sixty-five cents by the end of that year. Further, the coastwise longshoremen who had joined Local 8 received equal wages, unheard of in the era and due to the IWW's egalitarian streak—in contrast to the craft-based wage hierarchy of the ILA.[48]

Most of the IWW was thrown into utter turmoil as a result of wartime repression, but Local 8 maintained its power. In fact, although many contemporaries and historians consider the federal raids the beginning of the end of the IWW as a force, the ONI reported that, a year after the raids, "the shipping interests of the city generally recognize the power [of] the Local and are obliged to employ members of it exclusively. In many instances when stevedores are required a request is made direct to the [union's] headquarters."[49]

With the arrests of Nef, Doree, Fletcher, Walsh, and Rey, other members, albeit with less experience, stepped to the fore. Joseph Weitzen replaced Charles J. Cole as secretary of Local 8, while his fellow union member Archie Robinson ably chaired meetings in 1917. In 1918 Weitzen took over as chair, and William "Dan" Jones was elected secretary. Polly Baker served as port delegate, and William Green was assistant secretary. With the exception of Baker, all of these leaders were African American. In 1918 longtime activist George McKenna, an Irish American, took over the position of secretary of the local from Weitzen. The orderly switch in officials was an example of the democratic impulses of the IWW. No member was allowed, according to local bylaws and MTW constitution, to hold a post for more than a year. Due to the union's commitment to its founding principles of industrial unionism, democracy, and racial and ethnic solidarity, Local 8 persevered, though weakened, and even sought to extend its gains after the war. Indeed, the 1917 sugar strike revealed how deeply committed Local 8 was to industrial unionism as an ideology and the strike as a tactic; however, it also showed that the power of the union was limited severely by the even greater power of employers, especially when assisted by the government. And, having its first cadre of leaders removed from Philadelphia reverberated loudly in the years following the war. Just as the union had been a part of the wave of wartime militancy, taking advantage of the tight labor market, so too after the war Local 8 acted to impose its will upon hostile employers, as part of a national surge in strike activity.[50]

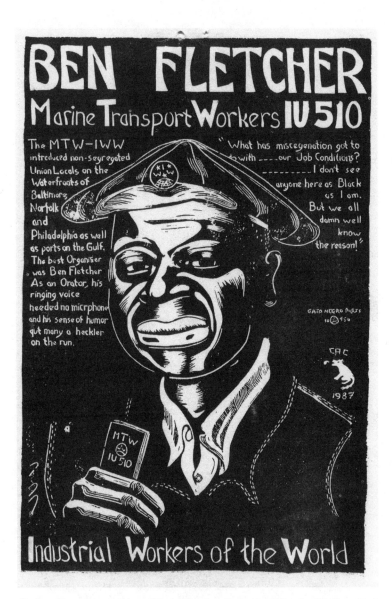

The text within the woodcut reads:

BEN FLETCHER

Marine Transport Workers IU 510

The MTW-IWW introduced non-segregated Union Locals on the Waterfronts of Baltimore Norfolk and Philadelphia as well as ports on the Gulf. The best Organiser was Ben Fletcher As an Orator, his ringing voice heeded no microphone and his sense of humor put many a heckler on the run.

"What has miscegenation got to do with ----- our Job Conditions? ---------- I don't see anyone here as Black as I am. But we all damn well know the reason!"

GATO NEGRO PRESS 10/450

CAC 1987

MTW IU 510

Industrial Workers of the World

Carlos Cortez's woodcut of Ben Fletcher (courtesy Charles H. Kerr Co.).

The IWW's favorite whipping boy, Mr. Block, fails to learn the core lesson of solidarity across ethnic and racial lines (courtesy Charles H. Kerr Co.).

Making up a sling of case oil on the apron of a pier, Philadelphia (source: Boris Stern, Cargo Handling and Longshore Labor Conditions, *Bulletin of U.S. Bureau of Labor Studies, no. 550 [Washington, D.C.: Government Printing Office, 1932], 45).*

Most longshoremen who worked on the sugar piers were African American, 1920 (courtesy Philadelphia City Archives; source: Frederic M. Miller, Morris J. Vogel, and Allen F. Davis, Still Philadelphia: A Photographic History, 1890–1940 *[Philadelphia: Temple University Press, 1983], 104).*

A Call to Solidarity!!

Local 8 of the Marine Transport Workers of Philadelphia, affiliated with the Industrial Workers of the World, call to the workers of all races, creeds, color and nationality to Unite.

If we would maintain our standard of living, and prepare for the final emancipation of the workers, we must organize our labor power upon an industrial basis.

We are the only organization in America which has a uniform wage for engineers, holemen, truckers, riggers, and water boys.

Of our three thousand and five hundred members, over two thousand are Negroes.

In this period of industrial depression and black reaction, only solidarity can save the workers.

Let workers of all races, creed, color and nationality, organize to liberate the class-war and political prisoners. Let us organize to build up a new Brotherhood for mankind where there is no race, class, craft, religious or nationality distinctions.

Workers: Organize, Agitate, Educate, Emancipate!

Marine Transport Workers Industrial Union, Local No. 8

INDUSTRIAL WORKERS OF THE WORLD (I. W. W.)

121 Catharine Street, Philadelphia, Pa.

The Messenger *frequently celebrated Local 8 in its pages due to the union's interracial and industrial unionist principles (source:* The Messenger *4 [April 1922]: 396).*

I. W. W. LONGSHOREMEN TIE UP SHIPPING IN PHILADELPHIA

"HOLD FAST, BUDDIE, WE GOT 'EM"

E. F. Doree's drawing exhorted black and white workers to "Hold fast, buddie, we got 'em" (source: One Big Union Monthly, July 1920, 7).

IWW prisoners before surrender at the Federal Penitentiary in Leavenworth (E. F. Doree in back row, second from right; Ben Fletcher in front row, second from right; Walter Nef in back row, fourth from left; Jack Walsh in front row, far left) (courtesy Walter P. Reuther Library, Wayne State University).

The port frequently was boosted by Philadelphia's business community (*source:* Philadelphia Chamber of Commerce Journal, *October 1916*).

Pier No. 78 South (McKean Street), one of the new, city-owned piers (courtesy Urban Archives, Temple University, Folder 10, Box 754, News Photographic Collection).

Philadelphia, one of the nation's premier ports, with ships lined up "in the stream," the Delaware River (courtesy Philadelphia City Archives).

5 *Onward One Big Union?*

Although they experienced wartime repression, Philadelphia's longshoremen approached the postwar era with guarded optimism. The raids and their leaders' imprisonments notwithstanding, their union continued to shape labor relations on the Delaware riverfront for years after the war in the face of powerful and increasingly coordinated employer-government attacks. Crucially, Local 8 still maintained job control, so anyone who wanted to work on the docks had to stick with the union. The continuing strength of Local 8 after World War I challenges the established historiography of the IWW that, for all intents and purposes, ignores the postwar era. While undeniable that many IWW outposts did not recover from the wartime repression, Local 8 emerged essentially intact. With a new leadership even more heavily black than the prewar years, the union continued to represent its large, now black-majority membership.[1]

The postwar years were a turning point in U.S. history. Many Americans, especially in parts of the labor movement and among some East European immigrants, became disillusioned with the outcome of World War I and looked to the Bolsheviks in Russia for inspiration. The combination of the Russian Revolution and a reenergized American labor movement translated into several years of unprecedented labor unrest. The manner in which Local 8 responded to these and other events—notably a concerted effort by corporate America and many in the government to suppress the labor movement via the Open Shop and Red Scare—explains how the union survived. Philadelphia's longshoremen were prepared, as true Wobblies, to continue their battle at the point of production, along with millions of other American workers. For half a decade after many historians have considered the IWW dead, Local 8 successfully resisted these antiunion, antileftist, and anti-immigrant trends.

The year 1919 witnessed the greatest strike wave in American history. Militant workers clashed with the equally determined opposition of employers and government. Alexander Bing, a labor mediator during World War I, claimed that the war "gave workers a realization of a strength which before they had neither realized nor possessed." The Seattle General Strike in January 1919 marked the beginning of a tumultuous year and demonstrated how fiercely worker radicalism would be suppressed by the combined opposition of business groups, city, state, and federal governments, and, at times, AFL officials. Enormous strikes in the steel, railroad, and coal-mining industries demonstrated the growing militancy of workers, as well as the superior power of their employer-government adversaries. In marine transport, the most notable event was the October strike in New York harbor. Initiated by ILA longshoremen in Brooklyn, this waterfront strike was the largest in the nation's history, affecting 150,000 workers in America's most important harbor. Yet, despite noteworthy efforts at maintaining racial and ethnic solidarity in the face of employer, and even their own union leadership's, repression, the strike failed, as did almost all of the large strikes of 1919.[2]

Local 8 extended its control of the waterfront through the tumultuous war years, despite the arrests of organizers Doree, Fletcher, Nef, Rey, and Walsh. In November 1918 the leaders of Local 8 were William "Dan" Jones serving as secretary, Joseph Weitzen as chair of the union meetings, Joseph Green as financial secretary, and William Ellis as recording secretary. All but Ellis, whose race is unknown, were of African descent. The job delegates/business agents were Lithuanian immigrant Paul "Polly" Baker and a black man named Schooles. All of these men were "clever and shrewd," according to the ONI, but not as experienced as the previous cohort, which contributed to Local 8's instability. Even after the wartime raids, the federal government maintained its surveillance of the IWW, including Local 8, and constantly watched for alliances between Wobblies and Bolsheviks. Local 8 was of particular concern to the government. One federal informant who had traveled nationally reporting on IWW activities wrote, "I was more than surprised to find that the I.W.W.s had gained more ground in Philadelphia than any other city in the United States, even more than in Seattle, and they are still gaining." This agent had reason for concern because Local 8 included "practically all the stevedores [another term used for deep-sea longshoremen] employed in this port, approximately 2500 men."[3]

In fact, despite hostile employers backed by the local and federal governments, Local 8 extended its power. All the deep-sea longshoremen in Philadelphia belonged to Local 8. The union's delegates visited any pier in the city as they pleased, despite employer antipathy. In 1919 no foreman or hiring boss could verbally abuse a man without a firm response from his workers. Significantly, the committee that represented the workers in discussions with employers had protected and, in some cases, increased wages. By the end of 1919 longshoremen made eighty cents per hour for a standard eight-hour day, $1.25 per hour for night work, time and a half for overtime, and double time during meal hours.[4]

Local 8 controlled the docks, including the Navy Yard and other government piers, except for some coastwise piers run by a handful of stalwart anti-IWW firms. The experience of Agent Joseph C. McKenna of the ONI is instructive. Posing as a longshoreman recently arrived from New York, he applied at the office of the stevedore firm M. P. Howlett & Son, two blocks from Local 8's hall. Agent McKenna was told that he could not get a job unless he belonged to the IWW; perhaps shockingly, the stevedore agreed to advance McKenna's union initiation fee directly to delegate Baker. Soon thereafter McKenna found work. A second agent reported that the stevedore contracted by the League Island Navy Yard also employed Wobblies exclusively. When stevedore Sheehan hired longshoremen, a walking delegate of Local 8 stood next to him at the pier gate and examined every worker; if a longshoreman was not wearing the current month's button, representing a fully paid-up member, the man was turned away. "In short," according to an ONI report, "the subject [Local 8] absolutely controls the labor along the water front." Integral to the success of Local 8 was lining up every waterfront worker, which during the war became majority black.[5]

Interestingly, some of these new longshoremen were West Indian immigrants. The United States purchased a series of Caribbean islands from Holland in 1917. Henceforth, residents of the (now) U.S. Virgin Islands could move freely to the North American mainland. As Winston James argues, because they were not raised in a Jim Crow society, Caribbean immigrants were more likely than African Americans to work with whites in radical organizations like the IWW. The U.S. government clearly took special interest in their presence on the Delaware. However, only one Local 8 member, Ernest Varlack, a native of St. Thomas, has definitively been identified as West Indian. James, though, contends that Meeting Chair Joseph Weitzen was West Indian because a report from the ONI referred to him as "colored" rather than as Negro or American.[6]

Far more of Philadelphia's new black residents, though, arrived from the American South—part of the famous Great Migration. According to demographers Daniel Johnson and Rex Campbell, "In terms of net population increase, the single most attractive state for northbound black migrants was Pennsylvania." Fully forty thousand Southern blacks moved to Philadelphia during the war. These migrants hailed primarily from the rural Lower South rather than the Upper South, as was the case with previous generations, including Ben Fletcher's parents. As Blanche J. Paget wrote in the Urban League's *Opportunity*, "Most of them were field hands or share-croppers who had lived in abject poverty." In Philadelphia Paget reported that male newcomers "often engaged in casual jobs such as that of longshoreman, a notoriously uncertain occupation," an observation confirmed by historians Lorenzo Greene and Carter G. Woodson. Black longshoreman Abraham Moses, for one, arrived in Philadelphia from Alabama in 1916, and his colleague James Fair moved from "down South" in 1917. The primary causes are obvious: the war-induced labor shortage opened up job opportunities in Philadelphia for African Americans that previously had been denied them on account of racism—combined, of course, with the horrific conditions blacks experienced in the South. The port's economic growth, the virtual end of European immigration, and Local 8's commitment to inclusion resulted in an increasingly African American workforce. From 1910 to 1920 the U.S. Census reported an increase of one thousand longshoremen in Philadelphia. While the number of European immigrants and native-born white longshoremen remained constant, black longshoremen rose to 2,388.[7]

But even as Local 8 strove to bring together this diverse workforce, the racial climate of the city and nation was fast deteriorating. Major riots occurred in Houston, East St. Louis, and just down the Delaware River in Chester, Pennsylvania, during the war. Nationwide lynchings of African Americans almost doubled from 1917 to 1918. Tensions continued to rise as ever more black people fled the South. While Philadelphia was hardly the only destination, the city famous for its liberal Quaker heritage drew a significant number of Southern blacks. As one migrant wrote in 1917, "I havent [sic] heard a white man call a colored a nigger you no [sic] now—since I been in the state of Pa." From 1910 to 1920 the black population of Philadelphia rose to nearly 135,000, with most of this increase after 1915. Tensions flared throughout the summer and fall of 1918, mostly over blacks moving into previously all-white neighborhoods, but also involving mobs of whites, including Navy sailors, randomly attacking blacks on streets and trolleys. Aptly, the IWW paper *Solidarity* reprinted a *New Republic* piece that had predicted in 1916 that "the Negroes would be forced to seek homes in what are now regarded as 'white' neighborhoods, and a clamor would be raised at each new extension of their dwelling area."[8]

The worst riot in Philadelphia erupted on July 26, 1918, when Adella Bonds, a black woman, moved into a house on the previously all-white 2900 block of Ellsworth Street. White policemen chatted with members of the white mob as bricks were thrown at the woman's house, located in South Philadelphia but not near the Delaware River (it is much closer to the Schuylkill). Over the next four days, one black man was killed (a police officer shot him by "accident"), two white people died, and hundreds more were wounded. Although white citizens initiated the violence, far more black people were arrested, yet again calling into question the impartiality of the city's police force. In fact, black citizens in the newly created Colored Protective Association "put the whole blame [for the riot] upon your [the city's] incompetent police force" and demanded both an end to discrimination and the hiring of more black policemen. Tellingly, the Reverend Richard R. Wright Jr. claimed that the head of police, in response to such protests, "started a tirade against the 'hordes of Negroes coming up here from the South' and told us we should keep them from coming here." The ongoing attacks by whites led Lovett Ford Whiteman, a black IWW organizer, to complain that "my people in this City are afraid of the Police."[9]

In contrast, the IWW continued to treat all waterfront workers equally. Local 8 did not simply accept workers of all racial and ethnic backgrounds; rather, it actively promoted solidarity through educational meetings and fostering black leadership. African Americans continued to play an important role in the union in the aftermath of Fletcher's imprisonment. Many other black members such as Joseph Weitzen, Charles Carter, Glenn Perrymore, Alonzo Richards, Amos White, and Dan Jones moved into leadership roles. At all meetings, blacks held at least half of the leadership positions—an African American generally held the chair, while a white member served as secretary. When an issue threatened to racially divide the members, the union discussed the matter at meetings instead of letting the issue fester.[10]

Despite these efforts, racial equality *always* was a contentious issue—particularly as hundreds of, perhaps as many as a thousand, Southern blacks entered the union's ranks. These new members did not have the same experience with industrialization, unionism, or white workers as had the original black members of Local 8. James Grossman explains the numerous reasons why most Southern black migrants did not join unions: racism among unions in the South and North, antiunion leadership within the black community, lack of familiarity with industrial work or unions, intimidation by employers, and the fact that most black migrants saw their situation in racial rather than class terms, so did not perceive their fellow white workers as allies. For instance, when James Fair arrived in Philadelphia and joined Local 8, it was not because he shared the IWW dream of building a new society; rather, he could not get a longshore job otherwise. Fair recalled, "I joined solely to get better wages and working conditions." The challenge for unions that strove for an interracial membership was to convince black migrants that a union with many white members could protect black workers' jobs and improve their conditions. Of course, as Southern blacks overwhelmed the native-born black community in Philadelphia, rising tensions among blacks further complicated the union's efforts. The loss of Fletcher, the leading black "old-timer," thus was doubly troubling for it came at such an inopportune moment. Without the support of these migrants, though, the union would be weakened severely, if not broken. In response to historian Herbert Hill's question about whether blacks were "amenable" to joining the union, organizer Jack Lever recalled decades later that "no, but we had as much success in organizing Negroes as whites; all in spite of the many Negroes from the South who could not read or write." Local 8's challenge incorporating Southern black migrants paralleled the experience in Chicago meatpacking.[11]

Related problems that Local 8 confronted were the possibilities of racial competition for work and black disunity. The U.S. Department of Labor's Division of Negro Economics mentioned such difficulties between Polish and black longshoremen in Philadelphia; the ONI noted the same rising conflicts. These tensions did not arise solely because of worker perceptions of competition. Historians Greene and Woodson write of "Irish and other foreign stevedores," that is, the hiring bosses, who attempted to limit the number of African American longshoremen in Northern ports. Given the wartime boom, this issue was less pressing, until, that is, a severe depression hit the nation's maritime economy after the war. Another potential source of disorder that the union confronted was that the black population in Philadelphia was hardly monolithic. There were significant differences among blacks in class, gender, regional background, and religion. Further, oral historian Charles Hardy documents frequent conflicts between blacks native to the city, who labeled themselves "Old Philadelphians," and blacks who had migrated from the South, who quickly outnumbered the "OPs" but felt distinctly second-class. Of course, the white workers in the labor force were divided in any number of ways, too. Lizabeth Cohen notes that "historians have overlooked the extent to which obstacles within [white] workers' own ranks contributed to their political [and economic] failures. Isolated in local neighborhoods and fragmented by ethnicity and race, workers proved incapable of mounting the unified action necessary for success." Any of these factors, only some unique to the docks, could upend Local 8.[12]

In addition to Southern blacks, a small group of Seattle Wobblies found their way to Philadelphia. In January 1919 thirty-five thousand shipyard workers launched what became the Seattle General Strike, which shut down the city for a week. In the aftermath, radicals of all sorts were brutally repressed. In the words of Harvey O'Connor, a participant in the strike, "In such situations, the police had an easy and obvious way to obtain victims. Raid the Wobbly Hall!" At least thirty-nine were arrested. After the strike the Waterfront Employers Association established the "Seattle Plan," an employer-operated hiring hall, backed up by a private police force and possibly with the tacit consent of the international officers of the ILA (who had threatened to revoke its local's charter for joining the strike). The employers' campaign effectively pushed many unionists and radicals out of Puget Sound. Further, at the war's end, Seattle joined the rest of the nation in a short but painful recession, causing unemployment to skyrocket.[13]

These Wobblies, likely single men without families, also threatened Local 8's unity. As an undercover agent quoted one Seattle Wob, "Once a wobbly always a wobbly. You can't make a capitalist out of him. So, if we don't show our strength here in Seattle, it is shown somewhere else." Many Wobblies were migratory workers, especially in the Northwest, where a worker might find a job on a harvest, in a forest, and on the waterfront in the same year. The men from Seattle were anointed "floaters" by the Philadelphians. These transplants invoked IWW bylaws, which stated that any person who held an IWW membership card could transfer automatically to another local, in contrast to AFL rules that required separate initiation fees. No doubt, the Seattlites had heard of Local 8's power. It appears that these floaters transferred into the local seamen's branch, as they often spent their days in the sailors' hall. They wanted, however, to work as longshoremen. Fred Thompson, the Wobblies' own historian, wrote of the phenomenon, describing the "110 cats [migratory farm workers of the IWW's Agricultural Workers Industrial Union] wintering in Philadelphia to lick the cream off [MTW] 510 struggles." In contrast, the members of Local 8 resided in Philadelphia year-round (although some also were new arrivals) and resented the floaters. This conflict illuminates one of the basic problems inherent in the IWW: form strong unions or foment revolution? Local 8 members clearly were focused on short-term, workplace issues, while the floaters in from Seattle recently had participated in one of the more radical moments in

U.S. history. How to reconcile these two objectives (pushing for higher wages and preparing for revolution) remained a source of disagreement in Philadelphia and among all Wobblies and would erupt again the following year in the Philadelphia Controversy.[14]

Numerous arguments broke out between the Philadelphians and Seattlites. The floaters had not found Philadelphia as profitable as hoped for, many working only two days a week. To alleviate their underemployment, the floaters wanted hiring to be doled out equally among all members with no distinctions made between local and migratory workers. Dan Jones, the black secretary of Local 8, replied that his branch would continue the already established system that distributed work among the members of Local 8. He argued that it was of primary importance to preserve Local 8's power, more difficult in Philadelphia (where labor surpluses were common) than in a smaller port like Seattle. Jones claimed that floaters were welcome to join Local 8, but if they did not, then they would have to be content with picking up extra work, beyond what the locals performed.[15]

The role that race played in this conflict is unknown, but racial tensions had flared in Seattle previously. The Wobblies from Seattle had no experience with a black-dominated labor movement. In fact, while organized labor in Seattle, overwhelmingly white, often is cited for its radicalism, when it came to the treatment of black and Asian workers, Seattle's white unionists acted in typically racist and exclusionary ways. Three hundred blacks had been imported as strikebreakers in Seattle's 1916 longshoremen's strike, which possibly increased the animosity of white Wobblies in Seattle to black workers. The ILA local in Seattle, with the support of dual unionist Wobblies, did accept blacks, yet they frequently suffered discrimination.[16]

Meanwhile, dockside employers undertook a campaign to increase port traffic. With its motto "Port of Philadelphia—better facilities, better rates, better all around, better use it regularly," the Chamber of Commerce hoped to make Philadelphia the nation's leading port. The U.S. Emergency Fleet Corporation moved its executive offices to Philadelphia, a nod to the fact that the city accounted for fully 36% of the entire nation's shipbuilding. However quixotic the goal of surpassing New York City, Philadelphia continued to perform quite well. In 1918 the value of the city's imports and exports totaled almost $550 million. This figure, though enormous compared to prewar levels, significantly undervalues the city's exports because it does not take into account shipments to U.S. armed forces in Europe. The following year the port set another record for maritime commerce, earning over $675 million. Thus, despite war's tumultuous impact on commerce, the port continued to prosper.[17]

As it sought to expand the port, the business community simultaneously worked to undermine Local 8, the IWW, and organized labor generally. Events paralleled those of other communities throughout the nation as businesses strove to roll back workers' wartime gains. To do so, organizations like the Chamber of Commerce and the National Association of Manufacturers championed Americanization and the open shop. These groups tried, and largely succeeded, in equating radicalism and unionism; thus, the loyal Local 8, or even the "patriotic" AFL, was un-American. That is, any attempt by laborers to organize, no matter what their conditions, was painted as disloyal. As a part of this conservative backlash, the IWW, the AFL, other left-wing and liberal organizations, immigrants, and German Americans all were labeled radicals, aliens, un-American, and traitors. The 1917 raids and 1918 prosecutions of IWW leadership foreshadowed this postwar repression.[18]

Part of employers' efforts to increase their power focused upon demonizing German immigrants and German Americans. As the leader of the Central Powers during World War I, Germany was depicted as an evil empire in the United States. Due to their national heritage, German Americans also were painted as the enemy and suffered tremendous harassment, beatings, and, in at least one case, a lynching. As historian Robert Murray, author of *Red Scare,* writes, "Indeed, anyone who spoke with an accent or carried a foreign name, German or otherwise, remained particularly suspect as American superpatriots continued to see spies lurking behind every bush and tree." Often, public officials and employers collaborated with newly created private organizations such as the National Security League, American Legion, American Defense Society, and American Protective League; the Protective League's Philadelphia chapter "examined" 18,275 people in 1918 alone. In the 1910s Philadelphia had tens of thousands of German-speaking residents, immigrants, and longtime citizens. Yet despite efforts to prove their loyalty, including buying large amounts of Liberty Bonds, anti-German sentiment in Philadelphia ran strong. The Philadelphia School Board banned teaching German in its schools, and the Philadelphia Orchestra stopped playing German music.[19]

There were few, if any, Germans or German Americans working as longshoremen in Philadelphia, but *all* immigrants or native-born Americans with immigrant parents were lumped together as "foreign" and in need of being (Anglo-)Americanized. The war had unleashed hostile, pent-up feelings of many native-born whites to immigrants and so-called white ethnics. Under the pretense of wartime emergency, a huge Americanization campaign was undertaken. However, the end of the war did not end nativism. Writing about the vibrant French Canadian population that was fiercely committed to preserving its cultural identity in Woonsocket, Rhode Island, Gary Gerstle vividly describes "the inclination of the American government, at both the national and state levels, to use its power to shape the political and cultural identities of its citizens" even after the war. Numerous examples on the Philadelphia waterfront exist but two, both taken from Local 8's 1920 strike, suffice. In one instance, the (New York) *Journal of Commerce and Commercial Bulletin* contrasted the strikes with "the broadminded and patriotic" marine workers who accepted the current wage scale and did not strike. The chair of USSB went further, declaring, "I believe that the merchant marine should not only be wholly owned by Americans but that its personnel should be entirely American." In 1920 more than a third of Philadelphia's dockworkers were not U.S. born, so their loyalties were questioned.[20]

Business interests allied with nativists and conservatives in seeking to equate membership in a labor union with being pro-German. Philip Jenkins points out: "The ultimate nightmare was that the Socialists and radicals would gain strength by focusing what was felt to be endemic opposition to military conscription, perhaps in alliance with German agents." These fears already had contributed to the mass arrests and trial of the IWW. Not surprisingly, many employers believed they could act patriotically and solve their labor troubles simultaneously by "Americanizing" their workforce. Milton D. Gehris, vice president of the John B. Stetson Company in Philadelphia, lauded Americanization: "They are imbibing American ideas and ideals and seem to sense the importance of doing good work and showing their loyalty to the company as they had not thought of doing before they had these school advantages. They are easier to deal with when questions of work and policy are to be considered." Elisha Lee, a vice president of the Pennsylvania Railroad seconded Gehris: "The foreign-speaking agitator and trouble maker, on the other hand, flourished and worked with an almost free hand. As a result, we were repeatedly confronted with labor troubles and evidences of hostile feeling as to the causes of which we could gather only the vaguest notions." Hence, making workers "Americans," defined here as speaking English, allegedly would eliminate labor unrest.[21]

Another aspect of this broad employer campaign was anti-Bolshevism. Robert Murray demonstrates that by 1919 "the implantation of the Bolshevik in the American as the epitome of all that was evil" had taken place. One Reading, Pennsylvania, Socialist observed, "The IWW and Bolshevism have replaced the Yellow Peril and Prussianism as the great menace." On this point, many diverse groups in American society, including the AFL, could agree. The federal government took the lead, with the avid support of employer and business associations, by arresting thousands of IWWs, Socialists, and others and deporting thousands more "radical" immigrants. In April 1919 the Philadelphia Chamber of Commerce praised the U.S. Attorney General's actions and urged him to continue.[22]

The third aspect of this hysteria, inextricably linked to the other two, was a fervent antilabor stance captured in the motto "Open Shop." In the words of historian Allen Wakstein, the open shop meant "militantly antiunion" and total employer control of the workplace, in opposition to the era's popular if ambiguous prolabor mantra: "Industrial Democracy." Proponents of the open shop, including the Chamber of Commerce, claimed that organized labor had been captured by a small cadre of radicals that fomented industrial discord, unfairly demanded a "closed" (union) shop, and generally acted in an un-American manner. The Industrial Committee of the Philadelphia Chamber of Commerce contended that the closed shop caused a significant decrease in productivity. Cramp's, Philadelphia's largest shipyard, led the city's open-shop movement, which accelerated after the war.[23]

These three themes—anti-German/immigrant hysteria, anti-Bolshevism, and the open shop—all could be placed under the rubric of "Americanism." With the active support of the Republican machine in Philadelphia, the Chamber of Commerce led the city's business community in advocating Americanism, which they contrasted with "those who foment industrial disorder." Included in the laundry list of those opposed to the "American Plan" were Wobblies, radicals, foreigners, those who preached un-American ideals, syndicalists, socialists, anarchists, and Bolsheviks. The national Chamber of Commerce, collaborating with many other public and private groups and individuals, succeeded in equating patriotism with the open shop and socialism with being un-American. These anti-immigrant, antiunion, antileftist sentiments found a champion in U.S. Attorney General A. Mitchell Palmer. In late 1919 the Philadelphia Chamber's Board of Directors wrote Palmer, nicknamed the "Fighting Quaker," endorsing his actions and "demanding that the Government continue its warfare against radicals . . . who preach and practice doctrines false to American ideals." Robert Murray concludes, "Never before had the nation been so overwhelmed with fear."[24]

Wielding these rhetorical weapons, Philadelphia shipping interests collaborated with the federal government to destroy Local 8. Continuing a practice begun during the war, the shipping companies, federal government, and ILA negotiated annual agreements regulating wages and hours for all North Atlantic and Gulf Coast ports. After the war, Philadelphia continued to be excluded from these discussions. For instance, in 1919 the New York Harbor Wage Adjustment Board maintained the wage scale from 1918 for coastwise longshoremen in every port save Philadelphia, which was ignored.[25]

Local 8 fought against these powerful forces. As far as the IWW was concerned, the Red Scare's opening shots were fired during the war, considering the 1917 raids that led to the imprisonment of one hundred IWW leaders. After the war the IWW's General Defense Committee (GDC) continued its efforts to free its leaders. E. F. Doree, one of the Wobblies convicted in Chicago and a GDC member, praised the members of Local 8 who voted to levy a $1.00 assessment upon themselves to aid the union's "Class War Prisoners." The editors of New Solidarity, the main IWW newspaper at the time, also praised Philadelphia longshoremen for "not [being] content with having job control . . . they have gone a step further" thereby demonstrating "the true Union spirit of Class Conscious-workers." The Philadelphia GDC met weekly to raise over $50,000 in bail money for imprisoned local leaders, as IWW headquarters laid the responsibility for raising money on the locals from which the prisoners came. Feige "Fanny" Nef, Walter's wife, played a prominent role in this effort, helping the local GDC raise enough money to secure the release of four of the six Philadelphians. The longshoremen and their families' ability to raise truly large amounts of money displayed their commitment to their imprisoned leaders.[26]

The repression of the IWW, though, continued. In the spring of 1918 Philadelphia's Chief of Police forbade the IWW from holding mass meetings to organize, instead permitting only business meetings. To overcome this latest hurdle, Genaro Pazos, leader of Philadelphia's seamen, held two or three business meetings every week, rather than bimonthly. On the federal level, the Commandant of the Fifth Naval District recommended "deportation in the case of [IWW] foreigners, induction into military service . . . in the case of citizens" as well as "the placing of informants in the ranks of the organization." The commandant also advocated "prosecution," as "the raid . . . has [had] an unquestionable moral effect upon the members in that a salutary fear of governmental intervention arises." Accordingly, the ONI continued investigating Pazos, and numerous informants and undercover agents engaged in surveillance of Local 8. Not surprisingly, historian Murray suggests that "by 1919, it was definitely unwise for a person to declare openly he was a Wobbly." Nevertheless, the longshoremen of Philadelphia continued to do so. Even on government piers, longshoremen still had to be fully paid-up members of Local 8 or they could not work.[27]

These activities in Philadelphia were part of the discussions at the national convention in May 1919, the first in three years. Charles Carter, a black longshoreman, and Robert V. Chestnut, a white one, represented Local 8, and Spaniard Pazos attended on behalf of Philadelphia's sailors. In one Bureau of Investigation report, an informant saw Carter give a "radical speech at the I.W.W. hall on Sunday, May 4th. It is reported that in his speech he referred to the President as a traitor and made other vicious remarks regarding the character of the President."[28]

Confirming longshoring's importance to the IWW and the international labor movement, the convention spent a lot of time discussing the marine transport industry. The GEB reported that "a move towards an international affiliation in this industry is on, and a Revolutionary International Marine Transport Workers Federation [non-Bolshevik] with over 100,000 members may be a fact in the near future." This vision harkened back to the 1890s, when English dockworkers, led by longtime IWW ally Tom Mann, first created an international maritime union, with a short-lived branch in Philadelphia. A letter from G. Malvido, secretary of the Organizing Committee of the Buenos Aires MTW, looked forward to "overthrowing our enemy, the vampires of capitalism." James Scott, secretary-treasurer of the MTW, claimed that the seventy-five thousand members of the Irish Transport Workers Union had expressed interest in the IWW. Pietro Nigra, an Italian MTW organizer based in Norfolk, released from Leavenworth just weeks before the convention, reported that seventy-five thousand Italians also desired to join the IWW. Pazos, who corresponded with sailors throughout the Atlantic, suggested that workers in Spain and Cuba were interested in the IWW, including the Barcelona-based syndicalist sailors' union, La Naval. Like American leftist unions, La Naval suffered greatly from repression and sought alliances.[29]

Other potential allies included A. Philip Randolph and Chandler Owen, the coeditors of the African American socialist monthly *The Messenger*. The magazine's twofold mission was to educate black workers of the need to join socialist labor unions and convince unions to expend greater effort in lining up blacks. Thus, the editors praised the IWW as it "fight[s] for the solidarity of labor without regard to national, religious or color line." Randolph and Owen continued: "Our fellow worker, Ben Fletcher, who was sentenced for twenty years along with Haywood, has read with much satisfaction and enjoyment *The Messenger* during the last few months, and many of the Radical and I.W.W. men in Leavenworth are subscribing for it. . . . It is hardly necessary to impress upon a convention of industrial workers the importance of propaganda among twelve million black fellow workers." The IWW claimed to know that signing up African American workers was vital, but only in Philadelphia was much effort expended, so Randolph and Owen's words fell, mostly, on deaf ears.[30]

The most pressing convention issue for Local 8 dealt with the centralization of all maritime workers into a single industrial union. In May 1919 IWW longshoremen, sailors, and others belonged to chartered groups on the Atlantic, Great Lakes, and Pacific and in Philadelphia. Many delegates favored uniting these groups into a single, national charter. According to the Bureau of Investigation's informant at the convention, Local 8 possessed "a large sum of money in their treasury, and it is the money that the rest of the I.W.W. are after. The delegates of Local 8 declare that they will not give in to the rest of the M.T.W. and that they will remain as they are today, i.e., to have control over their own affairs. This will cause a big fight at the convention and probably a split." No doubt, Local 8 was wealthier than most branches, as evidenced by its large contributions to the GDC. At its root, however, the main issue for Local 8—and for other branches, mostly from the Mountain and Pacific West—was resisting centralization in the IWW. The convention went on record in favor of marine transport consolidation as soon as possible and ordered the four MTW groups to call a convention.[31]

The MTW convention occurred a week later in Philadelphia. The meeting, chaired by Philadelphian J. Harrington, took place at the seamen's branch—not Local 8's hall. Secretary Dan Jones represented Local 8. The Bureau of Investigation agent in charge of all surveillance on the IWW in Philadelphia, Joseph McDevitt, believed that the purpose of the meeting was to convince Local 8 to affiliate with the new industrial union of marine transport workers. However, consolidation did not occur, for the Philadelphia dockers remained steadfast in their desire to retain local control of decisions and finances. This issue proved to be one of the most important reasons for Local 8's future problems with the national IWW.[32]

After the conventions, the longshoremen redoubled their efforts to organize the city's other waterfront workers. To start, Business Agent Baker claimed that he had lined up approximately seventy checkers, who kept tally of cargoes loaded and unloaded, and hoped to organize a checkers' branch. The union targeted several hundred longshoremen who worked on piers traditionally nonunion; by September the local had signed up over fifty of these and by November had extended their control to include, once again, the sugar piers. The leadership planned to reorganize the boatmen and lightermen, who previously belonged to Local 8. Further, the local continued to raise money for their imprisoned leaders. Supporters sold $5 "liberty bonds" and sent this money to national headquarters to help Fletcher, Rey, and Walsh get released on bond. The local also sent money directly to their imprisoned comrades in Leavenworth and their families in Philadelphia. Although the local remained active, they were well aware of the hostility they still faced; therefore, rather than holding their traditional one-day anniversary strike around May 15, the men held a more modest picnic.[33]

That summer MTW members held their annual elections and voted on national referendums, most importantly on consolidation. The MTW leadership, especially MTW 100 Secretary-Treasurer James Scott, heartily supported this initiative. The subject interested many outside groups, as well, including the federal government, employers, and private investigators. E. R. Carrington, vice president of the Thiel Detective Service, wrote a federal agent that "IWW Branch #100 (Marine Transport Workers of Philadelphia) is reported to have more 'Reds' among its members than all the rest of the IWW organization. They do not pay much attention to advice from Chicago headquarters and recently when a district officer was sent to Philadelphia and objected to their 'Direct action' ideas, they threw him down a flight of stairs and sent him to the hospital." Perhaps surprisingly, given Local 8's opposition, the referendum carried. The new union would be called (temporarily) Marine Transport Workers Industrial Union (MTWIU) 8. Branch 1 (i.e., Local 8) would pay 25 cents per capita to the industrial union headquarters, in New York City, in accordance with the outcome of another referendum. All of these measures clearly were designed to limit the power of Local 8. Crucially, the vote tallies were quite small, less than three hundred, though Local 8 had more than four thousand members. Thus, it appears that Local 8 boycotted the referendum, for if its members had voted not only would the numbers have been much higher, the results most definitely would have been different. These tensions soon exploded into the Philadelphia Controversy.[34]

In contrast, Philadelphia longshoremen participated in the MTWIU 8 referendums held in January 1920. Instead of boycotting the process, the Philadelphians dominated the vote, resulting in amendments to MTW bylaws: branches and districts elect representatives to MTW and national IWW conventions based upon membership, and MTW officer wages be set at the same rate received by workers in the industry. James Scott and Elmer Kennard, the New York–based MTW secretary-treasurer and general organizer, commended, perhaps sarcastically, "the Philadelphia district [which] has set a good example" and reminded members that "all members should vote as well as in Philadelphia." That the Philadelphians voted implied that they accepted consolidation, at least temporarily.[35]

In the meantime, the imprisoned members of Local 8 remained committed to Wobbly ideals. Jailed Wobblies often corresponded with activists, organizers, and unionists. Fletcher kept in touch with many blacks with socialist leanings, including Wobbly R. T. Sims, who organized black janitors in Chicago, as well as Randolph and Owen. Fletcher exchanged letters with Joseph J. Jones and William Monroe Trotter, two African American activists whom Fletcher had met while organizing in Boston. Trotter, the prominent editor of the black newspaper the *Boston Guardian*, took a hard line on demanding full equality for African Americans. In one letter to Jones, Fletcher contended: "I hold that the I.W.W. is all sufficient to get the 'goods.'" As evidence of Fletcher's continuing influence on the IWW, especially on race matters, Bill Haywood accepted Fletcher's advice and instructed Charles Carter, a black leader in Local 8, to attend a meeting of the National Brotherhood of Workers of America. The Brotherhood's founder, the aforementioned Wobbly and former Socialist Labor Party member Sims, wished to establish a black version of the United Hebrew Trades. In fact, three black longshoremen from Local 8 attended that convention, which refused seats to AFL delegates.[36]

Other jailed Philadelphians continued to demonstrate their commitment to the cause, as well. For instance, in August 1919, Nef and Simon Knebel, out on bail, attended an IWW picnic to raise money for "class war prisoners," despite a heavy police presence with orders to arrest anyone causing "problems." Knebel, Pazos, and a good number of Germans and Italians listened to Nef talk about his experiences in Leavenworth. In September Doree was released on bail. He quickly embarked on a month-long fundraising lecture tour from Toledo to Boston. On September 25 Doree spent time with his wife and son in Philadelphia before giving a talk on the Chicago trial and life in Leavenworth.[37]

Both to educate its members and organize more workers, the IWW held open forums every Sunday afternoon at a place called the People's House in South Philadelphia. At these meetings, current events, economics, industrial unionism, revolutionary movements, and other issues were discussed. On January 5, 1920, Jack Walsh, out on bail, spoke. While there is no report of what Walsh spoke about, no doubt he discussed the Red Scare. On January 2 the Department of Justice had raided "virtually every headquarters of known radicals in this city," according to the

Public Ledger. The following week, at Garrick Hall, the IWW scheduled Doree, Nef, and Walsh, as well as *Messenger* coeditor Randolph, followed by a dance.[38]

When Ben Fletcher was released on bail during an appeal, the *New Solidarity* proclaimed that "Ben Fletcher Is Out." The efforts to raise the money necessary to get Fletcher released on bond as well as to win a pardon had received nationwide attention, becoming a minor cause célèbre among African American radicals, thanks to the campaign in *The Messenger*. The magazine ran numerous articles on the case, maintaining that "Ben Fletcher is in Leavenworth for principle—a principle which when adopted, will put all the Negro leaders out of their parasitical jobs. That principle is that to the workers belong the world." Dozens wrote letters to Presidents Wilson and Harding on Fletcher's behalf. Peter Curtin, a foreman for the stevedore firm Murphy, Cook, "saw him [Fletcher] at the meetings of the longshoremen. He always counseled the men to be tolerant and to work for their ends by peaceful means." Of course, thousands of Local 8 members petitioned the president to release Fletcher, too.[39]

Immediately upon his release, Fletcher went on a speaking tour. One Wobbly, Nick Digaetano, an immigrant from Palermo who worked for Chrysler in Detroit, remembered seeing Fletcher: "The hall was at capacity, perhaps five hundred. I don't remember seeing any Negroes in the audience, perhaps there were some. Ben Fletcher was a good speaker." Afterward, Fletcher took up residence with his father and wife in the Grays Ferry section of Philadelphia, near the Schuylkill River. Fletcher remained committed to the IWW, writing in one letter that "the first and most important duty is for all of us to prepare ourselves for the final chapter in the life of Capitalism." He also joined in the IWW's weekly forums, giving a lecture on April 25 entitled "The Price of Progress," something he knew quite well. Fletcher helped raise money to get other Wobblies out on bail and returned to Baltimore to organize longshoremen there.[40]

The members of Local 8 entered the postwar era in a state of flux. Their leaders had been arrested, tried, convicted, and imprisoned. As the war in Europe ended, the civil war in the Soviet Union heated up, and a strike wave of unprecedented proportions rocked the United States. In the midst of and partially in response to these domestic and international events, American employers undertook a nationwide offensive to curtail worker power. Concurrently, federal authorities continued to repress radical unionists and immigrants in the Red Scare. This business-government alliance succeeded in equating the open shop with Americanization: belonging to the IWW meant betraying the United States. As a result, the entire IWW was badly, perhaps irrevocably, damaged. Within this whirlwind, the members of Local 8 maintained their solidarity, found new leaders within their own ranks, and focused on preserving their wartime gains. Given the severe repression of the Red Scare, Local 8's achievements are impressive. In the summer of 1920, the waterfront workers of Philadelphia were poised to join the tidal wave of postwar worker militancy. However, as this strike revealed, Philadelphia's longshoremen had been hurt by the assaults from without and conflicts from within. IWW historian Fred Thompson later wrote of this moment, "I hope this [strike] gets dug into by someone probing whether by 1920 Philadelphia longshoremen were more vulnerable than in earlier years." The next chapter will do just that.[41]

6   Riding the Wave of Postwar
Militancy: The 1920 Strike

The strike launched on May 26, 1920, was the largest the port
of Philadelphia ever had seen, with close to nine thousand workers out at
its peak. When the longshoremen put down their cargo hooks, more than
150 ships immediately were idled in the Delaware River, and another 100
soon were affected. This conflagration belonged to an enormous wave
of postwar labor conflict, in which truly mammoth strikes occurred in
many industries and were met by well-coordinated, powerful employer
counteroffensives. In contrast to many others, Local 8's strike was not
defensive in nature, though as with most of the others it failed to extend
the union's power or raise wages. Rather, after six long weeks Local 8
desperately called off its strike ("moving the strike to the job") to avoid
losing its precious hold on the waterfront's workers. The combination
of the imprisonment of Local 8's first-tier leaders, strenuous employer
offensive, high cost of living (which helped cause the strike and made
it hard to sustain), and the presence of thousands of Southern black migrants—as both strikebreakers and Local 8 members—explains why the
1920 strike was doomed.

The agenda of Philadelphia's dockers was similar to that of many
other workers, combining practical and political demands. The strikers
wanted higher wages to keep pace with the era's staggering inflation
and an eight-hour workday. Along with these "pork chop" issues, Philadelphia's longshoremen were flexing the muscles that they had built
during the war, that is, they deserved a greater share of the wealth and

power created by their labor. How much the city's black longshoremen were influenced by the race-based radicalism of the New Negro or Marcus Garvey's black nationalism is unclear. As did others, Philadelphia's black community experienced tremendous change due to the influx of many thousands of Southern blacks. Longshoremen of African descent in places as far ranging as New York City, New Orleans, and Port-of-Spain, Trinidad, became emboldened in this era, and Philadelphia's would have been, too, especially given the presence of the IWW.[1]

Similarly, the strike provided Philadelphia employers with another chance to increase their power. The precedent was set less than a week after the war ended, when Philadelphia's Brill streetcar workers struck to preserve their wartime gains. The company replaced all of the strikers and continued to lay off "undesirable" (i.e., union) workers. At the end of 1919 the Philadelphia Chamber of Commerce declared itself "against radical control of organized labor unions and in favor of the 'open shop.'" Not coincidentally, on April 27, 1920, the local chamber's Industrial Committee "met to discuss the growing menace of union labor." Aiding employers in the strike were the city and federal governments, most notably the USSB and the Department of Justice's Bureau of Investigation. As with their opponents, the language, tactics, and goals of Philadelphia shippers paralleled national trends, with the employers' sentiments being captured under the mantra of the open shop.[2]

Strike discussions, largely focused on issues of wages and hours, began on May 18. Deep-sea longshoremen received anywhere from eighty to ninety-five cents per hour depending on the cargo, plus time and a half for any shift over eight hours, as well as for all work performed on Saturday afternoons, Sundays, and holidays. The high cost of living, though, drove the longshoremen to seek a raise. As David Montgomery writes, "The continuing inflation of 1919–20 kept wage demands constantly in the forefront of workers' struggles" across the nation. Local 8 wanted a twenty-cent-per-hour wage increase for all port workers, "on account of the continued increase in the cost of living." Crucially, the IWW almost never distributed strike funds; moreover, rising inflation made it much harder to remain on strike for a lengthy duration. Thus, if the strike did not end quickly, strikers and their families would suffer dramatically and be that much more dependent on community support. The workers also wanted to reduce the workweek. A longshoreman's standard week was fifty hours; the workers wanted to drop the basic workweek to forty-four hours—eight hours a day Monday through Friday with a half-day on Saturday morning. Many industries had adopted an eight-hour day during the war, though the marine transport industry had not.[3]

Local 8 presented its demands on May 20, and the companies emphatically refused. Walter F. Hagar, a prominent grain trader and acting chair of the port employers' General Committee, called a meeting of the forty employing stevedores, steamship companies, other shipping interests, and the USSB on May 24, to discuss the issues. Tellingly, this committee responded "to the longshoremen of the port of Philadelphia," rather than to Local 8. Employers announced that they had decided unanimously to deny the requests, claiming an agreement already existed, not due to expire until September 30. The committee was referring to the annual agreement made between the major Atlantic shipping interests and the ILA. Of course, the IWW did not participate in these negotiations, but it did maintain oral agreements that often paralleled contracts in other North Atlantic ports. The employers contended that the cost of living had not increased since late 1919 and, if anything, had decreased; thus, they suggested that their workers work harder and buy more prudently.[4]

The shipping interests concluded their reply with their own complaints, blaming the leaders of Local 8 for riverfront problems. Employers claimed that the port "has suffered seriously during the past several weeks by a reason of a shortage of labor. This situation we feel is due in large part to the excessive initiation fee which is being charged by the Marine Transport Workers which we understand has been increased [recently] to $25.00" (to be examined more fully in chapter 7). Employers argued that this new initiation fee "is a great handicap to the development of the business of the port." Rather than increase wages and initiation fees, the shippers believed the longshoremen could make plenty of money "by working ten hours six days a week, or by working eight hours six days a week . . . without taking into consideration the extra allowance for night, Sunday and holiday work or the extra allowance in wages for loading grain, oil, etc." The employers concluded that "we cannot feel that the action which has been taken is approved by a majority of the men."[5]

The shippers' reply speaks to a number of interlocking issues. First, it makes clear that Local 8 still controlled the deep-sea longshore labor force and that the employers reluctantly acknowledged it. The union maintained influence over an area of the industry, hiring, that management viewed as its exclusive domain. Second, it shows that the port, which had boomed since 1916, still was doing quite well—so much so that more longshoremen were needed. Third, it demonstrates that the union was confident of its power—attempting simultaneously to control the labor surplus that traditionally gave employers an upper hand *and* to increase their own wages during an inflationary period. In this broadside, the shippers also revealed how they would attempt to break the strike: by splitting the leadership from the rank and file and blaming the radical IWW for creating problems in a supposedly agreeable situation.

In reply, the longshoremen chose to strike, choosing their moment well. Local 8 sent a committee back with an ultimatum that failure to raise wages would result in a strike. When the employers held firm, the longshoremen voted unanimously to strike, and E. F. Doree confidently reported that "all are enthusiastic," since the port was in the midst of another record-breaking year, as the value of shipping reached almost three-quarters of a billion dollars in 1920. On May 26 George F. Sproule, director of the city's Department of Wharves, Docks, and Ferries, announced that there were more ships in the port than ever before. Twelve schooners and 141 steamships anchored on the Delaware. Although much of the nation's economy was mired in a deep, if brief, recession, the port of Philadelphia still prospered, no doubt aided by the congestion of New York harbor, particularly after its longshoremen struck weeks earlier. In fact, fifty thousand harbor and shipyard workers were on strike nationwide in May. Philadelphia's government and shipping interests worked furiously to take advantage of these stoppages, especially the one in New York. The Board of Trade confirmed the port's remarkable growth by noting that fifty-nine shipping companies were operating in Philadelphia, compared to twenty-two in 1919. The *Public Ledger* reported that "exporters are confident that last year's [ships] total will be exceeded by 50 per cent." These hopes were buoyed by Sproule's claim of 117 more steamships and 6 schooners en route to Philadelphia. Thus, the strike immediately affected the loading and unloading of 276 ships.[6]

On May 27 the nearly four thousand deep-sea longshoremen of Local 8 established huge picket lines and promptly shut down the port. By the day's end Local 8 had proven that not only could it pull its own men off the docks but also that many unorganized workers followed the union's lead, further induced by the union waiving the initiation fee during the strike. All nonunion docks, including those of the Spreckles' Sugar Refinery, American Line, and Southern Line, were closed. Moreover, one thousand workers applied for membership in Local 8. That evening many coastwise longshoremen also threatened to walk off the job, so pickets were dispatched to convince them to join the strike and union.[7]

The city's leading port advocate, George Sproule, attempted to settle the strike. The two parties met for several hours with no compromise reached. Sproule, who left that same night for his summer home in Ocean City, New Jersey, lamented, "Never in the history of Philadelphia has the port enjoyed such prosperity as it had up until the strike was called yesterday," for even after just one day on strike, some ships were diverted to other ports.[8]

Local 8 received crucial support from some unexpected places. First, a delegate arrived from the AFL Marine Firemen's union, who announced his union's intention not to produce steam on any ship employing scab longshoremen. One of the strike leaders, Jack Walsh—out on bail from Leavenworth and despite enormous personal risk—reported that when the firemen's secretary spoke at the longshoremen's hall "cheers lift[ed] the room two inches. No damage done." The firemen, a longtime radical union in the somewhat conservative ISU, proved to be Local 8's most strident supporters. That same evening "came the great surprise." John Gannon, a ship delegate of the British freighter *Haverford*, entered the hall followed by thirty other members of the crew, all of whom belonged to the radical Shop Stewards Movement sweeping England. Gannon proudly declared that, in the name of international solidarity, they would not handle scab cargo. Walsh wrote, "Those British boys sure got a fine ovation." Finally, when stevedores held a meeting with their foremen, they announced their allegiance to the union; the foremen refused to work with strikebreakers throughout the strike.[9]

Within three days the strike completely shut down the port. Employers claimed that 147 steamships and 10 schooners were stuck at their berths, with 120 more scheduled to arrive in Philadelphia. The Philadelphia office of the USSB sent frequent strike reports to other ports and encouraged diverting ships. Local 8's ranks had swelled to over seven thousand, including many from coastwise piers. The strikers' ability to keep the port closed depended greatly on the tremendous effort of their ever-growing local, the solidarity of workers belonging to other unions, and the militancy of unorganized workers. The Wobblies maintained large picket lines and managed to convince almost all of the replacement workers to stop working without resorting to violence. After ten days on strike, no one had been arrested, a truly remarkable feat, given the bloody history of relations between Local 8 and police.[10]

Vitally, throughout the strike waterfront neighborhoods strongly supported the strikers in numerous battles with the police who were guarding strikebreakers, as evidenced by the thousands who joined in the melees. As Ben Fletcher recalled, "The I.W.W. button was a passport every where's hereabout. The town was electrified. If you were operating a Restaurant, Saloon Club, or other whatnot, where Longshoremen and Marine Transport Workers and their allies frequented, you were outspoken in your support of the I.W.W." Local businesses were dependent on their working-class neighbors for their livelihood and possessed many ties (ethnic, familial, racial, and religious) to the strikers; without local businesses extending credit, the strike could not have lasted. Of course, neither the strikers nor their merchants could hold out for long.[11]

Events at the Spreckles Sugar Refinery, long a contested space on the waterfront, demonstrated the depth of the conflict. Fourteen of the stranded ships held unrefined sugar that threatened to spoil if not unloaded soon. Thus, management sought to unload one ship's sugar with replacements. The ship's firemen promptly turned off the steam. Then management responded by bringing in steam from a powerhouse on shore. Union cooks and stewards aboard the ship then refused to serve food to the strikebreakers. Later that afternoon, Spreckles stopped work and sent the replacements home. Normally, Wobbly longshoremen worked the sugar docks and loaded eight sacks per draft; however, the strikebreakers sent anywhere from one to seven sacks out of the hold, making proper accounting impossible. Management decided that the extreme inefficiency of the replacements was prohibitive. Without any sugar, thousands of refinery workers might be laid off temporarily.[12]

Signs of some employers feeling the pressure of the strike were evident within a week. One newspaper reported that "many millions of dollars have been lost to the port" and feared that "all the gains the port has made in the last six months as America's second largest shipping center will be wiped out within a week or so unless the strike is settled at once according to the shipping owners." Some employers transferred clerks and other employees to the docks, while another firm sent a representative to the longshoremen's hall willing "to pay any price" to have four thousand cases of lemons unloaded. The membership voted to refuse all requests to unload any individual vessel until the strikers had achieved their demands from all employers.[13]

The strike's initial success caused steamship and stevedore interests to take a new tact, sending letters to the homes of all known strikers. In this second official communication, employers again addressed themselves "to the longshoremen of the port of Philadelphia" rather than to Local 8. The letter stated that "you [the longshoremen] are at present being kept away from your work . . . due largely to outside influences and that the majority are not in sympathy with this strike." Of course, the IWW had been the official representative of the deep-sea longshoremen for seven years, the strike had been voted for by Local 8 members, and it was run exclusively by "homegrown" leaders. Even John Keats, a USSB detective who worked closely with shipping companies, reported that "nothing has developed that would indicate foreign influence backing," while Director Cortelyou of the city's Department of Public Safety had "no information that would lead to believe that this is other than local strikes [sic]." The shipping interests concluded their letter by reiterating their determination not to give in to the demands and threatened to divert all ships.[14]

Although Local 8 responded to the employers' letter in its own newspaper, the members took the unusual measure of sending a letter to the stevedore of Murphy, Cook & Company. Murphy, Cook was the largest firm in the port and, like most others, employed Wobblies exclusively. Apparently, Mr. Murphy was held in high esteem by his "workers white and black," hence the longshoremen were disappointed that Murphy had not agreed with the strikers' "reasonable" demands, given the high cost of living and the fact that Murphy still would earn a profit even at the higher wage rates. If the strike failed, the longshoremen vowed to boycott Murphy's firm, which would prove devastating.[15]

The federal government, a major player, actively supported the employers throughout the strike. Created in 1916, the USSB had significant powers over maritime commerce, including labor relations. A week into the strike USSB Director of Operations Foley sent a telegram to all district agents, notifying them to refuse wage increases on the many vessels owned by the USSB but operated by private firms. Foley concluded that "the mater [sic] is of utmose [sic] importance." The board's Department of Investigation also coordinated its efforts with a host of federal and local agencies as well as shipping interests. By June 10 Captain Joseph E. Gately, the head of the USSB in Philadelphia, had become frustrated by the strike and, typically, blamed the leadership of that "outlaw affair," the IWW. Gately claimed that if the strike was not settled soon, he would either declare the port an open shop or recognize the ILA; the USSB maintained an equally antiunion stance during a longshore strike the same year in New Orleans. The ongoing support that the USSB gave to employers greatly strengthened them and later provided an opening for Local 8's rival, the ILA.[16]

As the strike dragged on, tensions among the strikers rose and fighting broke out. On the morning of June 7 mounted police broke up a demonstration of picketers at the Merchant & Miners' Pine Street Pier. Later that same morning, three hundred African American strikers attacked replacement workers unloading a boat at the Chestnut Street pier. The police believed that these black Wobblies also formed the core of the thousand "colored men" who attempted to prevent the *Osakis's* cargo of lemons from being unloaded at the Vine Street pier. A "flying mounted squad of fifty [police] dashed down Market Street, riding ten abreast at a gallop." Mayhem ensued when the mounties charged, armed with heavy riot sticks and revolvers. The police ran down picketers and arrested eleven. Subsequently, the police forbade anyone from congregating along Delaware Avenue and banned all pickets. With police assistance, employers secured more replacement workers.[17]

That week's waterfront violence escalated when an African American strikebreaker shot a Polish striker dead. When three black strikebreakers encountered pickets, a heated argument ensued, escalating when Louis Townsend, one of the strikebreakers, fired his revolver at the strikers. Townsend proceeded to run away, shooting randomly. He wounded two Polish boys, brothers, seated on the front steps of their home. Further along, Townsend shot another Pole as he exited a barbershop. Seeing Townsend running with a gun in his hand, Stanley Pavzlack, a striking Wobbly who lived just a few blocks away, attempted to get his family to safety. Instead, Pavzlack took a bullet in his chest and died instantly. Townsend was chased down, captured by locals at South Street, and turned over to the police. Pavzlack was buried at the union's expense, with hundreds of Wobblies in attendance. No accounts of this incident make race an issue, and the identities of most strikebreakers are nonexistent; some, but not all, were African American, while others were white college students on summer break. However, if white strikers transferred their anger of black replacements to all black people, then the strike would fail and Local 8's existence would be in jeopardy. Similarly, if black trust of fellow white strikers diminished, the strike and union also would collapse. Interracial unionism required constant vigilance, in Philadelphia and elsewhere.[18]

Given Local 8's composition, it is not surprising that employers tried to divide the strikers along ethnic and racial lines. On June 9 several stevedores met with Polish strikers and promised to employ Poles exclusively if they returned to work. The Poles refused. Then, African Americans, the largest group of longshoremen in Philadelphia, were approached, told that they had always been the best workers, and promised that only black workers would be employed. African Americans knew this familiar employer tactic. Not one black striker returned to work. Finally, Italian workers (whose numbers on Philadelphia's docks were tiny) were approached—and even offered $1.20 per hour—to break the strike, but, again, the employers were denied. Local 8 reprinted a circular that was found along the waterfront that encouraged the formation of an "Independent Union of Colored workers," another common employer strategy. This document asserted that white men received all of the easy jobs and were favored in Local 8. The union's own bulletin urged longshoremen to "Read this circular carefully. DON'T BE FOOLED. . . . If we ever permit ourselves to become divided on either race or nationality question we are bound to defeat."[19]

Despite employer and governmental efforts, the strike still went well for the workers, though victory would be harder to achieve the longer they were out. In a letter to Manuel Rey (still in Leavenworth), Ben Fletcher, out on bail and helping with the strike, claimed that after three weeks Local 8 boasted eighty-five hundred members. Fletcher also reported on the ongoing support received by Local 8 from other unions. Following the lead of the firemen, organized steam engineers refused to work with scabs. Moreover, local railroad and machinist unions pledged support. Fletcher told Rey that the Delaware remained full of ships from Port Richmond to Marcus Hook, with many more being diverted. Fletcher soon traveled to Baltimore, where he successfully convinced sailors on four ships to strike in sympathy. Still, the employers held firm—committed to dividing the union's leadership and rank and file and confident in the knowledge that the bosses had far deeper pockets than the workers so could hold out longer.[20]

Three weeks into the strike, stevedore Joseph Mooney invited a group of strikers to a meeting. The workers elected a committee of fifteen men, with representatives from the various dock trades. Mooney's committee, however, insisted on dealing with deep-sea longshoremen only. The strike committee, true to its industrial union ideology, refused to be split along craft lines, so the meeting abruptly ended. Subsequent meetings proved equally fruitless. The longshoremen remained committed to getting a wage increase, citing inflation data from the U.S. Bureau of Labor Statistics as proof of their urgent need. Even the probusiness New York *Journal of Commerce and Commercial Bulletin* reported that the cost of living still was rising in the summer of 1920; for instance, food—which made up almost 40% of a working-class family's budget—had increased 15% in Philadelphia over the last year. Having gone three weeks without a paycheck and suffering from inflation, many strikers could not afford to stay out much longer, and both workers and employers understood this pressure.[21]

The bosses' unyielding stance, rising number of replacements, and increasing desperation of the strikers sparked renewed violence. After three weeks several hundred strikebreakers, perhaps more than five hundred, worked the port, so the union renewed its efforts to impede them. Hundreds of strikers and sympathizers regularly hurled bricks and milk bottles at replacements and police, who responded with revolvers. A young girl, Rose Skopes, possibly a strike sympathizer, was shot during one fight. Goldie Stein, a Russian immigrant and innocent bystander, was killed in another. Dozens of strikers and strikebreakers were wounded. The union dispatched members to employment agencies to inform potential replacements of the strike, as some claimed ignorance when accepting the jobs; if men were new to the city, say African Americans arriving from the deep South, this claim is plausible.[22]

The USSB continued its efforts to break the strike and noted weakening in the strikers' ranks along racial lines and due to inflation. Federal Agent Keats tried to talk with "the most intelligent of the negroes," including strike leader Charles Carter, to no avail. Some Wobbly sailors worried that Walter Nef was not performing his job as forcefully as he could for fear of having his parole revoked. Most importantly, Keats talked to several black longshoremen whose determination was wavering, primarily due to the high cost of living. These men complained that this strike was different from previous ones (indicating they were veteran IWW longshoremen) because during past strikes they could live for a few cents a day. Of course, as with many strikes in the era, it was precisely this inflation that had caused the strike. Wobbly strikes were even more difficult, for rarely were strike funds distributed. Still, the agent noted that Nef was greatly pleased by the support of English sailors and dockers and promises from longshoremen as far away as Argentina that they would not touch hot cargo, either. Clearly, Manuel Rey and Genaro Pazos maintained many Atlantic connections, though what Local 8 really needed were allies closer to home.[23]

As it neared a month, the union became more desperate and changed its goal: forgoing a raise, Local 8 still demanded recognition as the union of all riverfront workers. At a June 24 meeting with employers, Polly Baker spoke of Local 8's stance on a fully unionized waterfront. One federal agent present astutely reported that Baker "did not seem to be as anxious about the money as they did to have [stevedore] Schell [and the few other holdout companies] recognize the Union." Employers were equally adamant about making the waterfront an open shop.[24]

Demonstrating their opposition to unions and the strike's impact on the city, the shipping interests received major support from the business community. The local Chamber of Commerce, in coordination with chambers nationwide and open-shop proponent Walter Drew of the National Erectors' Association, formed an Industrial Relations Committee, ostensibly "to protect the public from industrial warfare," but whose main purpose was promoting the open shop. It is no coincidence that the chamber's Executive Committee developed its labor strategy in May–June 1920, amid this strike. Support for the open shop was reaffirmed at the Manufacturers' Club, one of the "central" societies of the city's "manufacturing elite," according to Howell Harris, where leading businessmen "discuss matters of common interest."[25]

Maritime employers sponsored meetings with manufacturing, railroad, and other local leaders to pressure the city to break the strike. At one meeting more than two hundred participants unanimously agreed that the demands for a wage increase and closed shop be rejected. Notably, Alba Johnson, president of both the Baldwin Locomotive Works and the city's Chamber of Commerce, spoke of the need for further police on the waterfront to protect "American" workers. Harris refers to the Johnson-run Baldwin Works as "the strongest bastion of the Open Shop" in the city. Along with thirty other executives, Johnson met with the mayor and police chief. According to Anthony L. Geyelin, secretary of a "citizens' emergency committee" and chair of the Philadelphia Export Club, "We only wanted him [the mayor] to know the real seriousness of the longshoremen's strike which is now threatening results damaging not alone to the regular shipping interests but practically every other business of the city." Mayor Moore acknowledged "the grave conditions in this port" and pledged help, but refused to mediate or ask for state police. Over the next ten days, though, he dramatically increased city police on the docks.[26]

Declarations notwithstanding, the first dissension among employer ranks soon surfaced. At their daily meeting several employers complained that the strike had been mishandled. One stevedore, John Sheehan, believed that the strike could have been settled weeks ago, if only the shippers had asked the mayor to mediate. William J. Tracy, a state conciliator, and Captain Gately, USSB operations director in Philadelphia, agreed. Gately pointed out that numerous times the strike leaders had asked for a concession, no matter how small, to take back to the men. Gately noted that the coastwise longshoremen received fifty cents per hour, fifteen cents below the coastwise wage scale set during the war. Immediately after the federal government's wartime control ended, Philadelphia maritime employers promptly reduced wages to forty cents an hour. Worker discontent forced wages back to fifty cents. Since the strikers were anxious for a concession, Gately suggested coastwise wages be raised to sixty-five cents, which was not truly a concession (since coastwise longshoremen in all other North Atlantic ports received it). As many coastwise men recently had joined Local 8, this raise would be seen as an important gain, and the union was desperately looking for a way to snatch victory from the jaws of an increasingly likely defeat.[27]

In fact, the employers could not agree on much, except to refuse the longshoremen's demands. John Sheehan resigned from the subcommittee in disgust. Gately continued to wait on Darragh DeLancey of the National Industrial Commission in Washington, D.C., who had negotiated the North Atlantic agreement with the ILA. Stevedore Murphy remained concerned with only one issue—to "get the leaders." Although Murphy admitted to not knowing who the leaders were, he believed the federal government should prosecute them based upon the wartime Lever Act, for holding up food shipments to Europe.[28]

State mediator Tracy continued negotiating with the longshoremen. He believed that the leaders were of low intelligence, for he repeatedly told the strike committee that no raise would be forthcoming for the deep-sea longshoremen, who already received the eighty cents per hour that deep-sea longshoremen did in other North Atlantic ports. Tracy did, though, believe that the coastwise longshoremen were entitled to a return to sixty-five cents per hour and openly questioned why employers suddenly had reduced wages to forty cents (before returning them to fifty cents).[29]

The citizens' committee, really an organization of Philadelphia business interests, continued castigating the mayor. Along with the Chamber of Commerce, the self-proclaimed citizens' committee demanded that the governor deploy state police and that the local police better protect replacements by searching all picketers for guns and breaking up any assembly of strikers, the First and Second Amendments not withstanding. The USSB also was upset with how the police handled the strike, as the USSB was losing "many thousands of dollars each day the strike is prolonged," though the strikers were losing even more and were near their breaking point.[30]

The strike had cost the shippers $50 million, and the port was of major importance to the economic health of the city. For instance, the Philadelphia National Bank, with close to $200 million in assets, ran advertisements in the *Public Ledger* that testified, "Philadelphia—as a port is of vital interest at this time to manufacturers and merchants engaged in Foreign trade." The bank cited the continuing growth of the port as essential to the city, and, despite the strike, 1920 still was another record year. The strike also had major human costs: five people had been killed, over two hundred injured, and eighty arrested in more than twenty street battles. Still, the shippers incorrectly blamed "imported radicals" for the disturbances and the strike.[31]

Finally, on July 6, the longshoremen voted to give up. The break had come the day before. Thomas J. Grace, a stevedore who normally employed hundreds of longshoremen, managed to bring over half of the strikers, more than four thousand men, to the vicinity of their union hall and urged an end to the impasse. Speakers screamed out of the hall's second-floor windows to the crowd in the street, as men "clung to awnings, 'shinned' up trees and climbed the outside of the building to have a look." Quickly, the deep-sea longshoremen voted to return to work at the old rate of eighty cents per hour, $1 for Sundays and holidays, and $1.20 overtime, assuming the coastwise longshoremen received a raise to sixty-five cents per hour. Every striker was given a new work button for free, without paying monthly dues.[32]

Almost as soon as the strike ended, employers asserted their dominance. It soon became obvious that the only vessels on which coastwise longshoremen would earn sixty-five cents per hour would be the USSB's. The fervently antiunion Southern Steamship Company opposed raising wages, and every other coastwise operator followed its lead. Not surprisingly, the workers were upset, since they had been told that all coastwise shippers agreed to the increase. Union firemen, who had strongly supported the longshoremen, promised to walk out in sympathy if Local 8 resumed its strike. Captain Carey, port engineer of the USSB in Philadelphia, claimed that the firemen's action would be considered "outlaw" and threatened to bring in replacements from New York to keep fires running aboard ships. In another instance of employer firmness, when longshoremen returned to the Pennsylvania Sugar Refinery, they were told that their services were not needed—that the refinery had established a company union with people hired during the strike. Although these sugar docks were the only ones where replacement workers were not dismissed, the Wobblies were angry, having been assured that all strikers would get their jobs back. Local 8 was forced to accept the fact that certain piers remained open shop, indicating the limits of its powers—strongest on the deep-sea piers, much weaker elsewhere.[33]

Subsequently the USSB, much like private employers, resumed its push to decrease longshore wages. Three days after the strike, a USSB representative wrote to Admiral William Benson, Chair of the USSB, suggesting that the board decrease longshore wages in Philadelphia after October 1, when the National Adjustment Commission (a wartime creation) expired. Benson agreed, contending that wages had risen faster than the cost of living.[34]

With the strike over, the city's private and public interests resumed their plans for port expansion and the open shop. Mayor Moore boasted, "When the men return to work tomorrow, Philadelphia will witness the greatest activity that has been seen at the port in many years." Some businessmen even saw the strike as a blessing in disguise, as it forced a diverse mix of business groups and companies to unite. To assist the port's development, the City Council passed a motion to build more municipal piers and invest in new marine-transport technologies. Most Philadelphia shipping interests also concluded that they must push harder for the open shop if "Philadelphia [is to] know prosperity." After all, the *Philadelphia Chamber of Commerce News Bulletin* noted, "The long-shoremen's strike alone is estimated to have caused a loss of $50,000,000 in little more than a month." Thus, employers demanded the right to hire any worker, regardless of union affiliation, instead of being forced to deal with "walking delegates of the unions." The open-shop campaign also tried to make sympathy strikes illegal as "an attack upon innocent third parties and the public, and is indefensible and intolerable."[35]

Of course, the strike of Philadelphia dockworkers did not happen in a vacuum—it reflected and echoed the national postwar strike and lockout wave. As on the killing floors of Chicago's stockyards, Midwestern steel mills, and numerous other workplaces, U.S. workers were radicalized during World War I and pushed for both higher wages and greater control. For the most part, this wave, lasting from 1919 through the early 1920s, resulted in defeats for organized labor. Local 8's two significant postwar conflicts—the qualified defeat in the 1920 strike and crushing lockout in 1922—paralleled national trends, even as they challenge conventional thinking on the moribund state of the IWW after the 1917 raids.[36]

As for Local 8, the strike demonstrated simultaneously the power it had on the waterfront as well as the fragility of that hold. The more than four thousand deep-sea longshoremen who belonged to Local 8 were able to pull out more than four thousand others, mostly coastwise long-shoremen, and together they brought the port to a standstill for over five weeks. Local 8 withstood the pressure of its employers, who had the active support of the rival ILA, city government (the mayor, police, and Department of Wharves, Docks, and Ferries), the entire press of Phila-delphia, the state of Pennsylvania's Department of Labor and Industry, as well as the federal government's USSB and Bureau of Investigation. Nevertheless, the suddenness with which the strike ended and the fail-ure to achieve a single concession revealed that Local 8's power could be challenged successfully. The decision to call off the strike—just as the one to initiate it—preserved the power that the union retained but also acknowledged its limits.[37]

In the face of this opposition, Local 8 remained committed to its core principle of interracial, multiethnic solidarity. The racial situation during the strike turns the white stereotype of African American workers on its head. One of the reasons that white workers often denied black workers union membership was their alleged lack of commitment to unionism.

Obviously, the seven years of proud unionism on the part of thousands of black longshoremen disprove this notion. Yet it is undeniable that some African Americans refused to join unions because of the long history of racism in the labor movement, and Local 8 had to deal with hundreds of new members, predominantly Southern black migrants, who never had partaken in a strike. Similarly, in the 1919 Chicago stockyard strike black workers, new to the city and industrial work, proved essential in defeating the strike. In Philadelphia, however, black longshoremen (likely those with longer tenures on the docks) appeared more committed than their white fellow unionists. Both the local *Public Ledger* and the New York *Journal of Commerce* reported that the most militant strikers were "colored" and that it was the "white" members, likely East European immigrants, who wished to return to work. The newspaper also claimed that white strikers were intimidated by their black comrades. The press reports further indicate that black strikers took the lead in actively resisting black strikebreakers. Here is evidence of festering racial divisions among Local 8's membership that would grow in subsequent years. Also apparent is the militant "New Negro" whom many contemporaries saw rise after World War I. Moreover, hundreds of Local 8's black (and white) members were veterans of World War I and had been empowered by that experience. When employers tried splitting their workers along racial or ethnic lines, on June 9, the response was clear: none of the longshoremen would return to work unless all did. No doubt, the strike leadership, divided among African Americans, Irish Americans, and immigrants from Europe and the West Indies, countered employer efforts.[38]

Local 8 demonstrated its belief in industrial unionism through its commitment to the coastwise longshoremen. Under the aegis of the U.S. Railroad Administration, employers paid coastwise men sixty-five cents an hour. Following the termination of the Railroad Administration's authority, though, coastwise shippers in Philadelphia immediately dropped their unorganized longshoremen's wages to forty cents an hour. After the deep-sea longshoremen struck and pulled out the coastwise workers within a day, employers raised rates back to fifty cents an hour. Without the union it is unlikely that wages of fifty cents per hour would have resumed. Only if the four thousand or so coastwise longshoremen firmly believed in the ability of Local 8 to deliver would a heretofore unorganized body of workers remain on strike for five weeks. Furthermore, deep-sea longshoremen eventually dropped their own wage demands in order to concentrate on unionizing and raising coastal rates. The deep-sea longshoremen's strong commitment to industrial unionism was at least partially to protect themselves. In an industry in which commodities could be loaded at a nonunion pier—or an entirely different port—workers understood the need to form One Big Union. One poststrike flyer urged unionists not to work with replacements: "NO WORK WITH SCABS [is] our slogan."[39]

The change in Local 8's leadership definitely was an important factor in the union's defeat, as they clearly miscalculated the employers' response. Although Doree, Fletcher, Nef, and Walsh were out on bail and helped out, they no longer were the main leaders. All four could have had their bails revoked at any time, be returned to the federal penitentiary, and resume their ten-to-twenty-year sentences. Rather, the blacks Carter, Jones, and Varlack along with the Lithuanian Baker took over the primary leadership roles. None of these men ever had led a dispute of this magnitude. It was a tactical error to strike for wage increases in the aftermath of the huge and largely unsuccessful wave of strikes nationwide in 1919 and when employers already had mounted a powerful antiunion offensive locally. Clearly, this new generation of leaders, and the rank, believed in their ability to achieve wage increases and extend their dominion to previously nonunion coastwise piers. They knew the port of Philadelphia was booming but incorrectly gambled that employers would grant concessions, an enormous mistake.

Still, the strike ultimately failed because the employers had become far better organized. For instance, in 1913 to deal with the newly organized longshoremen on strike the shipping and stevedore interests formed an ad hoc committee, which suffered from internal dissension. Eventually, one employer forged a compromise with the strikers, despite the opposition of fellow employers. By contrast, in 1920 the steamship and employing stevedore committee was highly organized. The employers established subcommittees and granted these smaller bodies the authority to deal with their issues. The labor subcommittee and the committee of the whole steadfastly opposed any compromise despite suffering enormous losses. At least part of the reason for their strength was that the companies involved in the port's economy were much larger, national and multinational, firms. Furness, Withy & Company, a London-based shipping line, could afford to wait out a long strike because it possessed interests in many ports. Likewise, a shipping line such as the International Mercantile Marine could temporarily redirect its vessels to another port. The firmness in 1920 of William Holmes, general manager of Furness, Withy and chair of the strike subcommittee, differed markedly from the flexibility displayed in 1913 by Fred Taylor, owner of a local, family-owned and -run grain-exporting firm in Philadelphia and broker of the 1913 settlement. Moreover, the shipping interests successfully mobilized support from other businessmen in Philadelphia, as well as from the city, state, and federal governments, because it was clear that the interests of the port coincided with and were crucial to the city's economy. Finally, the employers' commitment to defeating the strike was confirmed by their willingness to accept fifty million dollars in losses. The increasing centralization and size of capital cannot be stressed enough.[40]

Although the strike proved unsuccessful, Local 8 was far from broken. Philadelphia's longshoremen maintained their union. The vote to return to work was an acknowledgment of defeat but can be seen in strategic terms, in order to fight (or strike) another time. The workers failed to achieve their aims, but they did not forfeit their wage scale or give up a single dock. The employers had not been able to split fully the union either along racial or craft lines. Local 8 had over seven thousand members and job control along much of the riverfront, but the employers had learned a powerful lesson about organization. Yet before the next union-employer conflict erupted in 1922, Local 8 found itself fighting for its survival. This time, though, it was due to internal divisions and the insurgent challenge of Communism. Arguably, the Philadelphia Controversy was as detrimental to Local 8 and the IWW as any open-shop campaign or federal raid.

7 *The Philadelphia Controversy*

In August 1920 the IWW suspended Local 8 for loading ammunition on a vessel allegedly destined for the enemies of the Russian Revolution. The IWW's national weekly *Solidarity* claimed that the union "would rather face death and dismemberment than stand the disgrace of having its members render any assistance in keeping its workers enslaved to the Moloch of capitalism." Thus, the largest and most durable IWW branch, as well as its only local with a significant black membership, was punished. Shortly after settling this matter, Local 8 was suspended again, this time for charging new members unconstitutionally high initiation fees. These two matters, lasting until November 1921, make up what became known as the "Philadelphia Controversy."[1]

The American Left, always at risk from external repression, underwent an internal crisis with the creation of the world's first socialist nation. In the decade leading up to World War I, America's radical Left had been dominated by the IWW. During the war, though, the Wobblies suffered from systematic repression. Many historians believe that this campaign deserves the primary role in the IWW's decline, even though the union's highest official membership occurred after the war.[2] Simultaneously, many people sympathetic to the Left found a new champion in the Soviet Union. To many, including some American Wobblies and Soviet leader V. I. Lenin, it seemed logical that the IWW fold itself into the new "Red International." After all, the Bolsheviks had achieved what leftist groups the world over had only dreamed about, namely overthrowing a capitalist state. Eventually, though, the IWW decided against aligning with the Soviet Union. How did Communism affect the IWW, and why did it, after a flirtatious courtship, reject the Communists? It was not, simply, because the IWW had been rendered powerless by a combined government-employer offensive. The brutal infighting among pro- and anti-Soviet Wobblies also resulted in the Philadelphia Controversy and foreshadowed a further decline in the IWW when the debate over central-ization crescendoed in 1924. These forces—domestic and international, internal and external—whipsawed Local 8 and the entire IWW.[3]

This chapter examines the complex interrelationships between the IWW and Communists and within the IWW over means and ends in order to see how the Philadelphia Controversy played a vital role in undermin-ing the IWW generally and Local 8 particularly. Ben Fletcher believed, as did Fred Thompson (the IWW's in-house historian for four decades), that the IWW-Communist conflict lay at the heart of the Philadelphia Contro-versy. The combination of Communist efforts to capture the mainstream AFL and eventual IWW rejection of Bolshevism resulted in a fierce split between these competing left-wing movements. As a result, Communists in the United States sought to undermine the IWW, beginning with its most powerful branch, Local 8. Further, this crisis revealed a deep fissure in the IWW over short- and long-term goals. Local 8's efforts to protect itself, during its second suspension, pitted the practical needs of the local to limit the labor supply against the revolutionary goal of bringing more workers into the fold. Of course, this issue was inherent in revolution-ary groups like the IWW but reappeared with a vengeance during the Philadelphia Controversy. The IWW's celebrated interracial branch also suffered from worsening race relations after the war; combined with the rise of Marcus Garvey's black nationalist movement, both of these events threatened to rip Local 8 apart along racial lines. As Wobbly organizer Claude Erwin put it, "There was not a large city in the U.S. that looked more promising from an organizational standpoint than did Philadelphia. Why did we lose this chance?" Analyzing the Philadelphia Controversy of 1920–21 and lockout of 1922 (in chapter 8) provides the answers.[4]

On August 5, 1920, word arrived at the New York headquarters of the MTW that the *Westmount*, docked in Philadelphia, was loading am-munition intended for General Wrangel, a leader of a White Russian army fighting the Red Bolsheviks in the Russian Civil War. The Soviet Bureau in New York threatened to publicize Local 8's "treasonous" act in the labor and radical press unless loading stopped immediately. James Scott, secretary-treasurer of the MTW and firmly pro-Soviet, promptly sent a telegram announcing that he and several members of the IWW GEB were coming to Philadelphia on important business. Scott arrived in Philadel-phia that same evening and demanded that a meeting be called the next day to "knock the men off" immediately or the branch would be expelled. Local 8 leaders protested that such a meeting could not be arranged on such short notice as, typically, two days were required to notify the thousands of members along miles of riverfront. Fletcher also asked Scott why Local 8 had not received word from the GEB in Chicago.[5]

Scott succeeded in convening a meeting the following day. He and two GEB members addressed the fewer than two hundred union members present at the hastily arranged meeting. The longshoremen informed Scott that they had not known the destination of the munitions, a reasonable possibility considering the countless tons of war materiel shipped out of the port since 1914. Many members—notably Assistant Secretary George Hellwig and rank-and-file leader Ernest Varlack, both of whom had been working in distant parts of the port—did not even hear of the gathering until the next day. Meeting Chair Sam White and others reiterated that a larger group was required, decided that they would not halt loading the *Westmount* until such a gathering occurred, and eagerly awaited instructions from national headquarters.[6]

The next day, August 7, the Chicago-based GEB revoked Local 8's charter. The board based its decision on the reports of the two board members who had visited Philadelphia as well as one received from Scott. New York's IWW branches had bombarded the GEB with numerous telegrams and printed an extra edition of their newspaper, *Fellow Worker*, all demanding expulsion. At its regular meeting on August 10, Local 8's members voted to await word from the GEB on the "powder question." On August 13 the local finally received a telegram from General Secretary-Treasurer Thomas Whitehead informing them of the expulsion, with notice that they could appeal at the next general convention the following May, fully ten months away. According to Local 8, "The Philadelphia Branch was at the height of its power when the controversy over the 'powder' question started."[7]

Philadelphia's longshoremen were expelled for "a crime against the working class," namely loading munitions aboard a ship that allegedly would supply Wrangel, a stunning charge in the IWW. Longshoremen and sailors were particularly conscious of international issues because of their work experience, or as one Wobbly put it, "To the marine worker the term industrial solidarity means international solidarity at one and the same time." Like many socialist groups, at first the Wobblies strongly supported the Russian Revolution. The GEB claimed as late as 1920 that "the I.W.W. views the accomplishments of the Soviet government of Russia with breathless interest and intense admiration." Thus, the longshoremen of Local 8 "betrayed the international labor movement by loading shrapnel shells consigned to the infamous Allied catspaw, Wrangel, for the purpose of drowning the Russian revolution in a sea of blood." Ironically, the editors of the *One Big Union Monthly* blamed the longshoremen's very success. Since Local 8 had job control, anyone who wanted longshore work had to join the IWW. At least some of the union's members, especially newer ones, were ignorant of the IWW and its history in Philadelphia. Accordingly, the IWW expelled Local 8; or, in Wobbly vernacular, the IWW "had bit off more than it could chew and we had to spit it out."[8]

There is simply no extant evidence to support or deny that the Whites were being supplied with weapons through Philadelphia or that Local 8 loaded any such vessel. In fact, it is far more likely that the United States supplied its forces, based in the Siberian port of Vladivostok, out of Seattle; Seattle longshoremen uncovered boxes of machine guns in crates marked sewing machines in late 1919. Most likely, the longshoremen were loading military supplies but its destination was—and is—unknown. Nevertheless, whether the longshoremen actually loaded ammunition and whether it was intended for Wrangel is not as important as the accusation, for, ultimately, what was at stake was the path the IWW would take: join the Communists who were sweeping through much of the Left worldwide or remain with an international group of anarchists and syndicalists that challenged, unsuccessfully, the Bolsheviks.[9]

On the same day that Local 8 received its expulsion notice GEB Chair George Speed arrived in Philadelphia. Speed—who had served time in Leavenworth with Local 8 leaders—had organized in Philadelphia frequently over the years, most notably in 1913 when he helped during the initial longshore strike. At their August 17 meeting the Philadelphians explained to Speed that they had been on poor terms with MTW headquarters ever since it had been moved from Philadelphia to New York the previous year. Many members complained of Scott's domineering treatment of the Philadelphians. In particular, Local 8's power to control MTW elections, based upon its enormous membership, irked Scott. According to veteran organizer Walsh, the Philadelphians refused to listen to Scott, whom they did not trust, but did tell Speed that they would stop loading if the GEB ordered it. In his report to the GEB, however, Scott never mentioned that Local 8 awaited word from Chicago. Speed then addressed the membership for over an hour about the importance of international labor solidarity. After Speed's talk, the membership unanimously passed a resolution boycotting all longshore work involving war materiel, ac-

companied by a notification of expulsion for anyone who loaded ammunition. The next morning Local 8's business agent Polly Baker went to
the *Westmount* and pulled the forty Wobblies working it.[10]

Still, it was another month before Local 8 was reinstated. George
Speed intended to convince the GEB to reverse its expulsion of Local 8
immediately. Speed argued that Local 8 had acted in the proper manner
(quitting work on the *Westmount* as soon as the members understood the
situation) and that he would not have approved of the local's expulsion
if he had been fully informed. Speed soon wrote Walsh, "I feel I made a
grievous mistake in our hasty decision." The newly elected GEB decided
that Local 8 should remain suspended for a while longer, in order to appreciate the gravity of the situation. But, the GEB also acknowledged
that "the Phil[adelphia] Dist[rict] is not wholly to blame" and decided
to take control of the MTW until new officers were elected. In October,
when the longshoremen returned to the fold, it seemed like the dispute
had ended.[11]

However, another issue drove a wedge between Quakertown's longshoremen and the national leadership. Local 8 blatantly violated the
IWW's constitutionally mandated $2 initiation fee. First implemented
in the spring of 1920, in August Local 8 still charged new members a $2
initiation fee and a $22.25 assessment. The reasons for this huge increase
are important to comprehend. The union had been hurt by numerous
events in 1920, including the maritime depression (resulting in a labor
surplus on the docks), the start of an employer open-shop campaign, the
arrival of dozens of Wobbly "floaters" from Seattle who wanted to use
the IWW universal transfer feature to become instant members of Local
8, and a defeat in Local 8's strike that involved upward of ten thousand
workers. In Local 8's document *The Philadelphia Controversy*, Doree
and Nef argued that the hike in initiation fee was needed to operate effectively as a union, especially in the aftermath of a massive strike in
which four thousand members temporarily had joined at a reduced rate
of $1.25. The longshoremen argued that, while the raise violated the
constitution, there was no important principle at stake; Local 8 believed
that it was more important to maintain a stable membership and treasury. Nevertheless, the IWW national leadership remained adamant that
Local 8 reduce its initiation fee. The Philadelphians held a meeting on
October 20, at a hall large enough to accommodate the entire membership, where they refused to compromise. Thus, although the "powder
question" had been resolved, this second issue again threatened Local
8's position in the IWW.[12]

What had been a conflict over solidarity with the Soviet Union had been transformed into a disagreement over the centralization of power within the IWW. The crux of the disagreement was over the potentially contradictory goals of maintaining job control while also advocating the overthrow of the capitalist system. That fall a series of increasingly adversarial telegrams traveled among Local 8 in Philadelphia, MTW headquarters in New York, and the GEB in Chicago. The MTW and GEB insisted that Local 8 immediately lower its initiation fee to $2 and charge no additional assessments to new members. Recently elected Local 8 Secretary Walter Nef responded that the Philadelphians would consider the issue but did not want to destroy the organization they had worked so hard to build. Local 8 suggested a national referendum be held on the issue. In response to Local 8's refusal to lower its fee, the GEB informed the Philadelphians that it had until December 1 to comply or else be suspended again.[13]

In a fascinating letter published in the main IWW publication *Solidarity*, E. F. Doree argued passionately for a high initiation fee in order to maintain job control along Philadelphia's waterfront. Doree claimed that forcing Local 8 to comply involved two issues: should the IWW continue to experiment regarding the structure and tactics of the union, and should work control be sacrificed over a technical issue that did not compromise a "first" principle? On experimentation, Doree recalled that in 1915 he and Nef helped form the Agricultural Workers Organization (AWO), which had revitalized the entire IWW. The AWO charter also had violated the IWW constitution, but the GEB, "acting as revolutionists and practical men rather than as ultra-constitutionalists, felt that the experiment was necessary." Doree maintained that the situation in Philadelphia paralleled the AWO's. As for the second issue, Doree contended that the IWW consistently had failed to maintain job control, except in Philadelphia. Local 8 believed that its continuing power depended upon limiting the entry of workers into the industry (notorious for large labor surpluses) and could be managed only through high initiation fees. With low fees, an overabundance of laborers, and irregular jobs, many workers joined, dropped out, and rejoined the union. In order to establish a powerful union, Doree contended, "it must be built upon a permanent membership who pay dues regularly." Few Philadelphians let their dues lapse in slack times because they would have to pay the high initiation twice. Clearly, Doree's argument follows those made by both AFL craft unions and the militant West Coast longshoremen in the 1930s—that to maintain power a union must have a closed shop and regulate those who can join the union. Eric Arnesen also has written about how "the particular structure of employment relations on the docks" made limiting labor surpluses that much more imperative for longshore unions.[14]

Considering its success, Doree suggested that Local 8 be allowed to continue its "experiment," at least until the next convention when the issue could be discussed by the entire organization. Doree condemned the mandatory low initiation fee, "this straight-jacketing of experiments," that had proven "a failure," for it neither supplied the IWW with sufficient finances nor encouraged members to stay in the union. In response to those who complained that high initiation fees hindered organizing, Doree asked, "Where are the members?" Doree contrasted the initiation issue with signing contracts that, according to him, violated basic IWW principles. The IWW, including Local 8, never signed contracts with employers because that would limit their ability to strike (either for their own benefit or in sympathy with fellow workers) and Wobblies must be able to do so. Of course, the counterargument is that by requiring such a high initiation fee, many workers could not afford the Wobblies' red card. In response, Doree claimed that a high initiation fee did not compromise the IWW's ironclad commitment to working-class solidarity; in fact, in *The Philadelphia Controversy* the authors argued that since a Local 8 member easily could make $40 in a week, the fee was not exorbitant. Doree concluded that, if forced to lower its fee, "the greatest shop-control organization of the I.W.W. will have passed away. The I.W.W. will have done what the bosses were unable to do."[15]

Not surprisingly, given its intransigence, Local 8 was suspended. Further, Ben Fletcher and Ernest Varlack, as members of the now-suspended branch, were denied their seats as secretary-treasurer of the MTW and member of the General Organizing Committee respectively, despite being "overwhelmingly elected" in recent balloting. Since Local 8 made up a large majority of the MTW membership, Fletcher's and Varlack's victories were givens. Thus, the second suspension conveniently kept Local 8 from taking control of the MTW. In its defense, Local 8 compiled "A Complete and Detailed Statement of All That Has Occurred," which they entitled *The Philadelphia Controversy*. The cover page of this booklet boldly declared, "The I.W.W. must now decide whether it shall be an industrial union in name only or whether it shall be an industrial union in fact. The day of test is here. We have sacrificed much for the principle of industrial unionism, now let's have it."[16]

The significance and contentiousness of the issue kept the Philadelphia Controversy alive within the IWW after the suspension went into effect. Doree's powerful letter actually was published in *Solidarity* several days after Local 8's was suspended. The debate raged on in the GEB and newspaper for several more months in letters and editorials. Though many condemned Local 8, E. W. Latchem, an AWO member, praised the longshoremen as "they are the only branch of the I.W.W. who have been successful in organizing and holding within the organization any large number of colored workers."[17]

Ultimately, the Philadelphia Controversy concerned how the IWW dealt with the most pressing issue facing socialist organizations worldwide—how to respond to Communist Russia—and occurred just as the IWW rejected Bolshevik overtures. Right after the revolution, support was nearly universal from the IWW and other left-wing organizations, believing that the Bolshevik takeover signaled the beginning of the overthrow of capitalist nations worldwide. Many Americans, both sympathizers and opponents of Bolshevism, saw the events in America during 1919, particularly the Seattle General Strike, as evidence that the United States might be swept into revolution as well. By the summer of 1920, though, most strikes had been defeated and the Red Scare continued, while support for the Bolsheviks waned. Like many on the Left, the IWW fractured into those in favor of and those opposed to the Soviet Union. In 1919 the Soviet Union flirted with the IWW and supported its "dual union" approach of organizing head-to-head against the more mainstream AFL. Concurrently, a pro-Bolshevik GEB sought to establish formal ties with the Soviet Union by urging the IWW to join the Soviet-dominated Third International (Comintern). Considering the GEB's Communist sympathies, when the allegation against Local 8 surfaced, the swift suspension of Local 8 makes sense.[18]

When a new, anti-Soviet GEB took over in late August 1920 it became clear that the IWW would not ally with the Soviet Union. That fall and winter a bitter debate ensued over affiliation with the Third International until the IWW decided against joining. By the end of 1922 the IWW also had chosen not to join the Red International of Labor Unions, a Soviet-led world federation of unions. Historian Melvyn Dubofsky believes that the Philadelphia Controversy was but one example of the IWW's increasing isolation from American and other radical groups embracing the Soviet Union. The Wobblies' opposition to the Communists was controversial—even if the Wobs' anarchistic fears of centralized, antidemocratic politics proved accurate in retrospect. Dubofsky also contends that due to the power it wielded, Local 8 "inevitably" came into conflict with the "putative" national leadership. That is, without its own power base, the GEB "clung to outdated revolutionary precepts" (e.g., very low initiation fees) rather than adapting to a changing postwar America (including an employer offensive as well as the rise of Communism). Dubofsky's multicausal analysis is insightful but not entirely clear; why did Local 8 and the national "inevitably" come into conflict? Why not, perhaps, encourage other locals to follow Philadelphia's model?[19]

Fred Thompson, the longtime in-house IWW historian, offers a different scenario—that Communism wracked the IWW from within and Local 8 was caught in the crossfire. In a 1982 letter Thompson speculated that the United States would not send arms to those fighting the Bolsheviks through Philadelphia: "I wonder why ship to Vladivostok [in Siberia] through an Atlantic port? There was a well-equipped American force in Siberia." Moreover, Thompson believed that Wobbly longshoremen who discovered a shipment would prevent it: "I am certain that any Philadelphia IWW who knew arms were being shipped to intervene in Russia would have used union channels and procedures [direct action] to stop it." After all, that was what Seattle Wobblies did. Thompson concluded that it would not surprise him if Communist sympathizers within the IWW "cooked up" the Wrangel arms story. Thompson's theory is seconded by Ben Fletcher, who claimed that when the Communists realized that they could not "capture the Port," that is, seize control of Local 8, they engaged in a "Liquidating Program upon orders from Moscow," though Fletcher provided no specifics. Fletcher wrote that IWW Secretary-Treasurer Thomas Whitehead, MTW Secretary-Treasurer James Scott, and three members of the GEB were "agents of Moscow." Another prominent IWW leader, George Speed, wrote in his 1924 memoir published in *Industrial Worker* that Communist members of the GEB and New York branches, including Scott, colluded to expel Local 8. Finally, in a brief but tantalizing report, the IWW General Office Bulletin reported in October 1920 that "when the [new] G.E.B. came into office, they were confronted with the turmoil of the Philadelphia situation; Communist influence being exercised within and without the organization." Although it is uncertain when he joined, Roy Brown, GEB Chair before September 1920, was an active Communist as late as 1930. While not definitive, clearly a number of important Wobblies, Scott likely included, joined the Communists' ranks by 1920 and wanted to bring the entire IWW with them; failing that, disruption of the IWW by Communists is plausible.[20]

Fred Thompson's contention seems the logical one, given the bitter fighting within the IWW over Communism. Thompson correctly suggests that, by late 1920, it was clear that nothing comparable to the Bolshevik Revolution would occur in Western Europe or the United States. Lenin arrived at the same conclusion, so he ordered Communists to enter mainstream labor movements in their respective nations. In the spring of 1920 his pamphlet *"Left-Wing" Communism: An Infantile Disorder* attacked Communist parties in West Europe for remaining outside of mainstream trade union movements and concluded that those working for Communism "must imperatively work wherever the masses are to be found." The Second Congress of the Communist International, held in Moscow in July–August 1920, adopted Lenin's position. However, most syndicalists present, including the British Shop Stewards' Movement and the IWW, opposed the new policy. Notably, even the (U.S.) United Communist Party delegation, represented by former Wobbly John Reed, voted against the measure because they believed that the AFL never could be turned leftward.[21]

In the United States the abrupt policy shift ordered by Lenin meant that all Communists, including those still in the IWW, must join the AFL. Only in industries in which no operative AFL union existed—timber and agriculture—would the Communist International "permit" the IWW to organize. In an unsigned "Instructions for Work in the United States," American Communists were informed that "a consistent effort [be] made to bring into line the revolutionary and semi-revolutionary groups outside of the general labor movement [AFL]"; the IWW was the first group targeted in this 1921 letter spelling out the Red International's mission in the United States. The marine transport industry, however, arguably fell into a third category, since the AFL's ISU and the MTW were of roughly equal strength in 1920–21. After a failed strike in 1921, ISU membership plummeted, many joining the MTW. The Communists were well aware of the MTW's power. A 1921 "Report on the IWW" commented, "Marine transport and textile organization being the only semblance of organized unions," those groups were targeted for recruitment. According to Fred Thompson, a debate took place as to whether the Communists should capture the MTW or ISU. Thompson contends that the ISU was endorsed, so Communists entered its ranks. Those Communists within the MTW "were told to encourage disruption there, rumor-mongering, waste of resources on things that wouldn't work, etc." Thompson wrote of the Communist Party's "game plan—same as their lies about the MTW in Philadelphia shipping arms to wrangle [sic], and other disruptive acts throughout the IWW."[22]

The ongoing Russian Civil War is the other factor at work. In the late summer of 1920 Wrangel led an offensive against the Red Army in the Crimea. By this time the Bolsheviks had defeated nearly all of their enemies, save Wrangel, so on August 19 the Politburo announced that "the Vrangel [Wrangel] front is to be recognized as the main one." In fact, the Bolsheviks were so fearful of Wrangel that they temporarily allied with another opponent, Nestor Makhno's band of Ukrainian peasant anarchists. The same fear that led Lenin and Trotsky to collaborate with Makhno easily could have led American supporters to jump on a rumor and transform it into something that had to be stopped immediately. Hence, the Philadelphia Controversy. By August 1920, the conflict between the rising Communists and declining IWW was intense, and the Comintern's official policy was to bore from within the AFL. The IWW did not attend future Comintern sessions, though Communists still worked to convert thousands of Wobbly longshoremen and sailors in Philadelphia and across the globe.[23]

Little is known about Communist infiltration of Local 8, but it seems clear that Communism had, at most, limited success. Unquestionably, members of Local 8 frequently debated the subject of Communism at their meetings; for instance, at one IWW open forum in December, William E. Smith, leader of the English-speaking Philadelphia branch of the United Communist Party, spoke. The IWW press printed ongoing discussions of Communism. Further, as a bustling port with a powerful IWW presence, a wide variety of people and ideas circulated. That is why numerous Spanish anarchist sailors and Seattle militants made Philadelphia their home. Yet, especially since Local 8 was a majority African American organization, Communist organizers found few converts. It was not until the 1930s that Communism attracted significant black support. Nevertheless, Fletcher claimed that a group of Communists (presumably East European immigrants, given the times) existed in Local 8.[24]

Considering that a majority of Philadelphia's longshoremen were African American with a few Afro-Caribbeans, a greater potential threat to Local 8 was the rising tide of black nationalism under the banner of Marcus Garvey's Universal Negro Improvement Association (UNIA). Black sailors and waterfront workers throughout the Atlantic world were essential links in the chain of information that people of African descent had forged for hundreds of years. Obviously, Jamaican-born writer, sailor, and Wobbly-turned-Communist Claude McKay knew Local 8 as he memorialized it in his novel *Home to Harlem*. Black maritime workers in the Atlantic, including Philadelphia, knew Garveyism well. After all, the UNIA was the largest black social movement of its time and displayed much strength in Philadelphia. In the summer of 1919 Garvey helped organize a Philadelphia chapter, Division 47, of the UNIA. The division's first leader was the Reverend James Walker Hood Eason (AME), who had grown disillusioned with the local NAACP's tepid response to rising racial tensions. Eason soon held the powerful Chaplain-General post and later still "Leader of American Negroes," the third highest position in the UNIA.[25]

Division 47 grew quite quickly and declined equally fast, mirroring the entire movement. Evidence of UNIA's popularity among Philadelphia's black population abounds. Despite the opposition of most of the city's black clergy and middle class, close to ten thousand people, overwhelmingly working class no doubt, joined in under a year, second only to New York. In 1920 Garvey called Philadelphia "one of our greatest strongholds." Over six thousand people attended a fundraiser at the Academy of Music for the Black Star Line, UNIA's shipping firm intended to transport people of African descent back to Africa. Black Star Line stocks were traded in the city. In the spring of 1920 the Black Star Line vessel *Yarmouth* arrived in Philadelphia from the West Indies. That fall the chapter raised $6,000 for Liberia. However, over the next two years, massive internal dissension, violence among the membership, including the murder of Eason while in New Orleans, and financial problems led to a destructive split in the local chapter. Division 47 never regained its earlier power.[26]

Generally, Local 8's black majority emphasized class solidarity across racial lines in an otherwise segregated city, but it is only reasonable that some black longshoremen were enticed by Garvey's powerful and popular ideas. Black longshoremen in New York, New Orleans, and Port-of-Spain, Trinidad, were active in the UNIA, and it would have wanted to gain influence in Local 8, one of the most powerful black organizations in Philadelphia. Having arrived from a foreign port of call, members of Local 8 would have unloaded the *Yarmouth* when it docked, noting the all-black crew and the entirely black passenger manifest. And some black longshoremen would have read Garvey's publications, particularly the widely distributed *Negro World*. Yet, there is but one reference to Garvey's influence in Local 8. A. Philip Randolph and Chandler Owens's black socialist monthly, *The Messenger*, reported in the summer of 1921, in the midst of Local 8's second suspension, that "alleged Negro leaders masquerading in the guise of race loyalty" urged black members to form an all-black longshoremen's union. While not mentioned by name, blacks calling for the voluntary segregation of their union fit the UNIA. Unequivocally, Garveyism was strong among working-class Philadelphia blacks. As the largest black social movement of the era, the UNIA deserves mention, and, no doubt, some blacks in Local 8 would have flirted with it. Still, its relationship to and potential as a threat to Local 8, while impossible to fully ascertain, seems to have been slight.[27]

Also clearly, voluntary segregation was highly unpopular among Local 8 members, even in 1920—a time of rising racial tension and growing Garvey influence. Given its leanings, that *The Messenger* compared segregated unionism to Jim Crow or "the Southern bugaboo" comes as no surprise. Both black and white Philadelphians opposed attempts to split their ranks; Randolph and Owens approvingly noted that separation of workers into different unions according to their race "has been routed by the plain, unvarnished workers. In the Marine Transport Workers Industrial Union, No. 8, there are 3,500 men, three-fifths of whom are Negroes." *The Messenger* reported that the attempt to form a black-only union "came from alleged intelligent Negroes outside of the union," so the membership decided to increase their efforts to remind the blacks among them of the advantages of interracial organization. Meetings continued to be run by an African American chair and a secretary of European descent. As black longshoreman James Fair recalled much later, "To my knowing at that time [1920s] the IWW was the only thing that was accepting negro or black workers . . . I mean freely. They would accept them and they did advocate just this thing, solidarity." Local 8 translated this notion from its union hall to the workplace, as Fair noted, "We worked decks together, we worked on the wharfs [sic] together, we worked in the hold together." This striving for equality even affected union members off the job. Prior to Local 8, black longshoremen faced the threat of violence when walking along the waterfront. However, with the advent of the union, blacks and whites worked and lived in some of the city's ever fewer mixed-race neighborhoods. Willy Krupsky, a Philadelphia docker himself and the son of a Russian immigrant who belonged to Local 8, recalled in a 1980 interview that he attended an interracial picnic, when just a young boy: "I went to this picnic, a longshoremen's picnic, so it had to be in the early twenties. . . . It was mixed, white and black were there, everybody knew one another, and we had a good time."[28]

The union's weekly series of Friday evening educational forums discussed a wide range of issues but focused on race. The first event, which hundreds of men and women attended, was entitled "The Relation of Organized Labor to Race Riots." The lecturer compared race wars to wars between nations, both of which benefited employers to the detriment of workers. In race riots, workers allowed bosses to consolidate their power. Using a "colorful" metaphor, one speaker claimed, "If the white and black working dogs [sic] are kept fighting over the bone of race prejudice, the artful, hypocritical yellow capitalist dog will steal up and grab the meat of profit." He went on to contend that the segregated locals of the ILA

played into the employers' hands. Numerous people that evening condemned the recent, brutal race riot in Tulsa, blaming the Ku Klux Klan
for doing the employers' dirty work. Thus, while the city and country's
racial climate deteriorated in the early 1920s, Local 8 provided its black
and white members with an alternative.[29]

Despite challenges from Communists and Garveyites, or possibly
because of them, Philadelphia's longshoremen wanted to remain in the
IWW yet believed that lower initiation fees would destroy their union.
Time and again since 1913, Local 8 had demonstrated its commitment
to the IWW, suffering greatly from its affiliation—leaders jailed, offices
raided, members spied on, and strikes crushed by a combination of private and public repression. Even after the war, the men participated in
a wide range of IWW activities, including conventions and fundraisers
for those imprisoned in the "class war." The ILA made frequent overtures in Philadelphia, the only non-ILA port on the Atlantic. Joining
the AFL would have made their union membership more palatable to
employers, especially during the war. Still, despite massive employer
opposition and increasing Red-baiting, the longshoremen remained committed to the IWW, if only they could preserve their local. Notably, the
black longshoremen's loyalty to Local 8 parallels the experiences of black
workers in other left-wing unions, such as the Alabama Sharecroppers
Union in the 1930s, as well as both the International Longshoremen's
and Warehousemen's Union and the United Packinghouse Workers in
the 1940s and 1950s.[30]

The longshoremen's insistence on maintaining an unconstitutional
initiation fee reveals how committed they were, first and foremost, to
each other, their local union, their leaders, and what they believed were
the "true" ideals of the IWW. Bruce Nelson astutely refers to the familial, ethnic, and neighborhood connections that tied longshoremen
together as "persistent localism." The membership did not place nearly
as much trust in the leadership of their industrial union or national organization, whom they believed to be either unnecessarily domineering
or Communist-controlled. Considering the MTW's and GEB's postwar
inadequacies and reversals over Communism, Local 8's lack of faith is
not surprising. The only GEB member whom the Philadelphians trusted
was George Speed, but even he could not convince the longshoremen to
lower their initiation fee. The longshoremen had fought many battles
against their employers and the government to preserve their union. In
the final analysis, in 1920 Philadelphia's longshoremen believed more
strongly in their local organization than in the organization at large.[31]

Nevertheless, Philadelphia's longshoremen wanted to return to the

fold, and the matter was discussed at the national convention in 1921.
Local 8 sent a mixed-race delegation to Chicago to argue their case, in
addition to delivering a letter from E. F. Doree, a nationally known organizer. The delegates discussed the suspension during "two days of earnest debate." George McKenna, active in Local 8 since 1913, spent half
a day facing questions insisting that his branch would lose job control if
it changed policy. Though divided, those present voted to stand by the
GEB. A second motion then passed allowing for the immediate reinstate-
ment of Local 8 as soon as it reduced its initiation fee. The convention
also upheld the suspension of a New York local of Italian bakers that
charged a $15 initiation fee. Local 8 was given ninety days to comply
or else the IWW threatened to establish a new branch in Philadelphia.
When Doree, back in Leavenworth, heard the news, he wrote his wife,
"It is hard to recall 15 years service in an organization and then, while
in prison because of activities in its behalf, to be thrown out. . . . But by
all means boys, stick, stand together. Let nothing separate you. You boys
of the marine industry, must build a better and stronger union. We are
with you in spirit if not in body."[32]

Local 8 continued to agitate, as it always had, at the point of production, even after the strike and despite its suspension. The union's power
continued to rest on the militancy of the rank and file, as illustrated by
a series of job actions undertaken over three main reasons: wages, work
conditions, and gang composition. For instance, when hold men (who
worked in cargo bays) were shortchanged in pay, they struck the following morning, with the deck and dock hands joining them. The company
agreed to pay not only the hold men their back wages but also all of the
strikers for the hour's time lost. When the captain of a ship refused to
let the longshoremen eat their dinner aboard the ship, all of the workers simply went home. The shipping company was forced to call up the
union hall and tell them to round up the gang, which would be allowed to
dine on the ship. Also, longshoremen frequently refused to handle drafts
(sling loads of cargo) that they, as experienced workers, believed were
too heavy to be safely moved. Often, these sorts of issues were mediated
without strikes, but it was not uncommon to call a quick strike in order
to have more workers placed on a gang.[33]

Most job actions, though, concerned who would or would not be allowed to work. When a boss fired a union man and the stevedore refused
to reinstate him, the rest of the work crew struck, along with all of the
longshoremen working a second ship at the same pier. The fired man
was rehired and paid for the wages he had lost. In numerous cases, Local
8 longshoremen successfully demanded, usually without resorting to a

strike, to have workers knocked off who had not paid up their membership dues. Longshoreman James Fair explained the process well: "We
wouldn't have a spontaneous strike as I recall, but we would have what
you might call a work stoppage you know on certain jobs, for instance
in those days we wouldn't have a check off system and men would be
working that was so far behind in their dues and they would stop and
call a job action because maybe the boss wouldn't knock those men off
or something like that." Fair's statement also reveals how longshoremen
viewed their actions—a quick "work stoppage" being a legitimate means
to enforce a specific union demand and different than a "strike." The
result of such tactics, similar to those deployed by Chicago packinghouse
workers, was that almost no foremen hired longshoremen who did not
wear the current button. The button system (a different one each month)
was a quick and easy method for regular longshoremen, hiring bosses,
and union delegates to ensure regular payment of dues, especially in an
industry where workers changed jobs as often as twice in a single day.
Polly Baker and Amos "White" Gardner, the local's two delegates, regularly walked "the front" and periodically forced foremen to fire longshoremen who had let their dues lapse, even midshift. During its suspension
the local remained committed to limiting the labor supply and had the
power to do so.[34]

On some levels, Local 8 never truly acknowledged that it had been
suspended, blaming the entire situation on a Communist-dominated
GEB, so it still actively supported the IWW. Local 8 continued to raise
money for IWW "class war" prisoners. Big Bill Haywood spoke in September at the Philadelphia Labor Lyceum to a crowd of twenty-five hundred people. A group called the Rebel Girls, named after the IWW's most
famous female organizer Elizabeth Gurley Flynn, led the gathering in
renditions of the "Internationale" and "Hold the Fort" and sold literature.
Haywood claimed that the meeting had more people than any other on
the East Coast and encouraged them to continue organizing.[35]

Further, despite the suspension, Local 8 worked with other Wobblies
to prevent coal from being shipped to Great Britain when miners there
struck. During Local 8's 1920 strike, sailors affiliated with the British
Shop Stewards' Movement had refused to work with replacement longshoremen. In fact, Jack Tanner, a leader of the movement, had spoken
at Local 8's hall. In addition to a common distrust of Communism, the
Philadelphia Wobblies and British Shop Stewards shared notions of international worker solidarity. Local 8's longshoremen gladly repaid their
debt to the British fellow workers.[36]

Nevertheless, Local 8 clearly suffered as a result of its 1920 strike and suspension. During the strike the local temporarily had lowered its initiation fee dramatically, and several thousand new members poured into the union. The increased competition among union men for jobs after the strike greatly hurt the older members, who got less work. This issue led to much conflict between old and new members. The old members did not see the recently joined ones as committed to the union. The local attempted to educate these new members by arranging a lecture series, publishing its own pamphlets, and providing free issues of *Solidarity, One Big Union Monthly, Industrial Worker, The Messenger*, and *The Liberator* (perhaps oddly, even during its suspension, Local 8 purchased many subscriptions to IWW and, surprisingly, pro-Communist publications).[37]

The weakening maritime economy also hurt Local 8, contributing to its desire to rejoin the IWW. The American Bureau of Shipping lamented "the slump" that the entire industry experienced after the war. Crucially, in 1921 the maritime economy in Philadelphia finally experienced this postwar depression. While the port's activity exceeded the prewar era, from 1920 to 1921 the value of the port's foreign trade, the docks that Local 8 controlled, plummeted close to $500 million. Contributing to the crisis was the decision by railroads to raise freight rates to Philadelphia by 40%; as a result, Philadelphia's grain exports dropped dramatically as merchants transferred their product to other ports. Far less activity in the port meant less work for Local 8's longshoremen, hence their position was much weaker than in previous years.[38]

One final factor that propelled Local 8 back to the IWW was increasing pressure from the ILA, which reappeared during the Philadelphia Controversy, seizing the opportunity to bring the important Atlantic port into its organization. Continuing a partnership initiated during the war, maritime employers and the USSB collaborated to bring the ILA into Philadelphia; the government and AFL still viewed Local 8 as a part of the IWW even if the IWW did not. The relationship grew even tighter as T. V. O'Connor, a former ILA president, assumed control of the USSB. For instance, O'Connor recommended to John McGrath of the Atlantic Coast Shipping Company that he contact A. J. Chlopek, ILA president, to discuss their plans to bring the ILA to Philadelphia. There are scattered references in correspondence between the MTW secretary in Philadelphia and Local 8 leaders in Leavenworth about the resurgence of the ILA.[39]

The ILA troubled Local 8 greatly. Philadelphia agents of the Justice Department's Bureau of Investigation reported that, since March 1921, hundreds of black Wobblies had joined a newly chartered ILA branch, #1116, led by African American organizer Glenn Perrymore, prominent in Local 8's 1916 strike. Lending credence to both Fletcher's and Thompson's allegations, Agent McDevitt believed that the defections resulted from disagreements over Communism and favoritism in hiring. Local 8 responded by issuing new circulars on the racism of the AFL. The presence of the highly respected black socialists Randolph and Owens at numerous IWW open forums that summer was no coincidence. Federal agents reported that, at business meetings and open forums, Wobblies had heated arguments, with some threats made against anyone who joined the ILA. Local 8 leaders believed that employers were, once again, trying to drive a wedge between the black and white longshoremen. In *The Philadelphia Controversy*, Local 8 reprinted one broadside found on the waterfront that encouraged black longshoremen to form an "Independent Union of Colored Workers," with the "backing" of the Employing Stevedores Committee (any Garveyite influence is speculation). Local 8 urged longshoremen to "beware of union disrupters."[40]

Local 8 managed to close ranks and rebuff this latest ILA challenge. Given Local 8's commitment to and history of interracial solidarity, the African American longshoremen could rest assured that they would be treated equally and with respect. There is little question that in the early 1920s Philadelphia blacks experienced discrimination outside of Local 8. Residentially and socially, de facto segregation existed. Away from the waterfront, black and white people rarely worked together. Most notably, the rebirth of the Ku Klux Klan throughout the nation reveals how racism was rampant and increasing. The Ku Klux Klan established an office in West Philadelphia in May 1921, and Pennsylvania became the Klan's stronghold in the Northeast. By late 1922 more than thirty thousand Philadelphians belonged to a dozen klaverns, with a hundred thousand members scattered throughout eastern Pennsylvania. Furthermore, most employers still refused to hire blacks. The AFL devoted little energy either to opening up its membership to blacks or protecting their interests, either. Perhaps most significant, Local 8's strong-arm tactic of expelling longshoremen who joined the ILA proved decisive. In August 1921 Local 8 revoked the memberships of Glenn Perrymore and thirty other black longshoremen accused of joining the ILA. As the longshoremen who joined the ILA discovered, the IWW still had a great deal of power on the Philadelphia waterfront. The lack of a Local 8 button meant, quite simply, no work on most docks. Finally, there were ideological considerations. James Fair, a black member of the local, remembered that "we would have our pep talks and what not and Fletcher, after he made a speech or something or another, solidarity, all for one and one for all." Within Local 8, Philadelphia's waterfront workers had an opportunity to improve their lives together, which explains their loyalty in the midst of worsening race relations and brutal fighting between the local and national over Communism and centralization.[41]

Finally, a year after being suspended, Local 8 was reinstated, as the longshoremen needed the support of the larger organization. The desire to rejoin the IWW was strengthened by threats from the ILA and weakened maritime economy. Hence, the Philadelphians agreed to IWW demands, namely to charge a $2 initiation fee, the constitutionally allowable maximum. On its front page, *Industrial Solidarity* hailed the return of the MTW's "most powerful subdivision, numbering several thousand members, and commanding complete job control on the waterfront." The paper went on to proclaim Local 8 "the most striking example ever seen in this country of the possibility of working-class solidarity between whites and Negroes."[42]

Historian Melvyn Dubofsky argues, essentially, that the IWW crumbled in 1917–18 due to massive employer and federal government repression. After the war the IWW stumbled on, near-death, as it were, because of government repression along with its own misguided policies and inability to adjust to the changing realities of the postwar era, which among other things led to the Communists' eventual dominance of the American Left. Hence, Dubofsky gives short shrift to IWW activities after the war. The continued power of Local 8, though, contradicts his claim that the IWW ceased to be an effective labor organization after the wartime raids. Fred Thompson offers a different theory. In 1972 he wrote that "the historians are quite in error in figuring the repression killed the IWW. I believe it was about as sturdy as it ever was in the summer of 1923, and that development from that point to its disruption in the 1924 split was its unfolding." Thompson's view is overly optimistic, though. Despite maintaining members comparable to prewar levels, Dubofsky is correct that the IWW never fully recovered from the wartime government and employer repression. Too, the rise of Communism sapped energy from the IWW. But, clearly, the IWW—in Philadelphia, the Great Plains, the Northwest, and elsewhere—still was quite active in the 1920s, and it is a gross oversimplification to suggest otherwise.[43]

Thompson's contention regarding the significance of IWW infighting also needs to be modified to factor in the Philadelphia Controversy, which proves that the IWW was in disarray prior to the 1923–24 centralization battle that Thompson believed crucial. After World War I, while the national IWW and soon all of organized labor was reeling from a combined employer-government offensive, Local 8 had persevered (despite the imprisonment of its leaders). Even after its failed 1920 strike, Local 8 maintained an enviable position. Considering that it was perhaps the most powerful local in the IWW at the time, the national organization should have done all in its power to ensure the continued health and allegiance of Local 8. That, however, did not occur. In fact, the GEB in Chicago and MTW leadership in New York did the exact opposite. At a time when the IWW should have been attempting to resuscitate its ailing organization by building on still vital branches such as Local 8, the IWW suspended Local 8 twice on debatable grounds. As IWW organizer Claude Erwin put it in 1925, "First and greatest, because it hinders greatest, is internal dissension."[44]

There is no single explanation for the Philadelphia Controversy. The depleted leadership ranks of the IWW resulted in a new crop of leaders on the GEB, which, according to Dubofsky, felt the need to assert its authority and contributed to organizational disarray. As many, including historian John S. Gambs, note, this leadership was decidedly pro-Soviet. The rise of Communism caused a fundamental realignment in left-wing circles, and Local 8 was caught in this whirlwind; by the time the IWW rejected Communism, the damage had already been done. The Philadelphians also had to contend with worsening race relations and a rising UNIA as well as employer, ILA, and governmental offensives. The men of Local 8 remained dedicated to the IWW first principles of industrial unionism and interracial solidarity, but refused to sacrifice their organization to the sectarian infighting that the (American) Left is famous for. The knockout blow to Local 8 would be delivered the following year, but the Philadelphia Controversy revealed serious cracks in Local 8's interracial armor and the entire IWW. Local 8 had survived its suspension; however, it could not do so if the membership turned on itself.

8 *Quakertown Blues:*
The Lockout of 1922

In 1980 James Moocke, a longtime Philadelphia longshoreman like his father before him, described his father's recollection of Local 8's last major clash with employers: "Of course back then it was like a war between labor and management. . . . It was a long strike. There was killings [*sic*]. Cops on horseback with billy clubs." Moocke referred to the ferocious lockout of October–November 1922, which resulted in Local 8 collapsing. From 1913 to 1922, despite numerous hurdles, the union forced employers to hire IWW members almost exclusively on deep-sea piers. By the fall of 1922 much had changed. Across the nation millions of American workers had struck after the war, and the great majority of these strikes ended in defeat. The marine transport industry proved no different. In America's largest ports—New York City, New Orleans, and San Francisco, to name three—workers launched major strikes, only to see their organizations torn asunder by ferocious employer counteroffensives, often with federal aid.[1]

In Philadelphia the struggling maritime economy and ongoing Great Migration meant that there were thousands more men willing to defy Local 8, whose postwar leaders proved less capable than the cadre jailed during the war. Sensing the turning tide, maritime employers locked out all Wobblies and then defeated the workers' desperate attempt to transform the struggle into a strike. Employers found thousands of replacements, including New Yorkers supplied by the ILA and African Americans from the South, some of whom belonged to Local 8 yet defied the union.

In particular, the large number of blacks who rejected the union—some losing confidence in Local 8, others, some new to the waterfront, some ignorant of it—was a deathblow. This racial split (whites sticking with the union, many blacks abandoning it), along with growing employer power and the mighty assistance of the U.S. government, clearly wanting to break the IWW and aid the ILA, explains how employers drove a fatal wedge into Local 8. Despite its radical, mixed-race leadership, large black membership, and proven commitment to racial equality, Local 8 still suffered from racial divisions, exacerbated by the Great Migration and rising segregation. The lockout indicates just how difficult it was to maintain an interracial union in this era. Philadelphia's riverfront never would be the same.

In contrast to Local 8's demand to reduce the workday to eight hours, many other American labor disputes were defensive. While the Philadelphians attempted to extend their power, the much larger railway, coal, and textile strikes of the same era "sought self-preservation . . . with those companies that still bargained" with them during the rising tide of open-shop campaigns. Though the New York and San Francisco waterfront uprisings of 1919 failed, longshoremen in New Orleans, the Gulf's largest port, struck three times after the war. The 1923 strike of the biracial Dock and Cotton Council failed to achieve a reduction in hours or an increase in wages and, more significantly, resulted in the collapse of the South's longest and most successful effort in mixed-race organizing. In fact, ILA-led strikes all along the Gulf Coast in 1923 were uniformly disastrous for workers. This wave of broken strikes combined with the national employer offensive (1919–23) provide the backdrop for events in Philadelphia.[2]

Similarly, the challenges that Local 8 experienced with black strikebreakers were significant if not unique. Due to the dramatic labor shortage during the war and effort to break unions afterward, many American workplaces became far more diverse, in terms of ethnicity, gender, and race. Previously employers had failed to split Philadelphia's longshoremen along ethnic or racial lines, but this tactic had proven effective elsewhere. Black strikebreakers and/or black workers unwilling to abide with unions proved decisive on the Seattle waterfront, in the Chicago stockyards, and throughout the Midwest's steel industry, to name just three contemporaneous examples. Many factors explain the willingness of African Americans to cross picket lines, including poverty, a lack of industrial experience, an awareness of discrimination among white-dominated unions and society, as well as a sense of gratitude to employers. Plus, the Great Migration meant a far greater supply of potential strikebreakers than ever before. The sentiment expressed by Claude McKay's character Zeddy in *Home to Harlem* applies: "I'll scab through hell to make mah living. Scab job or open shop or union am all the same jobs to me." As in New Orleans, this issue proved to be the crux of Local 8's 1922 clash.[3]

Philadelphia's employers, both on and off the river, had pressed vigorously for the open shop and Americanization since the war's end. In the spring of 1920 the Philadelphia Chamber of Commerce created an Industrial Relations Committee to promote the open shop, combat the "principles of Bolshevism and Revolution sweeping the world," and prevent the spreading of "un-American" ideals. The National Association of Manufacturers, the nation's most influential employer association, established an Open Shop Department the same year. Concurrently, the chamber and many other organizations pushed for the Americanization of immigrants. Milton D. Gehris, of the Philadelphia-based John B. Stetson Company, claimed that Americanization facilitated "loyalty to the company" and made immigrant workers "easier to deal with." Similarly, maritime employers—as well as the AFL seamen's union—pushed for the Americanization of the merchant marine. The American Bureau of Shipping editorialized: "The new Shipping Board in all of its actions has indicated a wholesome desire of having all its branches managed and operated on a 100 per cent American basis. So too has the principal organization, the American Steamship Owners Association." Thus, it is not surprising that longshore employers actively promoted the open shop and Americanization. Philadelphia shipping interests walked in lockstep with employers locally and nationally who actively worked to dismantle the power of organized labor.[4]

The members—or at least leaders—of Local 8, however, felt that they stood in a strong position vis-à-vis their employers. The longshoremen had been back within the IWW fold for close to a year. Despite the growing influence of the ILA, Ku Klux Klan, and UNIA, Local 8 appeared united. In the fall of 1922 the membership of Local 8 stood at thirty-five hundred, accounting for almost all of the deep-sea longshoremen in the port; of these, more than two thousand were African American. Importantly, the port had rebounded from the national depression and worldwide shipping slump. The entire American economy had been mired in a postwar depression through 1921 but the maritime sector had suffered more than most. After the war, ocean freight rates dropped, production costs rose, and new shipbuilding contracts plummeted. With European allies resuming much of their own production, total exports from Philadelphia in 1921 were less than a third that of 1920. Yet, in 1922, there was some cause for optimism. Grain exports, one of the city's main commodities, doubled 1920 figures and were two-thirds higher than 1921. In fact, 1922 was a record year for grain exports. With the port's activity—and the entire nation's economy—rising by mid-1922, union leaders incorrectly gambled that employers would quickly settle any work stoppage.[5]

Although Local 8 never signed contracts, it did reach "understandings" with its employers regarding wages and hours. A standard ten-hour shift for a longshoreman, under the 1921 "agreement," began when he reported for work at 7 A.M., continued until noon, when he had an unpaid hour for lunch, and then lasted until 6 P.M.; thus, if a longshoreman worked five full days plus Saturday mornings, he put in a fifty-five-hour workweek. At a meeting in September 1922 the men decided they should not have to work so many hours; after all, by the early 1920s many American workers worked eight-hour days. In early October the longshoremen voted to demand an eight-hour day. In typical Wobbly fashion, though, they would not negotiate with their employers. Rather, they would report for work at 8 A.M. (instead of 7 A.M.) and knock off at 5 P.M. (rather than 6 P.M.), thereby reducing the number of hours worked to forty-four a week (assuming an eight-hour workday Monday through Friday and four hours on Saturday). Accordingly, Local 8 business agent Polly Baker told employers, including the USSB, that workers sought a forty-four-hour week, with overtime rates for any additional hours worked.[6]

Local 8's demand for an eight-hour day was daring, given the nature of longshoring, which favored employers. That is, the men hired casually (by the job or shift) for manual labor that required little or no previous training (though experience dramatically improved productivity) had relatively little power to enforce their desires, as workers were easily replaceable. This already-skewed power dynamic was made worse since, in 1922, the nation was just emerging from the postwar recession, meaning that legions of unemployed people stood ready to replace strikers; the ranks of this so-called reserve army of labor were swelled further by the Great Migration. Though collective bargaining had become somewhat accepted in the industry, employers clearly dominated the relationship. In marked contrast, Local 8's demand suggests that it successfully limited entry into the workforce and felt confident enough to make such a bold demand.

The longshoremen bristled that they worked ten-hour days, and often much longer if a ship was under a tight schedule, while workers in many other industries worked eight- or nine-hour days. During their 1920 strike, the workers had demanded but failed to achieve an eight-hour day. Alonzo Richards, a popular and highly respected leader, spoke for many when he declared, "We have never had a square deal from the Bosses. We work hard and our work is dangerous as every one knows. We should have fought for an eight-hour day and had it long before this. Nearly every other class of men have it and why shouldn't we." One USSB agent, who called Richards "a very intelligent colored man," reported that his fellow black longshoremen "listen to him with rapt attention."[7]

In addition to long hours, the early hour at which work began caused much consternation. The men showed up at the hiring corner, in the vicinity of Front and Catherine Streets just one block from Local 8's hall, before 7 A.M. throughout the year, even during cold winter mornings or bad weather. (The location of the hiring corner was not accidental: all stevedores traveled to the union—rather than workers shaping up at individual piers.) Moreover, the men were forced to make themselves available daily without the guarantee of a job. One longshoreman, John Kelley, claimed that arriving at the hiring corner so early on a cold, winter morning had been an issue among the men for many years, particularly as they never knew if they would get a ship.[8]

The city's shipping interests immediately formed an emergency committee. The committee appointed A. L. Geyelin as chair and met at the offices of the British shipping firm Furness, Withy & Company in the Bourse building, a center for maritime firms. The committee quickly sought out Superintendent William B. Mills of the Department of Public Safety, who agreed to cooperate with the shippers, yet again. A representative from the committee reported to Mills twice a day throughout the conflict. Mills suggested that no one be allowed on any pier without a pass and that the shippers retain a lawyer, so if anyone trespassed, the law could be invoked promptly. In keeping with its open-shop sentiments, the committee refused to deal with Local 8. Finally, the committee resolved that unless the longshoremen reported to work on October 16 at 7 A.M., they would lock the men out.[9]

During the conflict important disagreements among workers emerged. Longshoremen with families particularly worried about the incurred hardships. With winter fast approaching, people needed to buy coal, a considerable expense. Some worried that they would lose more money by not working than they would make up with a new wage scale (from more overtime), and one of the USSB's agents reported that these issues might "break up the solid front of the Stevedores [longshoremen]." Nevertheless, at least at first, most supported the union. As close to five hundred men had joined in the last four months (or more likely rejoined after leaving for the ILA), Local 8 members felt confident. Employer divisions encouraged longshoremen like Otis Badhelor, who noted that three stevedores did not join the lockout.[10]

Wobbly leaders prepared the rank and file for the lockout. Initial discussions saw no progress, since the employers' committee refused to deal with the union. The local formed an eight-man strike committee, five of whom were African American. This committee told the membership to work at 7 A.M. but only if paid $1 an hour, the overtime rate, rather than sixty-five cents an hour, the normal day rate. Any longshoreman who worked for the basic rate would be considered a scab. For good reason, the union leaders worried that the ILA might try to use the situation to take over Philadelphia, the last major U.S. port without a significant ILA presence.[11]

On Monday morning, October 16, a large group of anxious longshoremen gathered at the union hall. Many left for the piers just before 7 A.M. and congregated in small groups along Delaware Avenue, planning to work only if paid overtime for the first hour. After 8 A.M. many returned to the hall. Having refused to start work at 7 A.M. at the basic rate, employers hired no one at 8 A.M. The USSB's informants, who turned in daily reports during the strike, noticed many arguments among the longshoremen but also strong support for the union. Apparently, the longshoremen at some docks had not gone on strike because their bosses had agreed to union demands; this situation, however, caused resentment among some not working. Most members, though, looked at the actions of these renegade stevedores as proof of employer disunity. Local 8 Secretary George Hellwig said things looked good, as the bosses needed a lot of workers and the warm weather meant the workers did not need coal soon. No pickets were dispatched and the hall was filled with longshoremen, as was the entire neighborhood, playing cards and shooting craps. Although no picket line went up for several weeks, groups of IWW-buttoned longshoremen placed themselves all along Delaware Avenue before 7 A.M. each day. By 8:05 A.M., after no union men were hired, most left the riverfront. The men were of two minds: they had to stick to their demands but also knew that employers wanted to break the union.[12]

Although they initiated the lockout, shippers suffered immediate challenges. Approximately five thousand longshoremen were out, idling more than thirty ships. To the shipping interests' chagrin, the United American Line issued a circular to other firms advising them to avoid Philadelphia. Philadelphia shippers feared that the recession would return and counted on grain exports to carry the port. The city traditionally exported a large amount of grain in November, at the close of the North American harvest, so it could not afford to have this commodity tied up for long. Their anxiety was heightened by stiff competition from Montreal, sending off grain before the St. Lawrence River froze.[13]

Replacements remained the primary concern throughout the lockout. Some Local 8 members took jobs as strikebreakers to act as union spies. For instance, after learning that the United American Line planned to charter a boat and hire strikebreakers in the nearby river town of Chester, four union men traveled there to prevent it, while Baker dispatched others to picket the United American Line pier. According to one USSB spy, many black unionists had not made "radical threats" against their employers until they learned of these strikebreakers but now claimed they would make it "damned hot for scabs." IWW members also traveled to Baltimore and Norfolk, but could not expect much support in either port, since the ILA controlled Baltimore's longshoremen and many IWW sailors had been blacklisted there, while the Wobblies had even less influence in Norfolk.[14]

The union also sent two organizers to New York to prevent the sending of ILA replacements. According to these men, both African American, the ILA was actively recruiting longshoremen. ILA Vice President Joe Ryan, who dictatorially ruled New York's longshoremen and collaborated with employers during the huge 1919 wildcat strike, boasted of ILA President A. J. Chlopek's offer to break the IWW in Philadelphia. The IWW issued a circular to New York's longshoremen in English and Italian describing the lockout and appealing both to class solidarity—"Their [Local 8's] success means your success"—and manhood—"Be men not Rats . . . Don't Scab."[15]

With the vital aid of the city and federal governments, employers developed their strategy to destroy Local 8. Accommodations for imported strikebreakers were provided courtesy of the USSB, which donated one of its vessels docked at the government-owned Pier 98 South. Matthis Moe, the shipping agent for Wessenberg & Company and chair of the Committee on Protection, essentially designed the city police's strategy for guarding strikebreakers. Each day Moe telephoned the police and sent a confirmation letter telling them what ships at which piers were to be worked the following day, so that the police could dispatch adequate protection on foot, horseback, and motorcycle. Moe also coordinated his actions with agents from the USSB's Division of Investigation. Agent Joseph Van Fleet suggested that the shippers should get an injunction against the union as soon as it committed an act of aggression. The committee sent him and another agent, who convinced the U.S. Department of Justice to cooperate. The shippers did not feel that the city and federal undercover agents were sufficient, so they also hired the Pinkerton

Detective Agency. Thus, arrayed against Local 8 stood Philadelphia's private shipping interests and organized business community, the USSB and Department of Justice, the Philadelphia police, and the legendary (or infamous) Pinkertons.[16]

Fundamental to the shippers' strategy was a Longshoremen's Employment Bureau based upon the "Seattle Plan," which had undermined the power of militant longshoremen there. To control the number of people eligible for work and eliminate the chaotic shape-up, in 1919 Seattle stevedores established a central hiring hall and required all potential workers to register. Through this system, Seattle employers succeeded in taking total control over hiring and eliminating any workers they deemed undesirable, namely radicals and unionists. Soon, Philadelphia shippers placed large job advertisements in the city's newspapers, and some AFL sailors were hired. The ads created dissension among the Wobblies, some of whom wanted to return to work, even if it meant forgoing their demands. Baker and other leaders reminded the rank and file that were it not for a strong union, with its direct-action tactics, they would not be getting the high wages they received.[17]

The role of the USSB was essential in defeating Local 8 and indicated how hostile it was to the IWW. First, the board allied itself with the shippers rather than remaining neutral, as a public institution might. Second, it supplied intelligence, spies, and resources to the employers and met daily with them. Third, the USSB donated one of its vessels, the *George E. Weed*, equipped with a commissary and sleeping quarters, to house hundreds of replacements. H. C. Higgins of the USSB's Operating Division hired the Burns Detective Agency, largest in the nation, and placed its agents undercover as stewards, since Higgins correctly suspected that the IWW tried infiltrating. During the lockout, the USSB opened up a Sea Service Bureau to hire sailors. Joining the open-shop crusade, the board refused to employ known Wobblies and tried to "Americanize" its crews, implying that Wobblies were not American. Finally, the USSB paid stevedoring firms on a cost plus 10% profit basis during the conflict, so the government bankrolled any expenses incurred by shippers. In essence, employers were federally subsidized to defeat Local 8.[18]

Desperate to force employers to accept the eight-hour day and maintain Local 8's power, union militants pushed to call a strike. There was an important split between those who were committed solidly to seeing the workweek reduced by any means necessary and those who wanted to return to work immediately, either content with the status quo and/or not confident in their ability to improve their lot. At their October 21 meeting many men, including much of the leadership, wanted to declare an official strike. To those who opposed this tact, Baker argued that were it not for the IWW, the men would be receiving forty cents an hour, as those on the unorganized railroad piers did, instead of sixty-five cents an hour. Alonzo Richards argued that the main issue was not wages or hours but the open shop. One USSB agent believed "that the general tone of the men today clearly showed that . . . they are going to fight." After much discussion, though, no vote occurred. The danger, of course, was that a division within the ranks would widen into a destructive (and possibly racial) rift. For now, the influence wielded by Local 8's leaders held the members together; in particular, Richards was important, as he was a veteran leader and commanded respect from the union's large black contingent.[19]

The keys, then, for Local 8 were to maintain unity while preventing employers from operating as usual. Local 8 deployed its members to "discourage" replacement workers. In a telling moment, at one meeting a "dark skinned negro" named Kelly said that there "sho will be trouble when they bring dem niggers off dat bunk ship [George E. Weed]." Kelly demonstrated the fierce commitment of many black longshoremen. Even though some, perhaps most, of the replacements were African American, Kelly did not let their common racial heritage divide him from his white fellow unionists. Further, by referring to African American strikebreakers as "niggers," Kelly was appropriating a term used by many whites for all blacks and redefining it to apply only to strikebreakers. Richards and "Plug" Dickerson, two black leaders, claimed that many of these replacements were inexperienced and, hence, no threat. If all the members believed as fervently as Kelly, Dickerson, and Richards, Local 8 stood a chance.[20]

As the lockout moved into its second week, the situation for Local 8 was decidedly mixed. Jake Schwartz, a strike leader, boasted to a USSB agent posing as an Associated Press reporter, that the Polish and Russian members could remain idle for some time because they had saved some money. The Williams Line broke ranks and agreed to union demands. And, IWW longshoremen struck the Pennsylvania Sugar Refinery in sympathy. However, employers already had hired over one thousand replacements, although they did not perform nearly as well as the experienced men, and ILA President Chlopek promised twenty-five hundred men from New York. Baker used Chlopek's statements to strengthen his men's resolve, but all knew that replacements, the mostly black locals and ILA New Yorkers, could break Local 8.[21]

The largest internal threat to Local 8's short-term success and long-term survival was the emerging split over calling a general strike, which broke along racial lines. Many opposed to stronger action were African American, while most in favor were European immigrants. Dissension allegedly went as high as Alonzo Richards, who believed that the timing of the conflict was poor, though he supported Baker. Another black leader and friend of Richards, Plug Dickerson, claimed that Baker was the "King Pin" and should be supported even though Dickerson hoped that a strike could be avoided. Nevertheless, that the disagreement divided black and white leaders and members did not bode well for Local 8. Though no evidence exists of how the black community viewed the strike, the status of several thousand well-paid men profoundly affected many thousands more black Philadelphians.[22]

At one marathon meeting, the longshoremen again discussed the eight-hour day, replacements, and calling a strike. The men considered reducing their demand to a forty-eight-hour week. Richards reported that the men hired by Furness, Withy had so badly damaged $40,000 worth of cargo that the consignee refused to accept it and that seventy thieves were found among the Italian ILA replacement workers, so the entire lot was sent back to New York. Richards said the men had worked too hard to build up their union to have it broken by a bunch of "green" workers. Then, to the members' surprise, John A. Moffitt of the U.S. Department of Labor appeared. Moffitt reported that most employers had no interest in dealing with the IWW, but that Murphy-Cook Company wanted to take back the union longshoremen at the old conditions. Moffitt urged the members to work for Murphy and use him as a wedge to force the other employers into line and encouraged Local 8 members to complain to their Congressmen because their employers ignored the eight-hour law (a reference to the eight-hour law for federal workers). After Moffitt spoke, George Speed denounced him, as all government representatives were subject to the shipowners, instead advocating a strike and "throw[ing] scabs overboard." Baker was applauded when he seconded Speed's assessment. Yet, a strike vote was voted down overwhelmingly when the sizeable black majority voted against it. The USSB's Operative #10 believed that the "negro stevedores [longshoremen] . . . [were] weakening" though they still strongly believed in the union. Shipping Agent Van Fleet heard from one informant that a "conservative element" talked of forming a new union, most likely a black-dominated ILA local.[23]

After hearing of the vote, the MTW leadership traveled to Philadelphia. Pat Ryan, MTW secretary-treasurer, and other New York–based Wobblies particularly hoped to strengthen the resolve of the black longshoremen. After the MTW leaders arrived, Speed left, disgusted at Local 8's reticence to strike. Without citing specifics, Speed believed that Dan

Jones, a black leader, acted duplicitously and that the Philadelphia situation was hopeless.[24]

By October 26 the shippers had workers for thirty-three ships, proving that they had little difficulty finding willing replacements. In addition to dockside police protection, a dozen officers on motorcycles escorted trucks carrying men from the Longshoremen's Employment Bureau to the docks. Crucially, many replacement workers were black members of Local 8.[25]

The deteriorating situation led the radicals to reconsider calling a strike. When the vote again went against the strike, those in favor became noticeably agitated. Operative #2 reported that he feared that "some of these people would not stop at bloodshed," and Baker worried that such violence would further weaken the union. The agent recommended increasing police along the riverfront and claimed that there was a movement among some of the blacks, along with a few white members, to oust the Lithuanian-born Baker, further evidence of racial splits. The following morning, many arguments erupted among the unionists. Those in favor of and opposed to a strike blamed Baker. Richards continued to support Baker, though some members wanted Richards to take charge. Richards had helped found Local 8, and, although he had flirted with the ILA, he believed strongly in the tactics and ideals of the IWW. As for Baker, he had given up on striking and was most concerned about keeping the union together.[26]

Surprisingly then, a successful strike vote occurred October 27. At the morning meeting Baker reported that the shippers remained determined not to deal with the IWW, but he hoped to arrive at settlements with individual firms. When MTW Secretary-Treasurer Ryan spoke, he was "howled down," and GEB member Ted Fraser could not convince the men to strike, either. Richards feared trouble and threatened to step down as chair. That afternoon, though, Baker somehow convinced the men to strike, claiming that the employers were weakening. Ryan, quite surprised, predicted that the black longshoremen would not hold out for "lack of backbone." Ryan also believed, as Speed had, that Dan Jones was colluding with the shippers.[27]

With the strike commencing, confrontations increased and radicals pushed for a general strike. Militants wanted to extend the strike from longshoremen to all maritime workers, particularly the seamen among whom a good number were Wobblies, but they needed permission from MTW headquarters. One striker reportedly believed that most black members opposed the strike and would not heed it. Richards and others again voiced concern that the ILA would take advantage of the situation. To help with the strike, Ed Lewis, a fiery soapbox orator, came in from Chicago and three other Wobblies arrived from Baltimore. E. F. Doree, just released from Leavenworth, also helped but not in a public capacity.[28]

Local 8 began its strike by deploying pickets all along Delaware Avenue and at the Longshoremen's Employment Bureau. The city's shipping interests had thirty-nine ships ready to load or unload, so many that Matthis Moe complained that the shippers needed still more police. Baker placed union men in the gangs of strikebreakers, inducing some replacements to quit working and join Local 8. Baker stopped holding meetings because he knew that the employers used undercover agents and feared that the radicals would provoke the police, complaining to Operative #2, "I cannot hold these fellows. They won't listen to me." When, in an effort to reduce the chance of a conflict, Baker ordered strikers not to display their IWW buttons on Delaware Avenue, black members complained that they might be attacked by other Wobblies. This fear confirms that many replacements were African American and most of the radicals white.[29]

Considering the high tensions and century-long history of labor and racial violence on the Philadelphia waterfront, it is not surprising that strikers clashed with replacement workers and police. On October 28 strikers attacked ILA scabs, Italians from New York. Another incident occurred near the Baltimore & Ohio Railroad piers where replacements were being escorted to work. More gravely, a police officer was shot and killed near the United American Line pier that night. The police blamed Local 8. Forty longshoremen were injured and four arrested. Trucks carrying strikebreakers were fired upon near Local 8's hall.[30]

The members' racial divisions and weak leadership might have been overcome by the return of Ben Fletcher and other veteran leaders but were not. One USSB agent, revealing his own prejudice, reported that the "coons [black longshoremen] are still wavering" yet most white members supposedly feared the blacks. This agent recommended that employers work on the black longshoremen, since they made up a majority of the union and were less committed to the strike: "The blacks are your line of attack, they are the weak sisters and can be worked on successfully, keep after them, harass them." If a few black leaders could be "eliminated," then the black majority would return to work; in fact many already had. At this moment the sentences of Fletcher, Walter Nef, and Jack Walsh, all veteran Local 8 leaders, were commuted. Not surprisingly, the Department of Justice opposed granting Fletcher clemency, as "he was a negro who had great influence among the colored stevedores [longshoremen], dock workers, firemen, and sailors, and materially assisted in building up the Marine Transport Workers Union which at the time of the indictment had become so strong that it practically controlled all shipping on the Atlantic Coast." Another agent reported that Walsh was "a clever, shrewd diplomat when it comes to handling a strike" and well respected among the men. Its spirits briefly revived, Local 8 boosted itself as the "last vestige of Industrial Unionism on the water-fronts of the United States" and called on workers in other ports to boycott vessels arriving from Philadelphia, as "scabs are plentiful."[31]

Philadelphia's shipping interests continued its offensive by establishing a company union. All men were advised to join the Employees and Employers Union, as it would provide "good conditions and representation of your own choosing," ignoring the long tradition of democratic elections in Local 8 and hinting that the employers would not impose their own leadership. A common tactic in the 1920s, company unions, like employer representation plans and work councils, claimed that workers and employers shared common interests and so should belong to the same organization. In actuality, company unions almost always were dominated by management and kept workers powerless. Often these organizations were used by employers to legitimize their efforts to reduce wages or institute other unpopular policies. This effort signaled the culmination of employer attempts to dismantle Local 8.[32]

Still, of greatest concern for the union was the exacerbation of racial divisions. USSB Agent Van Fleet believed that Local 8's lack of funds and the weakness of the black element would destroy it. Moe heard from one spy that many Polish longshoremen were upset that most of the union members who had returned to work were African American. Some Poles claimed that they would return to work, as well, so that the black longshoremen did not get all of the good jobs. Taking a page from Local 8's book, the employers printed circulars in English and Polish, claiming that Local 8 did nothing for "hard-working family men."[33]

Over the next ten days Local 8's strike collapsed. On November 13 USSB Agent Norton reported many strikers returning to work and the dramatic decline of pickets, although the police still maintained a large presence. The Sea Service Bureau had more applicants than positions. Agent Van Fleet reported that more unionists would return to work as the weather got colder and they would need money to buy coal. He also noted that many foremen who had supported the strikers by remaining at home since the lockout's inception also had returned to work. The USSB discharged some of its agents and returned the *George E. Weed* to normal duty. Strikers confirmed the obvious on November 18 by voting to return to work.[34]

Though numerous factors weakened the union in this seminal

confrontation, the ability of employers to recruit large numbers of replacements—and that many of these were African American, including Local 8 members—proved most important. The economic situation and ongoing Great Migration, which resulted in large numbers of unemployed (especially black) men, and the inevitable onset of winter also benefited employers. The shippers' superior organization, power, and initiative as well as crucial assistance from both the government and ILA contributed to their victory.[35]

It seems clear that the employers' primary goal was crushing Local 8. There was no reason that the employers could not have adapted their work schedules to accommodate an eight-hour day, as other ports and industries had. Plus, the lockout cost the employers far more than they would have had to pay for the extra two hours of overtime being demanded by their workers. Indeed, stevedores complained to USSB Agent Norton that they hired twice as many replacements, due to their inexperience, than they would have union men. In addition to wages, stevedores paid for the food and housing of replacements, as well as the major expense of hiring detectives and guards. Given these costs, Alonzo Richards's frequent claim that the shippers' priority was to break the union seems quite reasonable.[36]

The crux of the employers' successful strategy was securing replacement workers. The manager of the Longshoremen's Employment Bureau claimed to place twenty-five hundred men in the last two weeks of October. James Fair, a black member of Local 8, recalled:

> They were transporting in strikebreakers from different parts of the country to go down and take our jobs. . . . They would be loaded up on vans and they were transported to the ships, I mean to the docks and aboard the ships. Some having guns you know same as if they were the law and they would be these vans going down, they would be escorted by police escorts on motorcycles and a striker would have as much chance before the strikebreaker as a rabbit would have before a gunner.

In 1980 other longshoremen, who started working along the shore in the 1930s, vividly recounted hearing about the lockout in 1922 "to break the back of the IWW" and cited the instrumental role of the ILA replacements from New York.[37]

What Fair neglected to mention, but was widely noted in 1922, was that these replacements were mostly African American. Thomas Dabney, an Urban League expert on organized labor, wrote in 1928 that "the 1922 strike of the I.W.W. was broken by Negro strikebreakers brought up from the South by the U.S. Government on a Government ship." In addition to the government's role, Dabney detailed the other forces working to destroy Local 8: "The employers and certain [ILA] labor leaders conspired to accomplish this [destroying Local 8] by pitting the Negro against the whites." This tactic proved equally effective in meatpacking, steel, and other labor confrontations in the period. Historians Sterling Spero and Abram Harris caution, "Even where Negro unionists . . . struck side by side with white, the introduction of Negro strike-breakers . . . stirred up the same racial antipathies among whites . . . that existed when they struck alone." Given America's racist heritage and deteriorating race relations of the era, it proved far easier to destroy an interracial union than maintain one.[38]

Using black replacements, employers succeeded in dividing the membership, despite Local 8's efforts and ideals. This lockout was just one in a long series of employer efforts to destroy the union. The longshoremen were well aware of this goal; for years, in countless local speeches and circulars as well as in the IWW pamphlet "Colored Workers of America," Wobblies decried such employer tactics. As Fair reflected, "Ben Fletcher would tell us that we had to live together, we must work together. And his pet word was, all for one and one for all, solidarity was the main thing. And it sank in with a lot of us." On numerous occasions, Philadelphia Wobblies repulsed attempts by employers, the ILA, and Garveyites to split their ranks; in 1922, however, Local 8 failed to maintain its interracial unity.[39]

Worsening race relations greatly weakened Local 8. In the early 1920s African Americans suffered from growing racism. By 1922 the Ku Klux Klan claimed several million members nationwide, and local "white-on-black" violence erupted periodically (though not yet on the waterfront). Segregation (residential and other sorts) in Philadelphia was on the rise, especially as local whites perceived the Great Migration as an invasion. Within the black community, support for integration also was under attack. Ten thousand black Philadelphians (overwhelmingly working class) belonged to the UNIA, so likely embraced race separation; no doubt, thousands more, including some longshoremen, increasingly and not surprisingly questioned the commitment of any white person to an egalitarian society.[40]

Rising race hostility was compounded by the swelling number of African American dockers and residents in Philadelphia, many of whom were soft in their support of Local 8. From 1910 to 1920 the entire increase of one thousand longshoremen in Philadelphia, according to the Census Bureau, was black. The increase can be explained by the ongoing migration of Southern African Americans and immigration of black West

Indians, along with Local 8's inclusive policies. The pace of black migration had slowed after the war, but Charles Hardy, the premier scholar of the Great Migration to Philadelphia, estimates that ten thousand blacks arrived between the summers of 1922 and 1923. So, there were, quite likely, hundreds if not thousands of black migrants looking for work on the docks precisely when the lockout began. Some of the blacks who worked during the lockout had no reason to act in solidarity with white workers, given widespread racism and limited job opportunities; Clara Hardin, an early scholar of black migrants in the city, claimed that Local 8 was defeated by "Negro strikebreakers." Finally, many blacks in Local 8 who arrived during the Great Migration also had less commitment to and experience with unionism and the IWW. After being locked out for several weeks, these men streamed back to the docks, unwilling to stick with the union any longer.[41]

Part of the blame for Local 8's defeat must lie with the leadership, in particular Polly Baker and Alonzo Richards. First, anyone paying attention saw the obvious power of the employers and their nationwide successes in rolling back organized labor. Second, the IWW had suffered massive governmental repression at the city, state, and federal levels for years. Third, the IWW was being ripped apart over the issues of centralization and Communism. Fourth, Local 8's archrival, the ILA, willingly aided Philadelphia's shipping interests, which consciously fomented a confrontation with Local 8. Perhaps, as with other union leaders of the era, they felt that they had no choice, but it seems inane that Local 8's leaders encouraged a confrontation with employers. Maybe the crisis could have been averted by more experienced leaders, but none, Fletcher included, played a major role.[42]

On the destruction of interracial solidarity, again Baker and Richards deserve some blame. They understood, as the USSB's undercover agents did, the tremendous racial tensions brewing within their union. Both knew the absolute importance of racial solidarity as well as the employers' frequent attempts to exploit worker diversity. Nevertheless, Baker and Richards allowed their union to be split precisely along these lines. In 1925 Claude Erwin, an IWW activist, castigated the leaders of Local 8: "Instead of the I.W.W. members constantly keeping their hands on the pulse of their striking fellow workers and when they saw some of them weakening, call off the strike and get back on the job, they allowed it to drag along until some of the weaker [black] ones gave up and went back to work, thereby creating a [racial] split in their ranks." As before the arrival of the IWW, job competition among a diverse workforce in a racist society translated into racial animosity.[43]

Another factor was the ILA's willingness to scab, and boast about it, in order to displace its rival. The ILA greatly weakened Local 8 by providing approximately one thousand replacements. As Chair of the USSB, T. V. O'Connor proved his allegiance to his old union, by refusing to negotiate with the IWW and promoting the ILA, a more mainstream union. While the end of the lockout did not immediately result in the rise of the ILA, it achieved the necessary precondition: splitting Local 8.[44]

Though they made numerous mistakes, the longshoremen were defeated because the employers were stronger and intended to crush Local 8. According to James Moocke, a longshoreman for fifty years whose father had belonged to Local 8, the owner of Murphy-Cook declared, "Polly, you better not go on strike this time, because if you do, you're done." The employers succeeded in upsetting the interracial solidarity of the union. As James Fair put it, "Finally they [the employers] won out by breaking up the IWW in 1922," which was part of the larger decline in maritime unionism after World War I. Longshoremen in New York, San Francisco, New Orleans, Seattle, and other ports suffered similar fates, as did Philadelphia's Cramp's Shipyard union in 1923.[45]

Of course, the employers had a great many advantages, most notably their wealth. The longshoremen, having little in the way of savings and fearful of a cold winter, could not hold out as long as their bosses. In particular, men with families to support feared unemployment; the gender roles of these men (as family providers) conflicted with their class interests (their fellow workers and union). In contrast, the employers could afford to lock out the longshoremen and take large losses. The business of the port of Philadelphia in 1922 was close to $300 million. With so much money at stake, employers accepted a temporary slowdown in order to ensure their long-term power. The enormous sums at stake leads to a second, inextricably linked, issue.[46]

Employers had gained in size and power due to the war. The port's record-setting years brought more, wealthier, increasingly multinational shipping companies to the port. During the 1920 and 1922 clashes, representatives from large corporations took the lead. Matthis Moe, the chair of the employers' Committee on Protection, was the Philadelphia agent of the national Wessenberg & Company. He worked closely with Captain J. A. Sullivan, chief of police of the New York–based United American Lines. The shippers held their daily meetings at the British Furness, Withy & Company's Philadelphia offices. In addition, the mammoth railroad companies, the Pennsylvania, the Philadelphia & Reading, and the Baltimore & Ohio, collaborated in 1922. In contrast, during Local 8's initial strike in 1913, the employers' leader was Fred Taylor, who ran his family's local grain-export firm. The total value of the port of Philadelphia's imports and exports in 1913 was half that of 1922. As capital increased and became more concentrated, employer power increased dramatically.[47]

The employers also had the vital assistance of the state. The city government, especially its police, played a vital role in suppressing union activism. The local government also worked closely with the city's business interests to expand the port's facilities, spending almost $4 million in 1922 alone to construct new piers. Additionally, the federal government, through the USSB and Department of Justice, supplied sweetheart contracts, police, undercover agents, ships to house and transport strikebreakers, and vital information. The USSB provided a crucial link between employers and the willing replacements of the ILA, thanks to O'Connor. As Patrick O'Brien, an organizer for the ISU (AFL) commented, "The Shipping Board had decided to wipe the Wobblies out of the longshore end. . . . They are now doing all in their power to get them out of the cargo end there can be no doubt."[48]

From the summer of 1920 through the fall of 1922 Local 8 had faced their most serious challenges—the Philadelphia Controversy and a renewed employer onslaught. By the end of this period Local 8 had been twice suspended from and reintegrated into the IWW, only to be defeated in a brutal lockout—nine years of power destroyed by disagreements with their national organization and resurgent employers. The 1922 lockout shattered Local 8 by splitting its membership along racial lines. Yet, the events of these two years had not been preordained. Rather than serving as a resplendent example of a radical and egalitarian union, Local 8 was yet another example of the Wobblies' internal disarray as well as how employers dominated the 1920s nationwide. James Moocke recalled in 1980 what his father Joseph had told him about the aftermath of the 1922 strike—the IWW "went out of business." Not quite. David Montgomery writes, "As was typical of the great strikes of 1922, workers' militancy in the face of depression and a hostile government had saved their unions from destruction, but those unions emerged shrunken and humbled, in an open-shop environment." After employers wrested control of the waterfront, the IWW found itself, once again, battling the ILA.[49]

Conclusion:
Toward Radical Egalitarianism

In the aftermath of the lockout Philadelphia's deep-sea long-shoremen were cast adrift. The IWW no longer commanded the loyalty of the men, nor did it have the power to force employers to relinquish any of its perquisites. A number of Wobbly leaders, including Polly Baker, were blacklisted. Some longshoremen, mostly white and led by Jack Walsh, stuck with the IWW, periodically trying to reassert their dominance with little success. The ILA sought to fill this void but found that employers had little use for it, once the ILA had helped destroy the IWW. A third, independent union formed but made little headway. Meanwhile, work conditions deteriorated and segregated work gangs returned to the riverfront after a nine-year hiatus. After five years of total employer domination, the ILA managed to gain the support of Philadelphia's longshoremen, once it acknowledged the centrality of race and with the not-insignificant backing of the federal government. Nevertheless, the ILA did not promise—nor did it deliver—equality. Instead the ILA followed its all-too-familiar trajectory of corruption and segregation.

As throughout 1920s America, the open shop ushered in a host of technological changes intended to increase worker productivity, reduce worker power, and expand profits. In the two years following the lock-out, employers introduced new machinery, ships, and rigging that dramatically increased the amount of cargo that longshoremen could load; with the introduction of cranes, for instance, slings lifted much heavier loads. Claude Erwin, a Wobbly organizer, estimated that employers had increased longshoremen's productivity anywhere from five to twelve times with no increase in wages. Moreover, since loading or unloading a vessel was done faster, a longshoreman labored for fewer hours and, therefore, earned less than he had previously. In lockstep with employers, the city's harbor improvements facilitated the faster pace and heavier loads. The plan, at a cost in excess of $30 million, included the construction of a number of modern, mechanically advanced piers and grain elevators with much larger cargo capacities, according to local business leaders. The city continued its dredging and deepening of the Delaware and Schuylkill Rivers. Employers dramatically reshaped longshore work but, without Local 8, Erwin warned, "If you don't like it, or can't haul it, you can quit. There are others that will."[1]

Philadelphia longshoremen suffered from the lack of a strong voice in other ways, as evidenced by the return of the hated shape-up. Maud Russell, who chronicles the history of the ILA, describes the era as one of "rough and tumble labor relations. At the time of the IWW's 1922 collapse, management had a stranglehold on the lives of dock workers." When Local 8 represented the port's longshoremen, almost all employers went daily to the union hall to hire workers at three prearranged times. Without a strong union, however, the longshoremen were forced to wait around for hours, often in poor weather, for a chance to be hired in the reimposed shape-up (just as in New Orleans and San Francisco after unions were defeated). No issue was more important in waterfront relations. As Henry Varlack later recalled, the shape was "an evil form of hiring" because it was a "slave market, pitting one guy against the other"; considering that Varlack was of African descent, the choice of terms is apt. Employers took further advantage of their strength by literally stealing more than thirty minutes of work from the longshoremen every day. With no union present, bosses started shifts fifteen to twenty minutes before the agreed-upon hour and ended them after the official quitting time. The extra money went to the gang/hiring bosses. As Erwin noted wryly, "The men pay the drivers to drive them."[2]

Further, Philadelphia employers made the longshoremen work fifty hours a week before earning overtime. By contrast, in 1924, outside of Philadelphia, Atlantic and Gulf Coast longshoremen (assuming they worked every day) worked a forty-four-hour week, except those in Texas, who worked forty-eight hours. Since many, if not most, waterfront employers were national or international concerns, the same companies that operated in Philadelphia were willing to reduce the workweek elsewhere, but apparently only when forced to do so.[3]

Crucially, waterfront employers continued encouraging racial and ethnic competition and animosity among the ranks, via the shape-up and work assignments. In 1913, when it emerged, Local 8 had mandated that gangs, the basic unit of longshore work, be mixed race, which was just one example of the Wobblies' commitment to racial equality. But when Local 8 lost its grip, gangs became segregated again. In 1925 Erwin noted that "bosses pick and hire leaders, gangs of favorites, gangs of negroes, or whole gangs of whites." Employers used jobs to foster not simply racial competition but also racism among their workers. Erwin claimed that among the longshoremen, who were "comprised of negroes, Poles and a general admixture of other nations . . . there is a general suspicion and race hatred existing between the different nationalities," due to segregated gangs. The longshoremen were forced to accept the situation "because most of these men have families, dependent on them, and know no other work." So, when a Polish man was hired, frequently an unemployed African American worker might blame the Pole (rather than the hiring boss) for his troubles. Of course, the Philadelphia waterfront was hardly unique: writing about West Coast docks, Bruce Nelson comments that "the organization of work tended to harden the lines that separated one race and nationality from another." That Erwin does not simply describe gangs as white or black but specifies ethnicity (e.g., "Poles") fits with historians James Barrett and David Roediger's conclusion that "work gangs segregated by nationality as well as race could be and were made to compete against each other in a strategy designed not only to undermine labor unity and depress wages in the long run but spur competition and productivity every day."[4]

Deteriorating relations between black and white workers extended beyond the pier gates to waterfront neighborhoods. The Urban League's Thomas Dabney pointed out that "whereas before the I.W.W. was organized it was a common occurrence for Negroes to be set upon by white mobs on the water front, soon after the I.W.W. was organized Negroes could go about the water front all hours of the night without fear of molestation or harm." However, with the IWW defeated, "the relations between whites and blacks working on the docks and living in the community were in many instances bad." In the summer of 1923 a series of racial clashes occurred, including several South Philly street fights that pitted whites against blacks and an attempted lynching of two black men for allegedly insulting a white woman.[5]

Further evidence of declining race relations comes from Orrin Evans, a columnist for the local black paper, who wrote a very unflattering article about black neighborhoods in 1928. Describing one South Philadelphia area, Evans noted "a small Negro colony in the waterfront neighborhood of Delaware Avenue and Christian Street that out Souths sections of the South . . . completely isolated from the outside world and outside influences, lying close within their own shell of dialect, tradition and ideals. They come from primitive village life to the city . . . living in squalor and filth." The locale Evans derided for being particularly subject to Jim Crow was literally two blocks from the old Local 8 union hall. Thus, where once black and white longshoremen had worked, organized, and socialized in integrated groups, where blacks and whites once lived in the same waterfront neighborhoods, now blacks worked and lived increasingly segregated lives. Of course, the decline of Local 8 was but one factor, albeit an important one, in the increasing ghettoization of African Americans in Philadelphia that accelerated in the 1920s and took on its familiar rigid form by the 1930s. By the same token, rising racism and segregation in Philadelphia had contributed to the collapse of Local 8.[6]

Such problems inspired some to bring a union back, with one group of black men flirting with the ILA, while another created an independent organization, the Philadelphia Longshoremen's Union (PLU). The PLU was led by the veteran black Wobblies Ben Fletcher and Dan Jones and, curiously, had an all-black membership yet claimed to support racial inclusiveness. These black dockers easily could have aligned with the ILA but chose not to. Through 1926 the IWW, PLU, and ILA all failed to attract the allegiance of many longshoremen. In addition to the undeniable power of employers, the other main factor was ongoing racial tension, at least in part fomented by the bosses.[7]

Ultimately, the ILA gained the support of Philadelphia's longshoremen when, in 1927 and with the strong backing of the USSB, it secured an eight-hour day and union contract from employers. The former Wobbly turned ILA organizer Polly Baker proved essential. First, Baker ensured the black majority's support by agreeing to a "checkerboard" system of leadership, with blacks and whites equally dividing positions (just as Local 8 had practiced). Baker's strategy acknowledged black numerical strength and was a nod to the effectiveness of IWW policies. Then, with the strong arm of former ILA President and current USSB Chairman T. V. O'Connor, employers conceded to a union contract with an eight-hour day. Only the pragmatic militancy of Baker and power of the federal government forced employers to accept the return of a union.

The ascension of the ILA, though, did not result in many gains. Despite winning the eight-hour day, the rise of the ILA hurt Philadelphia's longshoremen. Many ILA members who had been in Local 8 did not like the contract. For instance, the rates for loading different types of cargo, including oil, were lower with the ILA than they had been previously.

More importantly, part of the contract stipulated that "the employer shall have the right to determine the size of the draft and truck-load." In other words, employers could place as much weight on a hand truck or in a sling as they liked, resulting in harder work conditions and higher rates of productivity with no concurrent rise in wages.[8]

The ILA contributed to racial tensions because of the very policies it practiced, particularly segregated work gangs. The Urban League's Dabney wrote that the "I.L.A. had members working in groups according to race e.g. whites working in groups together and Negroes working in separate groups." That the ILA segregated its members comes as no surprise, for it carried out such a policy in every other port, including Northern ones such as New York and Southern ones like Pensacola, Florida. Historian Bruce Nelson's recent work reaffirms the work of pioneer black labor scholars Sterling Spero, Abram Harris, and E. Franklin Frazier, all of whom reported that blacks belonged to the ILA but were segregated on the job; moreover, black ILA members were distinctly second-class and continued to be so for decades. Richard Neill, a white sailor who longshored in Philadelphia in the 1950s, remembers working in segregated ILA gangs; further, he recalls that black longshoremen always worked the more dangerous jobs. Kenny Green, a black ILA longshoreman who worked the river in the 1970s, also derided the racial separation of the men while (still) shaping up and the persistence of residential segregation, with white men living close by in South Philadelphia and black longshoremen commuting many miles to the riverfront.[9]

Within the ILA, problems went beyond the issue of race to its un-democratic tendencies, as embodied in the career of Polly Baker. Baker's 1927 decision to limit rank-and-file input by refusing to hold meetings at a crucial juncture in ILA Local 1116's history represented a serious departure from IWW Local 8; Baker's act was typical of the ILA but also repeated, tellingly, his approach near the end of the 1922 lockout. Hence, Baker revealed that, as a leader, he did not respect the democratic pos-sibilities of unionism even while promoting racial inclusion. Of the ILA, Nelson concludes that "there was no democratic procedure within the union, no grievance handling, and no effective advocacy of the members' interests. It appears that most ILA locals seldom met, and when they did it was only to ratify decisions made beyond the purview of the mem-bership." By 1931, elected leaders notwithstanding, Baker was the real power in Philly, and he remained an ILA vice president for decades. The Philadelphia ILA was thoroughly undemocratic, rarely holding meetings or asking the membership for its opinions. Esther Palazzi, who worked in Philadelphia for the National Maritime Union (CIO) in the late 1930s, remembered Baker as "corrupt, reactionary," quite a profound change from Local 8. Whether Baker gave up on democratic unionism, resigned himself to the imperfections of employer-ILA power sharing, or simply was opportunistic is unknown. His actions did bring a union back to the waterfront where none had existed for some years, so perhaps he viewed the ILA as better than no worker organization. Still, in the 1930s, first the Communist Marine Workers Industrial Union (MWIU) and then the International Longshoremen's and Warehousemen's Union (ILWU) (CIO) appeared, but both were routed by ILA thugs who used violence to "convince" MWIU and ILWU organizers to ship out. Later, after World War II, rank-and-file efforts to challenge establishment candidates met with similar, bloody fates. The legendary film *On the Waterfront* describes a thoroughly corrupt longshore union on the Hudson but it easily could have been set on the Delaware. Yet, the story of a once-powerful union, consisting of thousands of African Americans and European Americans, of native-born Americans and immigrants, deserves remembrance.[10]

Although ending in defeat, the story of Local 8's decadelong reign on the Philadelphia waterfront is remarkable, perhaps most importantly for the solidarity displayed in a racially diverse workforce. It is often the discovery of black Wobblies, specifically Ben Fletcher, that captures the imagination of those who hear of Local 8. After all, the Wobblies are far better known for their spectacular strikes, colorful songs, and free-speech fights than for durable, interracial unions that did the vital, if far less glamorous, work necessary to maintain a social movement.

The most basic objective of this book has been uncovering and analyzing how a diverse workforce established and maintained Local 8 for a decade as well as accounting for its collapse. Despite mammoth efforts by private and public forces to displace it, Local 8 did what few other organizations of that time—or ours, for that matter—could: forge an interracial alliance. The U.S. labor movement was well known at that time for its racism, and many historians have confirmed this view. So whether it was advocated by the highly respected Booker T. Washington or Claude McKay's character Zeddy, it was more common in the Progressive Era to find black men breaking strikes than leading them. That African Americans and West Indians not only tolerated but actively collaborated with Irish Americans, other native-born Americans of European descent, and a host of immigrants from Eastern and Southern Europe is practically unique. Prior to the IWW's emergence on the Delaware River, race relations were atrocious. Irish men fought and killed African Americans before the Civil War for jobs on the waterfront, and the situation had improved little in later decades. Only when Local 8 arose did this diverse and divided workforce come together.

Race matters always were central for Local 8, for both pragmatic and ideological reasons. On a practical level, it only made sense to forge an interracial union. In 1913 African Americans made up around 40% of Philadelphia's longshore workforce, and their numbers increased to close to 60% by 1920. White longshoremen needed the black longshoremen for the union to succeed and vice versa. Such pragmatic considerations motivated New Orleans dockworkers, Alabama coal miners, and Chicago meatpackers, as well as Philadelphia longshoremen. However, Local 8 and the entire IWW's commitment to equality went beyond the pragmatic to the ideological. The very first article of the IWW Constitution declared that this union was open to all workers, regardless of ethnic or racial heritage. This belief stemmed from the core socialist principle that all workers shared something in common—their separation from and animosity to their employers. Moreover, the IWW did, at times, acknowledge that black workers had distinct needs that required special consideration. Hence, the IWW addressed "Colored Workers" as a special group and frequently celebrated Local 8. And that is why no less a personage than W. E. B. Du Bois wrote in *The Crisis* that "we respect the Industrial Workers of the World as one of the social and political movements in modern times that draws no color line."[11]

Wobblies in Philadelphia understood that only a racially inclusive union could succeed on the Delaware riverfront. No one ever was denied membership because of his heritage. The union imposed integrated gangs on a waterfront that had been segregated, a system that had been supported by both employers and workers. From its inception, Local 8 maintained a democratic organization that distributed power among various ethnic or racial groups during negotiations, on meeting platforms, and in leadership positions. Most especially, Philadelphia native Ben Fletcher was hailed both by local black longshoremen as their champion and by the national IWW as a role model. Local 8's defeat in 1922, though, resulted in the end of its power. It was precisely because Local 8 had been split along racial lines that the lockout succeeded and the union lost its strength. Other factors, particularly rising employer power and government repression, also were important; still, employers consciously targeted the racial fault line as the union's weakest link. Despite all that Local 8 had done to fortify itself specifically from such attacks, it was racially divided, offering a cautionary tale of just how hard it is to create an interracial organization in a society where race has proven so polarizing. In the lockout's aftermath, race relations reverted to pre-IWW form. Black and white longshoremen soon worked in segregated gangs. In both the rise and decline of Local 8, as well as the later takeover of the ILA, race proved pivotal.

The book's second main theme assessed how Local 8 fought for short-term gains while maintaining a commitment to the IWW's long-term goals. Local 8 had great success with "pork chops" issues, a rarity in the IWW. On a day-to-day basis, the union spent its energy improving the work lives of its members. Deep-sea longshoremen benefited from dramatic wage raises (particularly overtime rates), less abusive bosses and conditions (once Local 8 eliminated the shape-up), and protection from arbitrary firings and excessive work. Longshoring still was hard and dangerous but it became far fairer and more remunerative. To achieve such results, the union called countless small strikes ("quickies") and held annual work stoppages around the anniversary of its creation. Five times in its ten-year reign Local 8 called out its thousands of members over issues of recognition, wages, hours, conditions, and worker control.

Concurrently, Local 8 remained committed to the IWW agenda, especially the new unionism that swept the world in this period, most readily evident in Local 8's use of direct-action tactics.[12] Local 8 leader and long-time IWW organizer E. F. Doree ticked off just a few of Local 8's many successful job actions lost to history, revealing the wide range of issues the longshoremen sought power over: workers struck three times in one day to have more men placed on their gangs unloading flour; gangs on two ships struck to have one fellow worker reinstated after being fired; a ship's gangs struck to be able to eat their dinner aboard rather than having to get off the dock; another ship's gangs struck to have the hold men's wages fully paid; longshoremen struck to have a foreman fired who supervised replacement workers during a previous strike; union members struck to have longshoremen who had worked during a strike fired; an untold number of strikes were called to have a man who had not paid up his union dues laid off; and countless other strikes were called to lighten cargo loads. The numerous actions cited by Doree are of import not only because they were attempts at controlling production but also because they demonstrate that the longshoremen used strikes—not contracts or formal negotiations—to get what they wanted. Shortly after their initial May 1913 strike, evidence of direct action on the job surfaced and continued for a dozen years. As Abraham Moses later recalled, "If you told one of them something, and they didn't like it, you know what they'd do? They'd run the load about half way up, cut the steve hold and walk off the ship . . . everybody walked off the ship and out the pier and went home." As with other syndicalists, Local 8 members knew where their power derived (on the job), strove regularly to expand their ranks via industrial unionism, and believed that they had to assert their power to achieve their goals.[13]

Although they did not emphasize revolution, it is wrong to assume that the longshoremen fought only for short-term gains. This issue is where Local 8 most frequently is viewed as not remaining true to the "real" IWW.[14] Local 8 did spend far more time on "bread and butter" issues, but it acted no differently than most Wobbly branches. As IWW historian Fred Thompson pointed out, it is wrong to "think that outside of Philadelphia IWW's sole concern was revolution: 8 hour day, employment sharks, shower baths, bedding furnished, quality of food, safety equipment and safety practices on the job, wage rates, job conditions in general—these were surely the focus of IWW everywhere." Thompson reminds us that "soweing [sic] radical ideas and catering to immediate objectives of workers are not contrary policies." Ben Fletcher took a similar approach: "People who spoke to me [Thompson] of Fletcher's speeches, stressed his linkage of far-flung hope to immediate organizational needs, and of organization as indispensable pre requisite for achieving any such hope." Similarly, when discussing "timber beasts" in the Northwest, to many the archetypal Wobblies, organizer Irving Hanson echoed this strategy: "Our basic approach was not to talk about revolution too much. We talked about immediate gains, union gains. . . . Meanwhile, the goal of an ultimate socialist society was stated quite plainly in our literature. We figured the people who were interested would read up on it." It is undeniable that many Local 8 members were far more concerned with pork chops than revolution. For these members, their commitment to Local 8 likely hinged on the fact that the militant union was able to deliver tangible benefits (and racial harmony). We will never know just how many Local 8 members were committed to revolution and how many just wanted a fatter paycheck, but it is certain that thousands of men fought on both fronts while belonging to the IWW. Of course, Local 8 repeatedly clashed with MTW officials in New York and IWW leaders in Chicago. These tensions were real and weakened both Local 8 and the IWW, yet the Philadelphians treated these disputes as familial. Philadelphia's longshoremen simultaneously struggled to improve their own lives and remain true to an organization advocating international class struggle.[15]

Beyond hoping for a commonwealth based on cooperation rather than competition, Local 8 saw more clearly than most organizations that such a society must encompass the entire racial and ethnic spectrum. The major economic, political, religious, and social institutions of early-twentieth-century America (all white dominated, as now) viewed true equality as a nonissue. Not surprisingly, as Melvyn Dubofsky insightfully argues, it was the most downtrodden—African Americans, immigrants, migratory and unskilled workers—who found the IWW most appealing. Where in the West the IWW's core support was among native-born male workers in the mining, timber, and agriculture industries often ignored by the AFL, in Philadelphia the IWW message resonated most strongly with the unskilled African American and immigrant waterfront workers. Hence the ideology of the IWW, in this instance a belief in a society not ordered on economic wealth but instead based upon equality, was indispensable to Local 8's success. That is why the men of Local 8 belonged to the IWW, were proud of their Wobbly noms de plume, and wore their membership, literally, on their lapels for ten years. The men of Local 8 were not simply loyal to the IWW, in many ways they were among its most committed.

In short, these unskilled and diverse workers put the ideology of radical egalitarianism into action. They were, arguably, the most successful local union in the history of the IWW, maintaining job control in the face of employer, governmental, societal, and, near the end, their own national union's fierce opposition. Their job control rested squarely on the local's ability to maintain a united front that depended on racial and ethnic equality. That they did so in an industry well known for racial and ethnic segregation is all the more noteworthy. In some ways, the Local 8/IWW model points the way to the CIO, in which blacks and "white ethnics" demonstrated their commitment to those unions that promoted equality. Of course, as the composition of the American working class becomes ever more diverse, the labor movement should work even harder to extend civil rights to all workers if it wants to play an influential role in society.

Perhaps no one is better qualified to discuss the intersections of race and class on the Philadelphia waterfront than Ben Fletcher. In his 1929 correspondence with historian Abram Harris, Fletcher wrote: "I have been identified with the Labor Movement—twenty years. . . . Nineteen of those years have been spent in the ranks of the I.W.W. and this long ago I have come to know that the Industrial Unionism as proposed and practiced by the I.W.W. is . . . the economic vehicle that will enable the Negro Workers to burst every bond of Racial Prejudice, Industrial and political inequalities and social ostracism." Local 8 demonstrates what can be accomplished when workers overcome racial and ethnic differences. It also is an excellent case study of the myriad, powerful forces that can defeat such efforts.[16]

NOTES

Introduction

1. McKay, *Home to Harlem*, 43–46.
2. Du Bois, *Philadelphia Negro;* Spero and Harris, *Black Worker.*
3. IWW surveys include Dubofsky, *We Shall Be All;* Foner, *Industrial Workers of the World;* Thompson and Murfin, *I.W.W.*
4. The simple classifications of "black" or "white" often are inappropriate, even though they are commonly used; see Roediger, *Towards the Abolition of Whiteness*, 181–98.
5. On Randolph, see Harris, *Keeping the Faith;* Pfeffer, *A. Philip Randolph.* On Harrison, see Perry, *Hubert Harrison Reader.* For more on Fletcher, see Cole, *Ben Fletcher;* Seraile, "Ben Fletcher."
6. Gambs, *Decline of the I.W.W.*, 135; Preston, "Shall This Be All?" 446. In the first major work on the IWW, Local 8 was not mentioned; Brissenden, *I.W.W.* In the second, Local 8 received several pages; Gambs, *Decline of the I.W.W.*, 135–37. Later historians gave Local 8 little more space: see Dubofsky, *We Shall Be All* (1988 ed.), 448–49; Foner, *Industrial Workers of the World*, 126–27. When a collection of essays on IWW local history was published, again Philadelphia was ignored; Conlin, *At the Point of Production.* Finally, there has been increasing interest in Local 8. The most important is Kimeldorf, *Battling for American Labor*, esp. 21–85. Also see McGirr, "Black and White Longshoremen in the IWW"; Kimeldorf, "Radical Possibilities?"; Kimeldorf and Penney, "'Excluded' by Choice; Cole, "Shaping Up and Shipping Out."
7. Nell Irvin Painter and Herbert Hill fired the first shots in this debate over whether labor history has a "race problem." If the field did, and I would concur, much has changed. See Hill, "Myth-Making as Labor History"; Painter, "New Labor History and the Historical Moment." The best recent contributions are Nelson, *Divided We Stand;* Kelly, *Race, Class, and Power in the Alabama Coalfields.*
8. Arnesen, "It Aint Like They Do in New Orleans"; Letwin, *Challenge of Interracial Unionism;* Halpern, *Down on the Killing Floor.*
9. Kelly, *Race, Class, and Power in the Alabama Coalfields.* On IWW efforts to organize blacks outside of Philadelphia, see Spero and Harris, *Black Worker,* 182–205, 329–36; Foner, "IWW and the Black Worker"; Green, "Brotherhood of Timber Workers."
10. Kimeldorf, "Bringing Unions Back In." My attempt to combine the best of the "old" institutionally focused and "new" social history-influenced labor

history follows Freeman, *In Transit;* Kazin, *Barons of Labor.* Eric Arnesen notes that "working-class organizations and perspectives are often slighted" in the growing and vibrant field of African American history. A review of the literature on Philadelphia's African Americans and white ethnic groups reveals the same deficiency; Arnesen, "Following the Color Line of Labor," 81.

Chapter 1: "The Workshop of the World"

1. U.S. Engineer Department, *Port of Philadelphia,* 1; Philadelphia Department of Wharves, Docks, and Ferries, *Port of Philadelphia* (1926 ed.), 13; Warner, *Private City,* 4–5, 11–13; Heinrich, *Ships for the Seven Seas,* 3–14.

2. MacFarlane, *Manufacturing in Philadelphia,* 45, 95–96; Licht, *Getting Work,* 4–7; Hugill, *Sailortown,* 178.

3. U.S. Engineer Department, *Port of Philadelphia,* 45–47, 340–41; Philadelphia Department of Wharves, Docks, and Ferries, *Port of Philadelphia* (1926 ed.), 31.

4. U.S. Engineer Department, *Port of Philadelphia,* 325, 340–41.

5. Scranton, *Figured Tapestry,* 1–8; Harris, *Bloodless Victories,* 29–36; Licht, *Getting Work,* 30–35.

6. The literature on longshore labor is voluminous. See Nelson, *Divided We Stand;* Arnesen, *Waterfront Workers of New Orleans;* Montgomery, *Fall of the House of Labor.*

7. Poole, *Harbor,* 138.

8. Barnes, *Longshoremen,* 57; Montgomery, *Fall of the House of Labor,* 90.

9. Callan, Shooting Script, LDOHP; Licht, *Getting Work,* xi.

10. Neill to author, December 12, 1995; Poole, *Harbor,* 139; Brennan, Shooting Script, LDOHP.

11. Quinn oral history, LDOHP; Larrowe, *Shape-Up and Hiring Hall,* 50–55; Davis, *Waterfront Revolts,* 19–20.

12. Varlack oral history, LDOHP; Bailey, *Kid from Hoboken,* 69–70; Nelson, *Divided We Stand,* 10, 39, 53.

13. Dabney, "Questionnaire for ILA Local 1116," Labor Union Survey, Pennsylvania, 1925–28, in National Urban League Papers, Box 89, Series 6E; Moses oral history, LDOHP; Quinn, Shooting Script, 7, LDOHP; Whatley, "African-American Strikebreaking," 525–58.

14. Dabney, "Questionnaire for ILA Local 1116," Labor Union Survey, Pennsylvania, 1925–28, in National Urban League Papers, Box 89, Series 6E; Hill, "Racial Practices of Organized Labor," 365–70; Whatley, "African-American Strikebreaking," 526–29, 544–48.

15. Barnes, *Longshoremen,* 129–30; Walsh testimony in IWW Collection, *U.S. v. Haywood et al.,* July 30, 1918, 9331, Folder 5, Box 114.

16. Brennan, Shooting Script, LDOHP; and Ushka oral history, LDOHP.

17. Philadelphia, *Annual Report of the Department of Wharves, Docks, and Ferries . . . 1914,* 18; MacElwee and Taylor, *Wharf Management,* 2, 9, 29, 32; Poole, *Harbor,* 145.

18. Barnes, *Longshoremen,* 131–32; Davis, *Waterfront Revolts,* 35–39.

19. *Philadelphia Inquirer,* June 3, 1898, 3; and June 4, 1898, 3; Fair interview, December 21, 1978, in Shaffer Papers, Box 3; *Afro-American,* July 23, 1920, 4; Poole, "Ship Must Sail on Time," 178, 185–86.

20. Fair interview, December 21, 1978, in Shaffer Papers, Box 3; Callan, Shooting Script, LDOHP; Walsh quoted in George, *I.W.W. Trial*, 158, in IWW Pamphlets.

21. Barnes, *Longshoremen*, 80–81; Simpson, Spence & Young, to Chas. M. Taylor's Sons, Inc., June 3, 1913; and Furness, Withy & Co., to Chas. M. Taylor's Sons, Inc., June 3, 1913—both in Taylor Papers.

22. Callan, Shooting Script, LDOHP; Foner, *Policies and Practices of the American Federation of Labor*, 14, 18; Barnes, *Longshoremen*, 82–92; Poole, "Ship Must Sail on Time," 181.

23. Montgomery, *Fall of the House of Labor*, 89–91; Davis, *Waterfront Revolts*, 11–12, 36–37, 46–48; Fern, "Good Man Gone"; Poole, "Men on the Docks," 144.

24. Nelson, *Divided We Stand*, 9, 12; Davis, *Waterfront Revolts*, 12, 21–24; Letwin, *Challenge of Interracial Unionism*, 154–56.

25. "Negro in Pennsylvania," (Baltimore) *Afro-American* (*Ledger*), June 13, 1914, 1; Johnson and Campbell, *Black Migration in America*, 76–78.

26. Manly, "Where Negroes Live in Philadelphia," esp. 11; Du Bois, *Philadelphia Negro*; Hardy, "Race and Opportunity," preface, 130–31.

27. Hershberg et al., "Tale of Three Cities," 469–70, 476, 479; Franklin, *Education of Black Philadelphia*, 12–21; 48–51; *Philadelphia Tribune*, April 26, 1913, 1; Jackson, *Ku Klux Klan*, 170–71; Jenkins, *Hoods and Shirts*, 36–39.

28. Du Bois, *Philadelphia Negro*, 98, 111; *Public Ledger*, April 13, 1913, cited in Foner, *Organized Labor and the Black Worker*, 126–27; Hardy, "Race and Opportunity," 70–71, 113–15.

29. Du Bois, *Philadelphia Negro*, 135, 330–33; Wright, *Negro in Pennsylvania*, 172, 186; Greene and Woodson, *Negro Wage Earner*, 108.

30. Ignatiev, *How the Irish*; Clark, *Irish Relations*, 144–45, 152.

31. Lane, *William Dorsey's Philadelphia*, 82–83; Clark, *Erin's Heirs*, 51–66.

32. Golab, "Polish Experience," 53.

33. Golab, "Polish Experience," 60–63, 70n4; Bodnar, *Workers' World*, 15–21; Lewandowka, "Polish Immigrant," 82, 89.

34. Bodnar, *Workers' World*, 13–14, 63–66; Cohen, *Making a New Deal*, 362–63; Gerstle, *Working-Class Americanism*, 1–5, 20–25.

35. Lane, *William Dorsey's Philadelphia*, xi–xiii; Steffens, *Shame of the Cities*, 134–38, 143–44; *Philadelphia Tribune*, February 15, 1913, 1; Geffen, "Violence in Philadelphia," 382.

36. Laurie, *Working People of Philadelphia*, 2–66; Salinger, "Artisans, Journeymen, and the Transformation of Labor," 62–63; Clark, *Irish Relations*, 144–45; Runcie, "Hunting the Nigs," 196–98; Nelson, *Divided We Stand*, xxxiv–xl, 13–15.

37. Laurie, *Working People of Philadelphia*, 62–66, 124–25, 151–58 (including quote); Ignatiev, *How the Irish*, 125–27.

38. Feldberg, *Philadelphia Riots of 1844*, esp. 19–20, 78–79, 89; Roediger, *Wages of Whiteness*, 133; Ignatiev, *How the Irish*, 40–59, 148–59.

39. Hershberg, "Free Blacks in Antebellum Philadelphia," 375–76.

40. Du Bois, *Philadelphia Negro*, 100; U.S. Census Office, *Thirteenth Census of the United States*, vol. 4: *Population 1910: Occupation Statistics*, 588–89; Moses interview, LDOHP; Lever interview, 15, BLMOHP; U.S. Census Office, *Fourteenth Census of the United States*, vol. 4: *Population 1920: Occupations*, 1194; Quinn, Shooting Script, 6–7, LDOHP.

41. Wright, *Negro in Pennsylvania*, 167–87, 195; Licht, *Getting Work*, 45–50;

U.S. Immigration Commission, *Reports of the Immigration Commission*, vol. 27: *Immigrants in Cities*, 358–59.

42. Greene and Woodson, *Negro Wage Earner*, 113.

43. U.S. Immigration Commission, *Reports of the Immigration Commission*, vol. 27: *Immigrants in Cities*, 356–59; Golab, "Immigrant and the City," 213–14, 219–21; Golab, "Polish Experience," 52–60; Licht, *Getting Work*, 13–14.

44. U.S. Immigration Commission, *Reports of the Immigration Commission*, vol. 27: *Immigrants in Cities*, 356–59; Licht, *Getting Work*, 13–14.

45. Golab, "Immigrant and the City," 213–15; Juliani, "Italian Community in Philadelphia," 233–62; Lane, *William Dorsey's Philadelphia*, 84–85.

46. Golab, "Immigrant and the City," 203–26; Licht, *Getting Work*, 13–14, 31, 49. See, for instance, Brennan, Green, and Moocke interviews, LDOHP.

Chapter 2: Wobblies Take the Docks

1. Fletcher, "Philadelphia Waterfront Unionism"; *Public Ledger*, May 17, 1913, 2; May 19, 1913, 1; May 20, 1913, 1; Montgomery, *Workers' Control in America*, 91–109.

2. Montgomery quoted in Nelson, *Divided We Stand*, 16.

3. Bernstein, "Working People of Philadelphia," 336–39; Laurie, *Working People of Philadelphia*, 85–107; Davis, *Parades and Power*, 134–35 (quote).

4. Rediker, *Between the Devil and the Deep Blue Sea*, esp. 77–115.

5. Laurie, *Working People of Philadelphia*, 124–25, 157–58.

6. Garlock, *Guide to the Local Assemblies of the Knights of Labor*, 450–60; Brecher, *Strike!* 44 (quote); Scranton, *Figured Tapestry*, 29–36, 50–51; Foner, *Organized Labor and the Black Worker*, 47–63; Lane, *William Dorsey's Philadelphia*, 68.

7. Barnes, *Longshoremen*, 101–10; Hobsbawm, *Labouring Men*, 217; *New York Times*, September 28, 1896, 8; *The Longshoreman*, June 1915, 1; Russell, *Men along the Shore*, 33–41.

8. McGirr claims that only 164 black longshoremen worked in Philadelphia in 1896, but she confuses the city's entire black longshore force with that in the Seventh Ward, the district that Du Bois examined in *Philadelphia Negro*, which obviously accounted for only some of the total. See McGirr, "Black and White Longshoremen in the IWW," 380; Du Bois, *Philadelphia Negro*, 101.

9. *Philadelphia Inquirer*, June 1, 1898, 8; Barnes, *Longshoremen*, 113.

10. *Philadelphia Inquirer*, June 3, 1898, 3; and June 4, 1898, 3.

11. *Philadelphia Inquirer*, June 4, 1898, 3; Durham, "Labor Unions and the Negro," 227–30; Greene and Woodson, *Negro Wage Earner*, 108; Barnes, *Longshoremen*, 5–7, 106–7.

12. Barnes, *Longshoremen*, 110–13; Lane, *William Dorsey's Philadelphia*, 68–69.

13. ILA, *Proceedings of the Twelfth Annual Convention: 1903*, 7; *The Longshoreman*, August 1913, 2; Reynolds and Killingsworth, *Trade Union Publications*, 94–100.

14. Spero and Harris, *Black Worker*, 199–200; Nelson, *Divided We Stand*, 38–44, 51, 61–64; Frazier quoted in Winslow, "On the Waterfront," 370–74.

15. Arnesen, "It Aint Like They Do in New Orleans," 57–60, 86–88; Lever interview, 14, BLMOHP.

16. Arnesen, "It Aint Like They Do in New Orleans," 57, 80; Roediger, *Towards the Abolition of Whiteness*, 127–80; *The Longshoreman*, October 1911, 2.

17. Russell, *Men along the Shore*, 91, 248–49.

18. Scranton, *Figured Tapestry*, 46–55; Fones-Wolf, "Employer Unity and the Crisis of the Craftsman," 449–55 (first quote); LaMar, *Clothing Workers of Philadelphia*, 25 (second quote); Harris, *Bloodless Victories*, 140–53 (last quote).

19. *Industrial Union Bulletin*, January 4, 1908, 4; July 20, 1907, 3; August 24, 1907, 3–4; *Solidarity*, July 9, 1910, 1; July 30, 1910, 1; September 3, 1910, 1; Burt and Davies, "Iron Age," 481–82.

20. *Solidarity*, June 3, 1911, 1; September 9, 1911, 1; September 16, 1911, 1; February 17, 1912.

21. Ben Fletcher in U.S. Census, 1910; Thompson to Brazier, January 4, 1967; and Brazier to Thompson, January 7, 1967—both in Thompson Collection, Folder 26, Box 12; *Solidarity*, July 27, 1912, 4 (second quote); August 10, 1912, 3; and September 28, 1912, 1 (first quote).

22. *Solidarity*, September 28, 1912, 1.

23. *Solidarity*, August 3, 1912, 4; August 24, 1912, 4; and September 7, 1912, 4.

24. *Philadelphia Inquirer*, April 8, 1913, 3; *Public Ledger*, May 5, 1913, 2; *Solidarity*, April 26, 1913, 1.

25. Disbrow, "Progressive Movement in Philadelphia," 311.

26. *Industrial Union Bulletin*, November 9, 1907, and July 25, 1908; Perry, "Transport Workers Join I.W.W."; *One Big Union Monthly*, April 1920, 41; Goldberg, *Maritime Story*, 38–40.

27. The Edward J. Lewis organizing Philadelphia's longshoremen was the same man that William Z. Foster mentioned as a top orator in one of his autobiographical works, *Pages from a Worker's Life*, 271.

28. *Public Ledger*, May 6, 1913, 3; and May 7, 1913, 6.

29. *Solidarity*, May 10, 1913, 1; and October 4, 1913, 1; Speed report in "Philadelphia," in IWW, *Proceedings of the Eighth Annual Convention: 1913*, 28. My understanding of Speed's racial ideology benefited from correspondence with John Holmes.

30. *Public Ledger*, May 7, 1913, 6; *North American*, May 17, 1913, 2; May 21, 1913, 4 (quote); and May 27, 1913, 8.

31. *North American*, May 27, 1913, 8; *Solidarity*, May 24, 1913, 2, 4 (quote); Thompson to Dawson, February 11, 1982, in Thompson Collection, Folder 6, Box 10.

32. *Solidarity*, May 24, 1913, 2; Spero and Harris, *Black Worker*, 333. Kimeldorf claims that the white longshoremen struck first and then the blacks followed. However, I have not found any evidence to support this claim; see Kimeldorf and Penney, "'Excluded' by Choice," 53.

33. Taylor to O'Neill, May 24, 1913, in Taylor Papers.

34. *Public Ledger*, May 17, 1913, 2; IWW, *Proceedings of the Eighth Annual Convention: 1913*, 5–7. On the conservatism of the ILA leadership, see Winslow, "On the Waterfront," esp. 376; Nelson, *Divided We Stand*, esp. chap. 2.

35. *North American*, May 22, 1913, 1, 4; and May 23, 1913, 1, 5; *Solidarity*, May 24, 1913, 4 (both quotes).

36. Steffens, *Shame of the Cities*, 134–38, 143–44.

37. Taylor to Furness, Withy & Co., May 26, 1913, in Taylor Papers; *Public Ledger*, May 24, 1913, 10.

38. Taylor to Furness, Withy & Co., May 26, 1913; and Taylor to Hampson, May 27, 1913—both in Taylor Papers; Whatley, "African-American Strikebreaking," 526, 529, 544–45; Norwood, *Strikebreaking and Intimidation*, 78–79.

39. *Public Ledger*, May 22, 1913, 1–2; *North American*, May 17, 1913, 2; and May 22, 1913, 1, 4; Norwood, *Strikebreaking and Intimidation*, 80–91.

40. *Solidarity*, October 4, 1913, 1, 4 (last quote); *The Longshoreman*, June 1913, 7; Dempsey to Morrison, September 25, 1913, in AFL Records, Reel 39.

41. Dabney, "Questionnaire for ILA Local 1116," Labor Union Survey, Pennsylvania, 1925–28, in National Urban League Papers, Box 89, Series 6E; Kelley, "We Are Not What We Seem," 80–81; Kelly, *Race, Class, and Power in the Alabama Coalfields*; Gregg, *Sparks from the Anvil of Oppression*, 15–16, 218–19.

42. *Public Ledger*, May 21, 1913, 1; and June 23, 1913, 2 (first quote); *Solidarity*, May 24, 1913, 4; Foner, "IWW and the Black Worker," 51 (second quote).

43. *North American*, May 18, 1913, 8; *Public Ledger*, May 20, 1913, 1; and May 21, 1913, 1.

44. Agent of Furness, Withy & Co., to Chas. Taylor's Sons, June 3, 1913, in Taylor Papers; *Public Ledger*, May 21, 1913, 1 (quote).

45. *Public Ledger*, May 22, 1913, 1–2; Montgomery, *Fall of the House of Labor*, 332.

46. *North American*, May 23, 1913, 1, 5; Kaplan, *Red City, Blue Period*, 107, 124.

47. Taylor to Furness, Withy & Co., June 3, 1913, in Taylor Papers; *North American*, May 30, 1913, 2; *Solidarity*, June 7, 1913, 4; and October 4, 1913, 1; Commercial Exchange of Philadelphia, *Fifty-Ninth Annual Report: 1913*, 149.

48. *Public Ledger*, May 22, 1913, 1; *Philadelphia Inquirer*, May 7, 1913, 2; *Journal of the Philadelphia Chamber of Commerce*, July 1913, 10; Philadelphia, *Annual Report of the Department of Wharves, Docks, and Ferries . . . 1913*, 7.

49. Taylor to Franklin, July 2, 1913; and Taylor to Furness, Withy & Co., June 3, 1913—both in Taylor Papers.

50. Taylor to Furness, Withy & Co., June 3 and June 11, 1913; Taylor to Franklin, June 26 (quote) and June 27, 1913—all in Taylor Papers; Arnesen, "It Aint Like They Do in New Orleans," 62–63, 82–83.

51. *Solidarity*, June 7, 1913, 4.

Chapter 3: There Is a Power in a Union

1. *Solidarity*, May 30, 1914, 2 (first two quotes); Peterson, "One Big Union in International Perspective," 42–44.

2. Fletcher to Harris, July 29, 1929, in Harris Papers.

3. Du Bois, *Philadelphia Negro*, 5, 98, 109–10, 145; Emlen, "Movement for the Betterment of the Negro in Philadelphia," 88–89; Golab, "Immigrant and the City," 210–12, 220–21, 226; Dubofsky, "Radicalism of the Dispossessed," 180–81, 192–93.

4. Washington, "Negro and the Labor Unions," 756–59, 764; Du Bois quote in

Whatley, "African-American Strikebreaking," 527; Nelson, *Divided We Stand,* xxxi–xxxiii.

5. Washington, "Negro and the Labor Unions," 756–59, 764; Arnesen, "It Aint Like They Do in New Orleans"; Arnesen, *Waterfront Workers of New Orleans;* Lewis, *In Their Own Interests,* 49–59.

6. Brundage, *Making of Western Labor Radicalism,* 1–6, 34–52, 154–63; Fair interview, December 21, 1978, 3, in Shaffer Papers, Box 3; Du Bois, "I.W.W."

7. Dempsey to Morrison, September 25, 1913, in AFL Records, Reel 39; Radzialowski, "Competition for Jobs and Racial Stereotypes"; Nelson, *Divided We Stand,* xxvii–xxix, 24; Barrett, *Work and Community in the Jungle,* 221–24.

8. Dempsey to Morrison, September 25, 1913, in AFL Records, Reel 39; U.S. Immigration Commission, *Reports of the Immigration Commission,* vol. 27: *Immigrants in Cities,* 356–59. This argument benefited from several discussions with Bruce Nelson.

9. Nelson, *Divided We Stand,* xxx–xxxi and all of part 1.

10. Moses interview, LDOHP.

11. Quote in Roediger, *Towards the Abolition of Whiteness,* 127–80; Letwin, "Interracial Unionism, Gender, and 'Social Equality'"; Shor, "Virile Syndicalism."

12. *Public Ledger,* May 20, 1913, 1; *The Longshoreman,* August 1913, 2.

13. Greene and Woodson, *Negro Wage Earner,* 113–14.

14. Taylor to Franklin, June 26, 1913, in Taylor Papers (quotes); *Solidarity,* August 22, 1914, 1; and October 4, 1913, 1; Montgomery, *Fall of the House of Labor,* 94–95.

15. Taylor to Furness, Withy & Co., June 11, 1913, in Taylor Papers; *Public Ledger,* December 1, 1913, 14.

16. Taylor to Furness, Withy & Co., June 11, 1913; Taylor to Franklin, June 26 and July 2, 1913—all in Taylor Papers; Roediger and Foner, *Our Own Time,* esp. 227–29.

17. U.S. Census Office, *Occupations of the Twelfth Census* [1900], 674–75; *Solidarity,* December 20, 1913, 2 (quote); Taylor to Franklin, June 26 and July 2, 1913—both in Taylor Papers; Cole, "Shaping Up and Shipping Out," chap. 3.

18. *Philadelphia Inquirer,* July 23, 1913, 6; and July 24, 1913, 3; *Public Ledger,* July 22, 1913, 17; Dempsey to Morrison, September 25, 1913, in AFL Records, Reel 39.

19. For more on segregated gangs prior to Local 8, see chapter 1. For after Local 8, see conclusion.

20. *Solidarity,* November 15, 1913, 4.

21. *Solidarity,* July 5, 1913, 1; and August 1, 1914, 1; Fones-Wolf, *Trade Union Gospel,* 180–81 (last quote).

22. Minutes of Shipping Interests' Meeting, June 10, 1913, in Taylor Papers; *Solidarity,* October 4, 1913, 1, 4; May 30, 1914, 1; and November 28, 1914, 1; *The Longshoreman,* October 1913, 4, cited in Brown, "I.W.W. and the Negro Worker," 67.

23. *Solidarity,* October 4, 1913, 1, 4; and May 30, 1914, 1; Dempsey to Morrison, September 25, 1913, in AFL Records, Reel 39.

24. IWW, *Proceedings of the Eighth Annual Convention: 1913,* 2–7.

25. IWW, *Proceedings of the Eighth Annual Convention: 1913,* 7–9.

26. *Solidarity*, May 30, 1914, 1–2; *Afro-American*, May 30, 1914, 1; Norris, *Ended Episodes*, 105.

27. *Solidarity*, May 30, 1914, 4; Ben H. Fletcher's Defendant's Card, Old German File 160053, Entry 31, Record Group 65; *Afro-American*, May 30, 1914, 1.

28. *Solidarity*, May 30, 1914, 1–2; and July 4, 1914, 4.

29. *Solidarity*, August 1, 1914, 1; and August 22, 1914, 1.

30. Philadelphia Department of Wharves, Docks, and Ferries, *Port of Philadelphia* (1926 ed.), 47; Norris, *Ended Episodes*, 96–117; *Philadelphia Inquirer*, May 29, 1913, 2; Cole, "Shaping Up and Shipping Out," chap. 3.

31. Philadelphia Department of Wharves, Docks, and Ferries, *Port of Philadelphia* (1926 ed.), 15; *The Longshoreman*, July 1914, 2 (second quote); *Solidarity*, July 4, 1914, 4 (first quote); and November 28, 1914, 1 (last quote).

32. *Solidarity*, November 28, 1914, 1; *Public Ledger*, December 1, 1913, 14; Mann, "Plea for Solidarity"; Peterson, "One Big Union in International Perspective," 42, 47.

33. *Solidarity*, April 11, 1914, 4; and May 23, 1914, 1.

34. *Solidarity*, October 3, 1914, 1.

35. *Journal of the Philadelphia Chamber of Commerce*, January 1915, 27; and July 1915, 12–13; Smith, *Influence of the Great War upon Shipping*, 26–30.

36. Walsh testimony in IWW Collection, *U.S. v. Haywood et al.*, July 30, 1918, 9317–20, 9337–42, 9345–46, 9352–53, Box 114.

37. Walsh testimony in IWW Collection, *U.S. v. Haywood et al.*, July 30, 1918, 9337–42, 9346, 9352–53, Box 114; Beffel, "Kin Takes over Walsh Funeral," in Beffel Collection, Box 5; IWW, *Proceedings of the Tenth Annual Convention: 1916*, 40–41, 150.

38. *Public Ledger*, January 28, 1915, 8; *Solidarity*, February 13, 1915, 1.

39. *Record* (Philadelphia?), February 10, 1915, in DWDF Clipping Book 1; *Solidarity*, February 13, 1915, 1.

40. *Solidarity*, February 20, 1915, 1.

41. *New York Times*, December 9, 1914; Smith, *Influence of the Great War upon Shipping*, 26–29; *The Longshoreman*, December 1915, 1.

42. Philadelphia Department of Wharves, Docks, and Ferries, *Port of Philadelphia* (1926 ed.), 15; Commercial Exchange of Philadelphia, *Sixty-Second Annual Report: 1916*, 35, 66–67; *Public Ledger*, January 5, 1916, 3.

43. *Public Ledger*, January 6, 1916, 20; Walsh testimony in IWW Collection, *U.S. v. Haywood et al.*, July 30, 1918, 9339, Box 114.

44. *Solidarity*, April 15, 1916, 1; and May 27, 1916, 1; Montgomery, *Workers' Control in America*, 95–97.

45. Avrich, *Anarchist Voices*, 394–95; *Solidarity*, April 15, 1916, 1; and September 23, 1916, 4.

46. Castellano, Cuevas, and Paredes testimonies in IWW Collection, *U.S. v. Haywood et al.*, August 8, 1918, 10793–802, 10809–10, Box 116; correspondence with Barry Carr of La Trobe University in Australia.

47. *Solidarity*, May 27, 1916, 1; Nelson, *Workers on the Waterfront*, 31–32; Cole, "Andrew Furuseth."

48. Guillel, Paredes, and Alonso testimonies in IWW Collection, *U.S. v. Haywood et al.*, August 8, 1918, 10789–93, 10803–9, Box 116; Nelson, *Workers on the Waterfront*, 48–50.

49. Paul Baker in U.S. Census, 1920; George McKenna in U.S. Census, 1910; McKenna testimony in IWW Collection, *U.S. v. Haywood et al.*, August 15, 1918, 12009–11, Box 117; *Solidarity*, April 15, 1916, 1.

50. *Press* (Philadelphia?), May 20, 1916, in DWDF Clipping Book 4; *Solidarity*, May 27, 1916, 1; and June 17, 1916, 1.

51. *Solidarity*, June 17, 1916, 1.

52. *Solidarity*, June 17, 1916, 1.

53. *North American*, June 16, 1916, in DWDF Clipping Book 4; Philadelphia Department of Wharves, Docks, and Ferries, *Port of Philadelphia* (1926 ed.), 91–94; *Public Ledger*, June 17, 1916, 6.

54. Pennsylvania Department of Labor and Industry, *Third Annual Report*, 1074; *Solidarity*, June 17, 1916, 1.

55. *Public Ledger*, July 14, 1916, in DWDF Clipping Book 4; *Solidarity*, July 15, 1916, 1.

56. *Public Ledger*, July 7, 1916, 1, 7; *Philadelphia Inquirer*, July 8, 1916, 4; *Solidarity*, July 15, 1916, 1 (first quote).

57. Gregg, *Sparks from the Anvil of Oppression*, 24–25; Hardy, "Race and Opportunity," 205–8. Kimeldorf contends that almost all of the unionists striking Southern were white, but I have not found any evidence to support his assertion; Kimeldorf and Penney, "'Excluded' by Choice," 56.

58. *Philadelphia Inquirer*, July 6, 1916, 1, 5; and July 7, 1916, 7.

59. *Public Ledger*, July 7, 1916, 7 (quote); and July 8, 1916, 4; *Solidarity*, July 15, 1916, 1.

60. *Solidarity*, July 15, 1916, 1.

61. *Solidarity*, July 15, 1916, 1; *Public Ledger*, July 7, 1916, 16.

62. *Solidarity*, September 9, 1916, 1; *The Longshoreman*, May–December 1916, 7.

63. Carter testimony in IWW Collection, *U.S. v. Haywood et al.*, August 15, 1918, 12018–27, Box 117.

Chapter 4: War on the Waterfront

1. Philadelphia Maritime Exchange, *Forty-Fourth Annual Report* (1919), 25; Collins, *Philadelphia*, 375; Heinrich, *Ships for the Seven Seas*, 165–68; Harris, *Bloodless Victories*, 202–5, including Chamber quote (202).

2. *Solidarity*, January 13, 1917, 1; Nef testimony in IWW Collection, *U.S. v. Haywood et al.*, 1918, 5968–75, Folder 4, Box 110; Hall, *Harvest Wobblies*, 107–9; Dubofsky, *We Shall Be All* (1988 ed.), 178, 315–18, 344.

3. Minutes of Meeting of the Organization Committee of MTWIU of the IWW Industrial Union #100, New York City, February 25, 1917; and "Summary of MTWIU 100," n.d.—both in Record Group 65, Old German File 160053; *Solidarity*, January 13, 1917, 1.

4. Doree testimony in IWW Collection, *U.S. v. Haywood et al.*, July 2, 1918, 5902–67, Folder 4, Box 110; Rosen interview, January 7, 1997; Doree interrogation in McDevitt report, September 25, 1917, in Record Group 65, Old German File 67-40; personal correspondence with John Reed Tarver.

5. Ben H. Fletcher's Defendant's Card and "Summary of MTWIU 100," n.d.—

both in Record Group 65, Old German File 160053; Lever interview, BLMOHP; Walsh testimony in IWW Collection, *U.S. v. Haywood et al.*, July 30, 1918, 9348–49, Folder 5, Box 114; *Solidarity*, February 10, 1917, 1; Spero and Harris, *Black Worker*, 192–94.

6. *Solidarity*, February 17, 1917, 1; U.S. Department of Labor, *Negro Migration in 1916–17*, 136.

7. *International Socialist Review*, April 1917, 615–17.

8. *Public Ledger*, February 10, 1917, 4; *Solidarity*, February 17, 1917, 1; *International Socialist Review*, April 1917, 616.

9. *Public Ledger*, February 9, 1917, 3; *Solidarity*, February 27, 1917, 3.

10. *Public Ledger*, February 22, 1917, 1, 9 (first quote); U.S. Department of Labor, *Negro Migration in 1916–17*, 136–37, 157; Kaplan, *Red City, Blue Period*, 106–7, 125.

11. *Public Ledger*, February 22, 1917, 1, 9; and February 23, 1917, 1, 15; *Solidarity*, March 3, 1917, 1, 4.

12. *Public Ledger*, February 26, 1917, 3; and February 27, 1917, 3; *Solidarity*, March 3, 1917, 1, 4; Kaplan, *Red City, Blue Period*, 83.

13. *Public Ledger*, February 15, 1917, 4; February 23, 1917, 1 (quotes), 15; and March 5, 1917, 3.

14. *Philadelphia Record*, March 26, 1917, and *North American*, March 15, 1917, in DWDF Clipping Book 7.

15. U.S. Department of Labor, *Negro Migration in 1916–17*, 136–37.

16. *Solidarity*, March 10, 1917, 2.

17. Collins, *Philadelphia*, 372–74.

18. Philadelphia Department of Wharves, Docks, and Ferries, *Port of Philadelphia* (1926 ed.), 15, 31 (quote); Collins, *Philadelphia*, 371; *North American*, March 7, 1917, in DWDF Clipping Book 7.

19. ONI, *Investigation of the Marine Transport Workers*, 14–17 (quote); *Philadelphia Inquirer*, April 12, 1917, in DWDF Clipping Book 7.

20. Preston, *Aliens and Dissenters*, 88–90; Foner, *Industrial Workers of the World*, 554–56; *Solidarity*, March 24, 1917, 1.

21. Shor, "IWW and Oppositional Politics," 78; Preston, *Aliens and Dissenters*, 90.

22. Doree and Nef testimonies in IWW Collection, *U.S. v. Haywood et al.*, July 2, 1918, 5902–10, 5941–54, 5981–83, Folder 4, Box 110.

23. Doree and Nef testimonies in IWW Collection, *U.S. v. Haywood et al.*, July 2, 1918, 5948–63, 5982, Folder 4, Box 110; Lever deposition, January 21, 1922, in Record Group 204, File no. 37-361.

24. Doree testimony in IWW Collection, *U.S. v. Haywood et al.*, July 2, 1918, 5942, Folder 4, Box 110; Anderson and Puller testimonies in IWW Collection, *U.S. v. Haywood et al.*, 1918, 11997, 11907, Folder 7, Box 117; *The Messenger*, March 1922, 377.

25. McDevitt report, November 9, 1917, in Record Group 65, Old German File 67-40; Lever, Petition for Clemency of Fletcher, April 29, 1922; and Olmsted, "In the Matter of the Applications of John J. Walsh and Ben H. Fletcher: Brief in Support of the Applications," 7—both in Record Group 204, File no. 37-479.

26. Lewis, *W. E. B. Du Bois*, 525–32.

27. Barrett, *William Z. Foster*, 71–73.

28. Doree and Nef testimonies in IWW Collection, *U.S. v. Haywood et al.,* July 2, 1918, 5934–35, 5978, Folder 4, Box 110; USSB, *Marine and Dock Labor,* 87.

29. *Solidarity,* June 2, 1917, 4 (first quote); Nef deposition, January 23, 1922, in Record Group 204, File no. 37-361.

30. Anderson testimony in IWW Collection, *U.S. v. Haywood et al.,* 1918, 11996, Folder 7, Box 117; Kane deposition, May 5, 1922, in Record Group 204, File no. 37-479.

31. Walsh testimony in IWW Collection, *U.S. v. Haywood et al.,* July 30, 1918, 9320, 9324, Folder 5, Box 114; ONI, *Investigation of the Marine Transport Workers,* 31.

32. USSB, *Marine and Dock Labor,* 27–29, 40, 75, 87; Heinrich, *Ships for the Seven Seas,* 168–69.

33. National Adjustment Commission, *Chairman's Report,* 156; Gompers, *Seventy Years of Life and Labor,* 1.425, 2.336–38; *The Longshoreman,* September 1917, 1; October 1917, 8 (quote); and November 1917, 4; Arnesen, *Waterfront Workers of New Orleans,* 222–28.

34. Goodwin to Gompers, June 21, 1917, in AFL Records, Reel 39; and Gompers to Goodwin, June 25, 1917, in AFL Records, Reel 39; National Adjustment Commission, *Chairman's Report,* 156–58 (second quote); *The Longshoreman,* August 1917, 2; ONI to Bielaski, September 28(?), 1918, in Record Group 65, Old German File 366145, Reel 12, *Federal Surveillance of Afro-Americans* (last quote).

35. Lever interview, 17, BLMOHP; Daniel to Bielaski, January 25, 1918, in Record Group 65, Old German File 67-40; Lewis, *In Their Own Interests,* 58–59.

36. *The Messenger,* March 1922, 377; McKenna and Puller testimonies in IWW Collection, *U.S. v. Haywood et al.,* 1918, 12014–15, 11910, Folder 7, Box 117; Gompers, *Seventy Years of Life and Labor,* 336–38.

37. ONI, *Investigation of the Marine Transport Workers,* 31–32; James, *Holding Aloft the Banner of Ethiopia,* 183–84.

38. Doree to Haywood, September 21, 1917, in IWW Collection, Folder 12, Box 99; Nef deposition, January 23, 1922, 2, in Record Group 204, File no. 37-361; Renshaw, "IWW and the Red Scare," 66; Seraile, "Ben Fletcher," 218–19.

39. McDevitt report, October 4, 1917, in Record Group 65, Old German File 67-40, Entry 31; Preston, *Aliens and Dissenters,* 119–20.

40. ONI, *Investigation of the Marine Transport Workers,* 32; Doree deposition, January 23, 1922, in Record Group 204, File no. 37-393.

41. "JAF-CZC, 371-361-3773, Nef et al.," in Record Group 204, File no. 37-479; Doree deposition, January 23, 1922, in Record Group 204, File no. 37-393; Preston, *Aliens and Dissenters,* 97–99, 118–22 (last quotes); Ellis, *Race, War, and Surveillance,* xvii–xix.

42. E. F. Doree to Chika Doree, June 18, 1922 (author's possession); Rosen, *Wobbly Life;* Preston, *Aliens and Dissenters,* 93–99.

43. Kane deposition, May 5, 1922; Daniel deposition, May 5, 1922 (third quote); and U.S. Pardon Attorney, "Memorandum for Mr. Burns, Chief, Bureau of Investigation," April 8, 1922, JAF-CZC (third quote)—all in Record Group 204, File no. 37-479, Box 985, 1853–1946; Fitts to Secretary of the Navy, January 3, 1918 (first quote); and Gibson to Fitts, February 18, 1918—both in Record Group 60, Box 2219, correspondence in *U.S. v. Haywood et al.,* File 188032, Straight Numerical Files.

44. "JAF-CZC, 371-361-3773, Nef et al.," in Record Group 204, File no. 37-479; Haywood, *Bill Haywood's Book,* 324–25, 367–68 (first and last quotes); George, *I.W.W. Trial,* 81–82, 157, in IWW Pamphlets; *The Crisis,* June 1919, 60; Renshaw, "IWW and the Red Scare," 66–67.

45. Fair interview, December 21, 1978, 8, in Shaffer Papers, Box 3; Haywood, *Bill Haywood's Book,* 328.

46. ONI, *Investigation of the Marine Transport Workers,* 27–30; Nef testimony in IWW Collection, *U.S. v. Haywood et al.,* July 2, 1918, 5976, Folder 4, Box 110; Guillel testimony in IWW Collection, *U.S. v. Haywood et al.,* August 8, 1918, 10790–91, Folder 3, Box 116.

47. ONI, *Investigation of the Marine Transport Workers,* 32; ONI to Bielaski, September 28(?), 1918, in Record Group 65, Old German File 366145, Reel 12, *Federal Surveillance of Afro-Americans.*

48. USSB, *Marine and Dock Labor,* 136–37; Arnesen, *Waterfront Workers of New Orleans,* 223–24.

49. ONI to Bielaski, September 28(?), 1918, in Record Group 65, Old German File 366145, Reel 12, *Federal Surveillance of Afro-Americans.*

50. McKenna testimony in IWW Collection, *U.S. v. Haywood et al.,* 1918, 12014–15, Folder 7, Box 117; *By-Laws and Rules of Order: Used in Business Meetings of the Marine Transport Workers Industrial Union no. 510 of the I.W.W.,* in IWW Collection, Folder 4, Box 70.

Chapter 5: Onward One Big Union?

1. Montgomery, "What More to Be Done?" 358 and n12. Sellars, *Oil, Wheat, and Wobblies;* and Hall, *Harvest Wobblies* also challenge the established historiography.

2. Brecher, *Strike!* 103–43 (quote); Winslow, "On the Waterfront."

3. ONI, *Investigation of the Marine Transport Workers,* 31–32 (first and last quotes); ONI report, October 28 [1919?], in Record Group 32, Case File 1494, Box 130; Leigh, "Memorandum for All Agents: Bolsheviki," November 22, 1918, in Record Group 165, "Bolshevism-I.W.W. Questionnaire," Box 4, Plant Protection Service–Philadelphia, 1917–1919, General and Special Staffs—Office of the Director of Intelligence (G-2).

4. Record Group 32, Case File 1494, Box 134; *New Solidarity,* January 24, 1920, 3; and January 31, 1920, 3.

5. ONI report, October 28 [1919?]; McKenna report, n.d.; and W.A.R. report, December 31, 1918—all in Record Group 32, Case File 1494, Box 130; ONI, *Investigation of the Marine Transport Workers,* 31 (quote).

6. ONI, *Investigation of the Marine Transport Workers,* 31–32; James, *Holding Aloft the Banner of Ethiopia,* 183–87 and n184.

7. Johnson and Campbell, *Black Migration in America,* 76–78; Paget, "Plight of the Pennsylvania Negro," 309; Moses oral history, LDOHP; Fair interview, December 21, 1978, 1, in Shaffer Papers, Box 3; Greene and Woodson, *Negro Wage Earner,* 308; U.S. Census Office, *Fourteenth Census of the United States,* vol. 4: *Population 1920: Occupations,* 1194.

8. Franklin, "Philadelphia Race Riot of 1918"; Scott, "Additional Letters of Negro Migrants," 461; *Solidarity,* August 12, 1916, 3.

9. Franklin, "Philadelphia Race Riot of 1918"; Hardy, "Race and Opportunity," 208–10 (first two quotes); Keats report, August 19, 1919, in Record Group 32, Case File 1494, Box 133 (last quote).

10. *The Messenger*, July 1921, 214–15.

11. *Philadelphia Inquirer*, April 6, 1980, "Today" section, 4; Lever interview, 15, BLMOHP; Grossman, *Land of Hope*, 210–17, 243–45.

12. U.S. Department of Labor, *Negro Migration in 1916–17*, 137; Record Group 65, Microfilm Reel 806, Case File no. 366145, October 29, 1918; Greene and Woodson, *Negro Wage Earner*, 114, 308–9; Gregg, *Sparks from the Anvil of Oppression*, 15–28; Hardy, "Race and Opportunity," xiv–xv; Cohen, *Making a New Deal*, 13.

13. O'Connor, *Revolution in Seattle*, 146–52; Friedheim, *Seattle General Strike*, 8–10, 160–65; Larrowe, *Shape-Up and Hiring Hall*, 89–94.

14. Friedheim, *Seattle General Strike*, 162; Thompson to Lecaualier, September 24, 1981, in Thompson Collection, Folder 3, Box 10.

15. Keats reports, May 7, 13, and 14, 1919, in Record Group 32, Case File 1494, Box 129; Saposs to Leiserson, May 20, 1919, in Saposs Papers, Folder 21, Box 24.

16. Frank, *Purchasing Power*, 27–28; Wright, "Organized Labor and Seattle's African American Community."

17. *Philadelphia Chamber of Commerce News Bulletin*, March 1, 1918, 1; May 1, 1918, 1; and June 15, 1920, 1; Philadelphia Maritime Exchange, *Forty-Fourth Annual* (1919), 6; Commercial Exchange of Philadelphia, *Sixty-Fourth Annual Report: 1918*, 35–36.

18. Arnesen, *Waterfront Workers of New Orleans*, 228–32; Harris, *Bloodless Victories*, chap. 7.

19. *Philadelphia Chamber of Commerce News Bulletin*, May 15, 1918; December 1, 1919, 10; and February 2, 1920, 2; Murray, *Red Scare*, 14–15; Jenkins, "Spy Mad?" 207, 216; Harris, *Bloodless Victories*, 225.

20. *Journal of Commerce and Commercial Bulletin*, June 5, 1920, 1; and June 8, 1920, 5; Gerstle, *Working-Class Americanism*, 43–46.

21. Jenkins, "Spy Mad?" 209; Philadelphia Chamber of Commerce, *Americanization in Philadelphia*, 7, 36–37.

22. *Philadelphia Chamber of Commerce News Bulletin*, April 15, 1919, 4; Jenkins, "Spy Mad?" 226; Murray, *Red Scare*, 17.

23. Wakstein, "Origins of the Open Shop Movement," 460, 469; *Philadelphia Chamber of Commerce News Bulletin*, May 15, 1920, 1; Harris, *Bloodless Victories*, 85–90, 263–75; Fine, *"Without Blare of Trumpets,"* 70, 220–21.

24. *Philadelphia Chamber of Commerce News Bulletin*, December 1, 1919, 1 (second quote), 6; and July 15, 1920, 1, 5 (first quote); Murray, *Red Scare*, 190–209, 278–81.

25. Squires to Wright, October 9, 1919, New York Harbor Wage Adjustment Board, Minutes of Meetings, 1917–19, "Railroad Administration," in Record Group 32 (Northeast Regional Archives), Box 1, Entry 51; "Agreement and Wage Scale, 1918–19 ILA Local 791" (New York), "ILA," in Record Group 32 (Northeast Regional Archives), Box 4, Wage Disputes, 1918–19 of New York Harbor Wage Adjustment Board, Entry 53; Winslow, "On the Waterfront," 357–59.

26. Rosen interview, January 7, 1997; Keats reports, May 21, 24, and 28, 1919, in Record Group 32, Case File 1494, Box 129; *New Solidarity*, December 14, 1918, 4.

27. Welles to Bielaski, September 19 and October 19, 1918, in Record Group 65, Old German File 160053; Daniels to Burke, October 6, 1919, in Record Group 65, Bureau Section (Entry 32), File 202600-95; Murray, *Red Scare*, 31.

28. Stroud report, May 19, 1919, in Record Group 65, Old German File 160053; *New Solidarity*, May 10, 1919, 1.

29. *Industrial Solidarity*, May 27, 1919; *New Solidarity*, July 26, 1919, 1.

30. *Industrial Solidarity*, May 27, 1919.

31. Stroud report, May 19, 1919, in Record Group 65, Old German File 160053; Saposs to Leiserson, May 20, 1919, in Saposs Papers, Folder 21, Box 24; *Industrial Solidarity*, May 27, 1919.

32. McDevitt report, May 26, 1919, in Record Group 65, Old German File 160053; Friedman and Keats reports, May 29, 1919, in Record Group 32, Case File 1494, Box 129.

33. *New Solidarity*, June 28, 1919, 4; September 13, 1919, 7; and November 15, 1919, 1; Keats reports, May 29 and June 16, 1919, in Record Group 32, Case File 1494, Box 129.

34. Carrington to Flynn, June 18, 1919, in Record Group 65, Old German File 160053; *New Solidarity*, June 28, 1919, 4.

35. *New Solidarity*, February 14, 1920, 3.

36. Fletcher to Jones, August 21, 1919, and September 6, 1919; Sims to Jones, August 26, 1919—all in Record Group 65, Old German File 36727; *One Big Union Monthly*, December 1919, 23–24; Spero and Harris, *Black Worker*, 116–19.

37. Keats report, August 23, 1919, in Record Group 32, Case File 1494, Box 133; Busha report, October 3, 1919, in Record Group 65, Bureau Section File 202600-95; *New Solidarity*, September 20, 1919, 3.

38. Record Group 32, Case File 1494, Box 134; *New Solidarity*, January 24, 1920, 3; Post, *Deportations Delirium of Nineteen-Twenty*, 110.

39. *New Solidarity*, February 14, 1920, 3; Seraile, "Ben Fletcher," 223–25.

40. Digaetano oral history, BLMOHP; Fletcher to Hampel, December 31, 1919; Fletcher to Phillips, February 11, 1920; Clark report, April 19, 1920—all in Record Group 65, Old German File 29434; *New Solidarity*, April 2, 1920, 4; *One Big Union Monthly*, May 1920, 54.

41. Thompson to Halstead, March 20, 1976, in Thompson Collection, Folder 6, Box 10.

Chapter 6: The 1920 Strike

1. Elkins, "Black Power in the British West Indies"; Nelson, *Divided We Stand*, 31–38; Arnesen, *Waterfront Workers of New Orleans*, 228–36.

2. *Philadelphia Chamber of Commerce News Bulletin*, January 2, 1920, 1; and May 15, 1920, 1; Harris, *Bloodless Victories*, 250–54.

3. "To the Chairman of the Stevedores and Brokers Committee, Stevedores of the Port of Philadelphia, Pa. and Vicinity," "Phila—Longshore Strike," in Record Group 32 (Northeast Regional Archives), Box 23, Entry 54, General Records of Marine and Dock Industrial Relations Division, August 1917–September 1920; *Solidarity*, June 5, 1920, 1; Montgomery, *Fall of the House of Labor*, 396–97.

4. "To the Members of the General Committee," May 20, 1920, "L Phila—Longshore Strike," in Record Group 32, Box 23, Entry 54; "To the Longshoremen of

the Port of Philadelphia, PA," May 25, 1920, in Record Group 32, Case File 1494, "Longshoremen's Strike—Phila 1920," Box 135.

5. "To the Longshoremen of the Port of Philadelphia, PA," May 25, 1920, in Record Group 32, Case File 1494, "Longshoremen's Strike—Phila 1920," Box 135.

6. Philadelphia, *Annual Report of the Department of Wharves, Docks, and Ferries . . . 1920*, 3; *Journal of Commerce and Commercial Bulletin*, May 27, 1920, 4; *One Big Union Monthly*, July 1920, 5 (first quote); *Public Ledger*, May 26, 1920, 15.

7. *Solidarity*, June 5, 1920, 1, 4.

8. *Public Ledger*, May 28, 1920, 6.

9. McDevitt report, June 26, 1920, in Record Group 65, Old German File 160053; *Solidarity*, June 5, 1920, 1, 4 (quotes).

10. "Delaware River District (Labor Reports)," May 29, 1920, in Record Group 32, Box 7, Entry 54; *Solidarity*, June 5, 1920, 1, 4; and June 12, 1920, 1, 3.

11. Fletcher to Harris, August 8, 1929, in Harris Papers.

12. *Public Ledger*, June 1, 1920, 3; *Solidarity*, June 12, 1920, 1, 3.

13. *Public Ledger*, May 30, 1920, 2 (first quote); *Solidarity*, June 12, 1920, 1.

14. Keats report, June 11, 1920, in Record Group 32, Case File 1494, Box 135; *Public Ledger*, June 4, 1920, 3; and June 5, 1920, 19; *Solidarity*, June 12, 1920, 3.

15. IWW to Murphy, June 6, 1920, "Longshoremen's Strike—Phila 1920," in Record Group 32, Case File 1494, Box 135.

16. Telegram of Foley, Director of Operations, June 4, 1920; DeLancey to General Comptroller, June 4, 1920; Friedman to Cosgrove, June 8, 1920; Keats to Meehan, June 10, 1920; Wilson report, June 10, 1920—all in "Longshoremen's Strike—Phila 1920," in Record Group 32, Case File 1494, Box 135; American Bureau of Shipping, *American Merchant Marine*, 10; *Journal of Commerce and Commercial Bulletin*, June 5, 1920, 1.

17. *Public Ledger*, June 8, 1920, 15; and June 9, 1920, 9.

18. McDevitt report, June 17, 1920, in Record Group 65, Old German File 366145, Reel 12, *Federal Surveillance of Afro-Americans; One Big Union Monthly*, July 1920, 7–8.

19. *One Big Union Monthly*, July 1920, 7; Doree and Nef, *Philadelphia Controversy*, 16–17, in IWW Collection, Box 170.

20. Keats reports, June 11 and 13, 1920, in Record Group 32, Case File 1494, Box 135.

21. Keats report, June 13, 1920, in Record Group 32, Case File 1494, Box 135; Doyas report, June 14, 1920, in Record Group 65, Old German File 34527; *Solidarity*, June 19, 1920, 1, 3; June 26, 1920, 1, 3; and January 1, 1921, 4; *Journal of Commerce and Commercial Bulletin*, June 22, 1920, 3.

22. *Public Ledger*, June 17, 1920, 3; June 19, 1920, 1; June 23, 1920, 3; and June 28, 1920, 3.

23. Keats reports, June 17 and 24, 1920, in Record Group 32, Case File 1494, Box 135.

24. A.G.B. reports, June 24 and 25, 1920, in Record Group 32, Case File 1494, Box 135; *Public Ledger*, June 23, 1920, 3.

25. *Philadelphia Inquirer*, July 1, 1920, in Record Group 32, Case File 1494, Box 135; *Public Ledger*, June 10, 1920, 17; June 19, 1920, 15; and July 1, 1920, 1;

Fine, *"Without Blare of Trumpets,"* 220–21; Harris, *Bloodless Victories,* 75–76, 263.

26. A.G.B. reports, June 25, 28, and 29, 1920; and MacLeod to Benson, June 28, 1920—both in Record Group 32, Case File 1494, Box 135; *Public Ledger,* June 29, 1920, 12; and June 30, 1920, 3; Harris, *Bloodless Victories,* 142–43.

27. A.G.B. report, June 30, 1920; and IWW to Murphy, June 6, 1920, "Longshoreman's Strike—Phila 1920"—both in Record Group 32, Case File 1494, Box 135; *Public Ledger,* June 30, 1920, 3.

28. A.G.B. report, July 1, 1920, in Record Group 32, Case File 1494, Box 135.

29. I.J.C. report, July 2, 1920, in Record Group 32, Case File 1494, Box 135.

30. *Public Ledger,* July 1, 1920, 1, 3; July 3, 1920, 6; July 5, 1920, 1; MacLeod to Mills, July 6, 1920, in Record Group 32, Case File 1494, Box 135 (quote).

31. *Public Ledger,* May 27, 1920, 19; and July 2, 1920, 1.

32. *Public Ledger,* July 6, 1920, 1; and July 7, 1920, 4; *One Big Union Monthly,* August 1920, 53.

33. A.G.B. reports, July 7, 8, and 9, 1920; and DeLancey to MacLeod, July 9, 1920—all in Record Group 32, Case File 1494, Box 135; *Solidarity,* July 17, 1920, 1.

34. DeLancey to Chair, USSB, July 9, 1920; and Chair, USSB, to DeLancey, September 2, 1920, "Longshoremen's Agreement"—all in Record Group 32, Box 1, Entry 54; Kennedy, *Over Here,* 258–59.

35. *Public Ledger,* July 8, 1920, 3 (first quote); *Philadelphia Chamber of Commerce News Bulletin,* June 15, 1920, 1, 3, 5.

36. Halpern, *Down on the Killing Floor,* 44–72; Kelly, *Race, Class, and Power in the Alabama Coalfields.*

37. Thompson to Halstead, March 20, 1976, in Thompson Collection, Folder 6, Box 10.

38. *Public Ledger,* July 2, 1920, 1; Fletcher to Harris, August 8, 1929, in Harris Papers; Tuttle, *Race Riot,* 208–41.

39. Thompson to Halstead, March 20, 1976, in Thompson Collection, Folder 6, Box 10; *Solidarity,* July 17, 1920, 3 (quote).

40. *Journal of Commerce and Commercial Bulletin,* July 3, 1920, 2; Heinrich, *Ships for the Seven Seas,* 165–68.

Chapter 7: The Philadelphia Controversy

1. *Solidarity,* August 14, 1920, 2.

2. Dubofsky, *We Shall Be All;* Foner, *Industrial Workers of the World.* The exception is the IWW's own history, Thompson and Murfin, *I.W.W.*

3. Not surprising, given the chronology they emphasize, few historians examine how Communism affected the IWW. Kimeldorf's *Battling for American Labor* does not, either, so the standard remains Gambs, *Decline of the I.W.W.*

4. Erwin, "Philadelphia," in IWW Collection, Box 32-1.

5. Fletcher (quote) and Jones depositions in Doree and Nef, *Philadelphia Controversy,* in IWW Collection, Box 170; *Solidarity,* August 21, 1920, 4; and October 2, 1920, 4.

6. Hellwig, Varlack, and Gardner depositions in Doree and Nef, *Philadelphia Controversy.*

7. Telegram of Whitehead to Jones, August 13, 1920; and "Philadelphia Controversy: A Brief History" in Doree and Nef, *Philadelphia Controversy* (quote); *Solidarity*, October 2, 1920, 4; *Fellow Worker*, August 12, 1920, 1, in IWW Collection, Folder 22, Box 79.

8. "Philadelphia Controversy: A Brief History" in Doree and Nef, *Philadelphia Controversy*; *One Big Union Monthly*, September 1920, 6 (quotes); Latchem Report, in IWW, *Proceedings of the Fifteenth Annual Convention: 1923*, 9 (second quote); Gambs, *Decline of the I.W.W.*, 76–77.

9. O'Connor, *Revolution in Seattle*, 158–59; Foglesong, *America's Secret War against Bolshevism*, esp. chaps. 4, 6, and 7.

10. Walsh and Baker depositions and Minutes of Local 8 Meeting, August 17, 1920—both in Doree and Nef, *Philadelphia Controversy*; *Solidarity*, August 28, 1920, 3.

11. Speed to Walsh, August 29, 1920, in Doree and Nef, *Philadelphia Controversy*; *Solidarity*, October 2, 1920, 4 (second quote).

12. Doree, Varlack, and Nef report to GEB in Doree and Nef, *Philadelphia Controversy*; *Solidarity*, October 16, 1920, 4; Kimeldorf, *Battling for American Labor*, 56.

13. Nef to Hardy, September 22, 1920; Hardy to Nef, September 9, 1920; Brown and Hardy to Philadelphia Branch, October 20, 1920; Nef to Hardy and Brown, November 3, 1920—all in Doree and Nef, *Philadelphia Controversy*.

14. *Solidarity*, December 4, 1920, 3; Arnesen, "It Aint Like They Do in New Orleans," 65; Hall, *Harvest Wobblies*, 186; Nelson, *Workers on the Waterfront*, 163–66.

15. *Solidarity*, December 4, 1920, 3.

16. Fletcher, "Branch Suspended—Fletcher Not Seated," and General Executive Board to Nef, December 4, 1920, in Doree and Nef, *Philadelphia Controversy*.

17. *Solidarity*, December 11, 1920, 2; December 18, 1920, 3; January 1, 1921, 3–4 (quote); January 15, 1921, 2; March 19, 1921, 2; and April 2, 1921, 2.

18. Howe, Coser, and Jacobson, *American Communist Party*, 25, 75–76; "Comintern Exhortation to the Industrial Workers of the World and to Others, 1920," in CPUSA Records, Delo 18, Reel 1.

19. Gambs, *Decline of the I.W.W.*, 75–85; Dubofsky, *We Shall Be All* (1988 ed.), 448–49 (quotes); Draper, *Roots of American Communism*, 315–17, 416n46.

20. Thompson to Dawson, July 30, 1982, in Thompson Collection, Folder 3, Box 10; Fletcher, "I.W.W. and Negro Wage Workers," in Harris Papers; *Industrial Worker*, July 23, 1924, 3; Gambs, *Decline of the I.W.W.*, 79, 91 (last quote).

21. Thompson oral history, 13, 17–18, LDOHP; Johanningsmeier, *Forging American Communism*, 161 (quote, emphasis original); Draper, *Roots of American Communism*, 244–58.

22. Unknown author to Cock, "Instructions for Work in the United States"; and "Labor Union Movement in America," 1921, in CPUSA Records, Delo 81, Reel 5; Thompson to Philips, April 16, 1977, in Thompson Collection, Folder 1, Box 10 (first quote); and Thompson to Carlson, January 29, 1981, in Thompson Collection, Folder 12, Box 12 (second quote); Draper, *American Communism and Soviet Russia*, 178; Nelson, *Workers on the Waterfront*, 54–67.

23. Mawdsley, *Russian Civil War*, 262–71 (quote); Thorpe, *Workers Themselves*, 140–41, 168; "Statement of the Communist Party of America to the Executive

Committee of the Communist International," 1921, in CPUSA Records, Delo 39, Reel 2.

24. McDevitt reports, December 4, 1920; and Busha, December 27, 1920—both in Record Group 65, File 202600-278; Kelley, *Hammer and Hoe.*

25. Hardy, "Race and Opportunity," 221–22; Nelson, *Divided We Stand,* 31–33; Stein, *World of Marcus Garvey,* 145–50.

26. Hardy, "Race and Opportunity," 221–25; Stein, *World of Marcus Garvey,* 78, 171–85; *Negro World,* March 7, 1925, 2.

27. *The Messenger,* July 1921, 214–15; Stein, *World of Marcus Garvey,* 166, 175; Nelson, *Divided We Stand,* 31–38; Elkins, "Black Power in the British West Indies"; Arnesen, *Waterfront Workers of New Orleans,* 228–36.

28. *The Messenger,* July 1921, 214–15; Fair interview, December 21, 1978, 3, in Shaffer Papers, Box 3; Dabney, "Questionnaire for ILA Local 1116," Labor Union Survey, Pennsylvania, 1925–28, in National Urban League Papers, Box 89, Series 6E; Krupsky oral history, LDOHP.

29. *The Messenger,* August 1921, 234 (quote); and October 1921, 262–63.

30. Kelley, *Hammer and Hoe;* Nelson, *Workers on the Waterfront;* Halpern, *Down on the Killing Floor.*

31. Nelson, *Divided We Stand,* 26, 45.

32. IWW, *Proceedings of the Thirteenth Annual Convention: 1921,* 7–9, 15, 20, 53–54, in IWW Collection, Folder 1, Box 3; *Solidarity,* May 21, 1921, 1 (first quote); E. F. Doree to Chika Doree, May 22, 1921.

33. *Solidarity,* January 1, 1921, 3–4.

34. Doree, "Open Letter to I.W.W.," in Doree and Nef, *Philadelphia Controversy;* Fair interview, December 21, 1978, 3, in Shaffer Papers, Box 3; *Solidarity,* January 1, 1921, 3–4; Cohen, *Making a New Deal,* 339–40.

35. *Solidarity,* September 25, 1920, 2.

36. Hardy and Fisher to Nef, October 18, 1920, in Doree and Nef, *Philadelphia Controversy;* McDevitt report, September 24, 1920, in Record Group 65, Old German File 36190; Thorpe, *Workers Themselves,* 135–41.

37. Doree, "Open Letter to I.W.W.," in Doree and Nef, *Philadelphia Controversy.*

38. Philadelphia Department of Wharves, Docks, and Ferries, *Port of Philadelphia* (1926 ed.), 15; U.S. Board of Engineers, *Port of Philadelphia,* 340–41; American Bureau of Shipping, *Bulletin,* January 1921, 3; and May–June 1921, 3.

39. O'Connor to McGrath, June 15, 1922, in Record Group 32, Box 1407; Stockinger to Neff (*sic*), June 26, 1921; and Stockinger to Walsh, July 31, 1921—both in Record Group 65, File 4-2-3-14; McCartin, *Labor's Great War,* 65, 174.

40. Busha reports, July 15 and 16, 1921; and McDevitt report, June 18, 1921—all in Record Group 65, File 202600-1617; "Beware of Union Disrupters," American Bureau of Shipping, *Bulletin,* 10, August 31, 1920, in Doree and Nef, *Philadelphia Controversy.*

41. McDevitt reports, August 20 and 27, 1921, in Record Group 65, File 202600-1617; Fair interview, December 21, 1978, 3, in Shaffer Papers, Box 3; Jackson, *Ku Klux Klan in the City,* 170–73, 240–43; Hardy, "Race and Opportunity," 130, 197–98, 219–21.

42. *Industrial Solidarity,* October 29, 1921, 1; and November 5, 1921, 1 (quote).

43. Thompson to Bopp, February 15, 1972, in Thompson Collection, Folder 14, Box 11; Dubofsky, *We Shall Be All* (1988 ed.), 443–49; Sellars, *Oil, Wheat, and Wobblies*; Hall, *Harvest Wobblies*.

44. Erwin, "Philadelphia," *General Office Bulletin*, January 1925, 7.

Chapter 8: The Lockout of 1922

1. Moocke oral history, LDOHP; Nelson, *Workers on the Waterfront*, 50–62; Nelson, *Divided We Stand*, 25–38; Arnesen, *Waterfront Workers of New Orleans*, 217–52.

2. Montgomery, *Fall of the House of Labor*, 407–9 (quote); Montgomery, *Workers' Control in America*, 91–109; Arnesen, *Waterfront Workers of New Orleans*, 244–52; Arnesen, "It Aint Like They Do in New Orleans," 80.

3. McKay, *Home to Harlem*, 48; Whatley, "African-American Strikebreaking," 526, 545; Taylor, *Forging of a Black Community*, 52–58; Halpern, *Down on the Killing Floor*, 44–72.

4. *Philadelphia Chamber of Commerce News Bulletin*, January 2, 1920, 1; and September 15, 1921, 1; Fine, "*Without Blare of Trumpets*," 220–21; American Bureau of Shipping, *Bulletin*, September–October 1921, 3–4; Philadelphia Chamber of Commerce, *Americanization in Philadelphia*, 36.

5. *The Messenger*, February 1922, 360; American Bureau of Shipping, *Bulletin*, January 1921, 3–4; Commercial Exchange of Philadelphia, *Sixty-Eighth Annual Report: 1922*, 40–41; Philadelphia Maritime Exchange, *Forty-Eighth Annual* (1923), 6; *Philadelphia Chamber of Commerce News Bulletin*, August 15, 1922, 15.

6. Operative #2 report, October 13, 1922; and Van Fleet report, October 14, 1922—both in Record Group 32, "October 1922" Folder, Case File 1494, Box 135. All references are to this folder unless noted.

7. Operative #2 reports, October 13 and 16 (quotes), 1922.

8. Operative #2 reports, October 13 and 16, 1922.

9. Van Fleet report, October 14, 1922.

10. Operative #2 report, October 14, 1922; Operative #10 report, October 15, 1922.

11. Operative #10 report, October 15, 1922; Operative #27 report, October 15, 1922; Committee from "Philadelphia Details," October 31, 1922.

12. Operative #10 reports, B.U.; and Operative #2, October 16, 1922.

13. McDevitt and Van Fleet reports, October 16, 1922; Commercial Exchange of Philadelphia, *Sixty-Ninth Annual Report: 1923*, 76.

14. Operative #10 report, October 17 (quotes) and 18, 1922; Baltimore Report, October 23, 1922.

15. Unknown author report, October 17, 18, and 23, 1922; *Marine Worker*, November 15, 1922, 2; and December 1, 1922, 2.

16. Van Fleet reports, October 16 and 20, 1922; Norton report, October 18, 1922; Committee on Protection to Mills, October 16, 1922.

17. S. C. Loveland Company to President, U.S., November 13, 1922, "Labor and Labor Conditions—Longshoremen and Stevedores: Philadelphia, PA," in Record Group 32, File 621-3-8, Box 1407, Subject-Classified General Files, 1920–1936,

Entry 7; Operative #10 and informant report, October 18, 1922; "Strike News Bulletin no. 1," November 7, 1922, in IWW Collection, Folder 2, Box 70; Larrowe, *Shape-Up and Hiring Hall*, 92–93.

18. Mack to Sheedy, October 24, 1922, "Stevedoring Files (O'Connor's Office) Philadelphia," in Record Group 32, Box 14, Entry 13k; Van Fleet report, October 20, November 2 and 3, 1922; American Bureau of Shipping, *Bulletin*, September–October 1921, 3–4.

19. Unknown New York author report, "Steamers in Port," October 19, 1922; Operative #10 reports, October 19 and 20, 1922; Operative #2 reports, October 19, 20, 21, and 22 (quote), 1922; Van Fleet reports, October 23 and 24, 1922.

20. Operative #2 report, October 22, 1922 (quote); Operative #10 report, October 22, 1922; Roediger, *Towards the Abolition of Whiteness*, 148–58.

21. Operatives #2 and #10 reports, October 23, 1922; Van Fleet report, October 24, 1922.

22. Operative #10 report, October 23, 1922. The *Philadelphia Tribune* was typically silent.

23. Operative #10 reports, October 24 (quote) and 25, 1922; Operative #2 report, October 24, 1922; unknown Philadelphia author report, October 24, 1922 (quotes); Norton report, October 25, 1922; Van Fleet report, October 26, 1922 (last quote).

24. Unknown New York author reports, October 25 and 26, 1922.

25. Van Fleet reports, October 26 and 27, 1922; Steamship Interests of Philadelphia Committee of Ways and Means to Mills, October 26, 1922; Higgins to Watkins, October 27, 1922.

26. Operative #2 report, October 27, 1922; Operative #10 report, October 27, 1922; Van Fleet report, October 28, 1922.

27. Operative #10 report, October 27, 1922; unknown New York author report, October 28, 1922 (quotes).

28. Operative #10 reports, October 28 and 29, 1922; Operative #2 report, October 28, 1922; Rosen interview, January 7, 1997.

29. Operative #10 report, October 29 and 30, 1922; Operative #2 report, October 30, 1922; Moe to Mills, October 30, 1922.

30. Operative #10 report, October 28, 1922; Sullivan to Van Fleet, October 30, 1922; *Public Ledger*, October 31, 1922.

31. Sullivan to Van Fleet, October 30, 1922 (first three quotes); Foner, *Organized Labor and the Black Worker*, 159 (Fletcher quote); Operative #2 report, October 31, 1922 (Walsh quote); "To the Members of the Marine Transport Workers I.U. 510," November 4, 1922 (last quote).

32. Van Fleet report, November 3, 1922; "To Longshoremen of Philadelphia," n.d.; Brandes, *American Welfare Capitalism*, 119–34; Nelson, "Company Union Movement."

33. Van Fleet reports, November 2 and 3, 1922; agent of Sullivan to Van Fleet, November 3, 1922; "To Longshoremen of Philadelphia," n.d.

34. Norton reports, November 8, 13, and 20, 1922; Van Fleet reports, November 13, 14, 16, 17, and 19, 1922.

35. The historiography draws different conclusions than I do. McGirr completely ignores the fundamental role of race in the 1922 lockout, not discussing that most strikebreakers were black or that racial solidarity collapsed. In contrast,

Kimeldorf goes to the opposite extreme, asserting that racial considerations were solely responsible; in seeking to give agency to black workers, he ignores the roles of employers, the federal government, Local 8's relationship with the IWW, and the rival ILA. See McGirr, "Black and White Longshoremen in the IWW," 378–79, 396–400; Kimeldorf and Penney, "'Excluded' by Choice."

36. "Philadelphia Longshoremen Locked Out," n.d., in IWW Collection, Box 170; Publicity Committee, "Bulletin no. 2," in IWW Collection, Folder 2, Box 70; Norton report, October 31, 1922.

37. Mulhall report, November 3, 1922; Fair interview, December 21, 1978, 2, 10, in Shaffer Papers, Box 3; Okavage, Krupsky, and Hopper oral histories, LDOHP (last quote).

38. Dabney, "Questionnaire for ILA Local 1116," Labor Union Survey, Pennsylvania, 1925–28, in National Urban League Papers, Box 89, Series 6E; Spero and Harris, *Black Worker*, 65.

39. "Colored Workers of America," in IWW Collection, Box 158.

40. Kimeldorf and Penney, "'Excluded' by Choice," 61–62.

41. U.S. Census Office, *Thirteenth Census of the United States*, vol. 4: *Population 1910: Occupation Statistics*, 589; U.S. Census Office, *Fourteenth Census of the United States*, vol. 4: *Population 1920: Occupations*, 1194; Hardy, "Race and Opportunity," 100, 135; Hardin, "Negroes of Philadelphia," 62–63.

42. Montgomery, *Fall of the House of Labor*, 403–10.

43. Erwin, "Philadelphia," 7–9.

44. *Marine Worker*, December 1, 1922, 2–3.

45. Fair interview, December 21, 1978, 3, in Shaffer Papers, Box 3; Moocke oral history, LDOHP; Arnesen, *Waterfront Workers of New Orleans*, 244–52; Nelson, *Workers on the Waterfront*, 50–74; Harris, *Bloodless Victories*, 263–69.

46. Philadelphia Maritime Exchange, *Fifty-Fifth Annual* (1930), 30.

47. Philadelphia Maritime Exchange, *Fifty-Fifth Annual* (1930), 30.

48. Philadelphia Maritime Exchange, *Forty-Eighth Annual* (1923), 6–7; Commercial Exchange of Philadelphia, *Sixty-Ninth Annual Report: 1923*, 40; O'Brien to Furuseth, October 29, 1922, in Olander Papers, "1922 Sept–Oct" Folder, Box 89.

49. Moocke oral history, LDOHP; Montgomery, *Fall of the House of Labor*, 423.

Conclusion

1. Erwin, "Philadelphia," 8; Bernstein, *Lean Years*, 52–54; Philadelphia Department of Wharves, Docks, and Ferries, *Port of Philadelphia* (1926 ed.), 31, 46–49, 97–99; Philadelphia Maritime Exchange, *Fifty-First Annual* (1926), 8–10.

2. Russell, *Men along the Shore*, 248; Erwin, "Philadelphia," 8–9; Varlack and Ushka oral histories, LDOHP; Stern, *Cargo Handling*, 83; Arnesen, *Waterfront Workers of New Orleans*, 254; Nelson, *Workers on the Waterfront*, 104–5.

3. "Longshoremen—Atlantic and Gulf Ports," 128–29.

4. Erwin, "Philadelphia," 8; Jones, "Mixed Union," 812; Moses oral history, LDOHP; Nelson, *Workers on the Waterfront*, 82; Barrett and Roediger, "Inbetween Peoples," 16.

5. Dabney, "Questionnaire for ILA Local 1116," Labor Union Survey, Pennsyl-

vania, 1925–28, in National Urban League Papers, Box 89, Series 6E; Kimeldorf and Penney, "'Excluded' by Choice," 64–65; Hardy, "Race and Opportunity," 130–31.

6. Evans cited in Hardy, "Race and Opportunity," 130; *The Messenger*, July 1921, 214–15; Manly, "Where Negroes Live in Philadelphia."

7. Jones, "Mixed Union," 812; Cole, "Shaping Up and Shipping Out," chap. 9.

8. *Industrial Solidarity*, January 19, 1927, 1.

9. *Industrial Solidarity*, January 19, 1927, 1; correspondence with Neill, November 5 and December 12, 1995; Spero and Harris, *Black Worker*, 200; Nelson, *Divided We Stand*, 61–64; Green oral history, LDOHP.

10. ILA, *Proceedings of the Twenty-Eighth Annual Convention: 1927*, 135–36; Palazzi interview; Kovnat oral history, LDOHP; correspondence with Neill, September 16 and 29, 1995; Neill, "Passing through the Port of Philadelphia"; Nelson, *Divided We Stand*, 53–54.

11. Du Bois quote in Foner, *Organized Labor and the Black Worker*, 159.

12. Montgomery, *Workers' Control in America*, 91–109; Nelson, *Workers on the Waterfront*, 6.

13. *Solidarity*, January 1, 1921, 3–4; Moses oral history, LDOHP; Taylor to Franklin, June 26, 1913; and Taylor to Furness, Withy & Co., June 11, 1913—both in Taylor Papers; Brissenden, *I.W.W.*, 100–101.

14. Dubofsky, *We Shall Be All* (1988 ed.), 448–49; Gambs, *Decline of the I.W.W.*, 135–38; McGirr, "Black and White Longshoremen in the IWW," 378–79.

15. Thompson to Halstead, March 20, 1976 (first quote); and Thompson notes on Asteroff's paper, May 10, 1976 (second quote)—both in Thompson Collection, Folder 6, Box 10; Bird, Georgakas, and Shaffer, *Solidarity Forever*, 40 (last quote).

16. Fletcher to Harris, July 22, 1929, in Harris Papers.

BIBLIOGRAPHY

Archival Collections

AFL Records—American Federation of Labor Records, Part I: Strikes and Agreements File, 1898–1953. Frederick, Md.: University Publications of America, 1985.

Beffel Collection—John N. Beffel Collection. Walter P. Reuther Library, Archives of Labor and Urban Affairs, Wayne State University, Detroit.

Beffel Papers—John Beffel Papers. Tamiment Institute Library, New York University, New York.

Carey Papers—George V. Carey Papers. Labadie Collection, Department of Rare Books and Special Collections, Harlan Hatcher Graduate Library, University of Michigan, Ann Arbor.

CIO Records—Congress of Industrial Organizations Records, 1935–36. Department of Archives and Manuscripts, Catholic University of America, Washington, D.C.

CPUSA Records—Communist Party USA Records, Manuscript Series 21,966. Manuscript Division, Library of Congress, Washington, D.C.

DWDF Clipping Book—[Department of] Wharves, Docks, and Ferries, Clipping Books. Philadelphia City Archives, Philadelphia.

Hall Manuscript—Covington Hall Manuscript. Walter P. Reuther Library, Archives of Labor and Urban Affairs, Wayne State University, Detroit.

Harris Papers—Abram Lincoln Harris Papers and Correspondence. Moorland-Spingarn Research Center, Howard University, Washington, D.C.

Inglis Papers—Agnes Inglis Papers. Labadie Collection, Department of Rare Books and Special Collections, Harlan Hatcher Graduate Library, University of Michigan, Ann Arbor.

IWW Collection—Industrial Workers of the World Collection. Walter P. Reuther Library, Archives of Labor and Urban Affairs, Wayne State University, Detroit.

IWW Pamphlets—Industrial Workers of the World Pamphlets. New York Public Library, New York.

IWW Vertical File—Industrial Workers of the World Vertical File. Reference Center for Marxist Studies, New York.

Marine Workers Historical Collection—Marine Workers Historical Collection. Tamiment Institute Library, New York University, New York.

NAACP Collection—National Association for the Advancement of Colored People Collection. Manuscripts Division, Library of Congress, Washington, D.C.

National Urban League Papers—National Urban League Papers. Manuscripts Division, Library of Congress, Washington, D.C.

Olander Papers—Victor Olander Papers and Correspondence. Chicago Historical Society.

Record Group 32—Records of the United States Shipping Board, Record Group 32. National Archives, Washington, D.C., and Northeast Regional Archives, New York City.

Record Group 60—Records of the Department of Justice, Record Group 60. National Archives, Washington, D.C.

Record Group 65—Records of the Federal Bureau of Investigation, Record Group 65. National Archives II, College Park, Md.

Record Group 118—Records of the U.S. Attorneys and Marshals, Record Group 118. National Archives, Mid-Atlantic Regional Archives, Philadelphia.

Record Group 165—Records of the War Department, Record Group 165. National Archives, Mid-Atlantic Regional Archives, Philadelphia.

Record Group 174—Records of the U.S. Department of Labor, Record Group 174. National Archives II, College Park, Md.

Record Group 204—Records of the Office of the U.S. Pardon Attorney, Record Group 204. National Archives, Suitland, Md.

Saposs Papers—David J. Saposs Papers. Archives Division, State Historical Society of Wisconsin, Madison.

Seraile Collection—William Seraile Collection. Walter P. Reuther Library, Archives of Labor and Urban Affairs, Wayne State University, Detroit.

Shaffer Papers—Deborah Shaffer Papers. Archives Division, State Historical Society of Wisconsin, Madison.

Taylor Papers—Fred W. Taylor Papers. Historical Society of Pennsylvania, Philadelphia.

Thompson Correspondence—Frederick W. Thompson Correspondence and Papers. Walter P. Reuther Library, Archives of Labor and Urban Affairs, Wayne State University, Detroit.

Urban League Papers—Urban League of Philadelphia Papers, Urban Archives. Temple University, Philadelphia.

Government Documents

Albrecht, Arthur Emil. *International Seamen's Union of America: A Study of Its History and Problems.* Bulletin of the United States Bureau of Labor Statistics, Miscellaneous Series, no. 342. Washington, D.C.: Government Printing Office, 1923.

National Adjustment Commission. *Chairman's Report* [1918]. Washington, D.C.: Government Printing Office, 1919.

Office of Naval Intelligence. *Investigation of the Marine Transport Workers and the Alleged Threatened Combination between Them and the Bolsheviki and Sinn Feiners.* Record Group 174, General Records, 1907–1942 (Chief Clerk's Files), Entry 1, Box 89, Folder 201580, December 23, 1918.

Pennsylvania Board of Commissioners of Navigation for the River Delaware and Its Navigable Tributaries. *The Port of Philadelphia: Its Facilities and Advantages.* Harrisburg, Penn.: Wm. Stanley Ray, 1914.

Pennsylvania Department of Labor and Industry. *Second Annual Report of the Commissioner of Industry of the Commonwealth of Pennsylvania.* Harrisburg, Penn.: J. L. L. Kuhn, 1918.

———. *Third Annual Report of the Commissioner of Industry of the Commonwealth of Pennsylvania.* Harrisburg, Penn.: Wm. Stanley Ray, 1916.

[Philadelphia]. *Third Annual Message of Rudolph Blankenburg, Mayor of Philadelphia, vol. 2: Containing the Reports of the Departments of Public Works, Wharves, Docks, and Ferries, City Transit for the Year Ending December 31, 1913.* Philadelphia: n.p., 1914.

[———]. *Annual Report of the Department of Wharves, Docks, and Ferries of the City of Philadelphia for the Year Ending December 31, 1913.*

[———]. *Annual Report of the Department of Wharves, Docks, and Ferries of the City of Philadelphia for the Year Ending December 31, 1914.*

[———]. *Annual Report of the Department of Wharves, Docks, and Ferries of the City of Philadelphia for the Year Ending December 31, 1920.*

[———]. *Annual Report of the Department of Wharves, Docks, and Ferries of the City of Philadelphia for the Year Ending December 31, 1922.*

Philadelphia Department of Wharves, Docks, and Ferries. *The Port of Philadelphia: Its History, Advantages, and Facilities.* Philadelphia: n.p., 1926.

———. *The Port of Philadelphia: Second in the United States.* Philadelphia: n.p., 1921(?).

[U.S. Bureau of Investigation, Department of Justice]. *Federal Surveillance of Afro-Americans (1917–1925): The First World War, the Red Scare, the Garvey Movement.* Frederick, Md.: University Press of America, 1985.

U.S. Census Office. *Occupations of the Twelfth Census of the United States, 1900.* Washington, D.C.: Government Printing Office, 1902.

———. *Thirteenth Census of the United States Taken in the Year 1910, vol. 4: Population 1910: Occupation Statistics.* Washington, D.C.: Government Printing Office, 1914.

———. *Fourteenth Census of the United States Taken in the Year 1920, vol. 4: Population 1920: Occupations.* Washington, D.C.: Government Printing Office, 1923.

———. *Negroes in the United States, 1920–1932.* Washington, D.C.: Government Printing Office, 1935.

U.S. Department of Labor. *Negro Migration in 1916–17.* 1919. Reprinted New York: Negro Universities Press, 1969.

———, Division of Negro Economics. *The Negro at Work during the World War and during Reconstruction: Statistics, Problems, and Policies Relating to the Greater Inclusion of Negro Wage Earners in American Industry and Agriculture.* 1921. Reprinted New York: Negro University Press, 1969.

U.S. Engineer Department, Board of Engineers for Rivers and Harbors, War Department. *The Port of Philadelphia, Pennsylvania, including Camden, N.J., Chester, Pa., Wilmington, Del.* Port Series, no. 4. Washington, D.C.: Government Printing Office, 1922.

U.S. Immigration Commission. *Reports of the Immigration Commission, vol. 1: Abstracts of Reports of the Immigration Commission; vol. 4: Emigration Conditions in Europe; vol. 27: Immigrants in Cities.* 1907–1910. Reprinted New York: Arno/New York Times, 1970.

United States Shipping Board [USSB]. *Marine and Dock Labor: Work, Wages, and Industrial Relations during the Period of the War.* Washington, D.C.: Government Printing Office, 1919.

Convention Proceedings

Industrial Workers of the World. Convention Proceedings, 1905–28.
International Longshoremen's Association. Convention Proceedings, 1903–31.

Business Records

American Bureau of Shipping. *The American Merchant Marine.* N.P.: American Bureau of Shipping, 1933.
———. *Bulletin.* Monthly publication of the American Bureau of Shipping.
Commercial Exchange of Philadelphia. Annual Reports, 1913–24.
Philadelphia Chamber of Commerce. *Americanization in Philadelphia.* Philadelphia: Walther, 1923.
———. *Philadelphia: Its Past Achievements, Present Greatness, and Future Possibilities.* Philadelphia: Philadelphia Chamber of Commerce, 1929.
———. *Philadelphia Yearbook: 1917.* Philadelphia: Philadelphia Chamber of Commerce, 1917.
Philadelphia Maritime Exchange. Annual Reports of the Board of Directors, 1916–30.

Newspapers and Journals

Afro-American, Baltimore
Call, New York
Crisis, New York
Fellow Worker, New York
General Office Bulletin, Chicago
Hawsepipe, New York
Industrial Pioneer, Chicago
Industrial Solidarity, Chicago
Industrial Union Bulletin, Chicago
Industrial Worker, Seattle
International Socialist Review, Chicago
Journal of Commerce and Commercial Bulletin, New York
Journal of the Philadelphia Chamber of Commerce
Longshoreman, Erie, Pa., and Buffalo, N.Y.
Marine Worker, New York
Marine Workers Voice, New York
Messenger, New York
Negro World, New York
New Solidarity, Chicago
New York Times

North American, Philadelphia
One Big Union Monthly, Chicago
Philadelphia Chamber of Commerce News Bulletin
Philadelphia Inquirer
Public Ledger, Philadelphia
Solidarity, New Castle, Pa., and Chicago
Trades' Union News, Philadelphia
Tribune, Philadelphia

Oral Histories and Correspondence Conducted by Author

Bolmarcich, John P. Philadelphia. July 23, September 25, October 8, October 16, October 19, and November 16, 1995.

Neill, Richard D. Cape May, N.J. September 16, September 29, November 5, and December 12, 1995.

Palazzi, Esther. New York, N.Y. July 13, 1995.

Rosen, Ellen Doree. Great Neck, N.Y. January 7, 1997.

Other Oral History Material

Barrett, T. "Hook," and Harry Cox. "Labor on the Delaware: The Longshore Experience." June 12, 1980. Delaware River Oral History Project [LDOHP], Independence Seaport Museum, Philadelphia.

Bey, Abudllah. "Labor on the Delaware: The Longshore Experience." July 22, 1980. Delaware River Oral History Project [LDOHP], Independence Seaport Museum, Philadelphia.

Brennan, Francis. "Labor on the Delaware: The Longshore Experience." January 20, 1981. Delaware River Oral History Project [LDOHP], Independence Seaport Museum, Philadelphia.

Callan, Bob. "Labor on the Delaware: The Longshore Experience." January 20, 1981. Delaware River Oral History Project [LDOHP], Independence Seaport Museum, Philadelphia.

Curran, Joseph. "The Reminiscences of Joseph Curran." 1964. Oral History Collection, Columbia University.

Digaetano, Nick. Interviewed by Jim Kenney and Herbert Hill. June 17, 1968. Blacks in the Labor Movement Oral History Project [BLMOHP], Walter P. Reuther Library, Archives of Labor and Urban Affairs, Wayne State University, Detroit.

Fair, James. Interview. December 21, 1978. Deborah Shaffer Papers, Archives Division, State Historical Society of Wisconsin, Madison.

Green, Kenny. "Labor on the Delaware: The Longshore Experience." June 12, 1980. Delaware River Oral History Project [LDOHP], Independence Seaport Museum, Philadelphia.

Kovnat, Sam. "Labor on the Delaware: The Longshore Experience." n.d. Delaware River Oral History Project [LDOHP], Independence Seaport Museum, Philadelphia.

Krupsky, Bill "Willy." "Labor on the Delaware: The Longshore Experience." June

29, 1980. Delaware River Oral History Project [LDOHP], Independence Seaport Museum, Philadelphia.

Lever, Jack. Interviewed by Herbert Hill. May 29, 1968. Blacks in the Labor Movement Oral History Project [BLMOHP], Walter P. Reuther Library, Archives of Labor and Urban Affairs, Wayne State University, Detroit.

McGinnes, Dennis. "Labor on the Delaware: The Longshore Experience." June 2, 1980. Delaware River Oral History Project [LDOHP], Independence Seaport Museum, Philadelphia.

Moocke, James. "Labor on the Delaware: The Longshore Experience." July 18, 1980. Delaware River Oral History Project [LDOHP], Independence Seaport Museum, Philadelphia.

Moses, Abraham. "Labor on the Delaware: The Longshore Experience." n.d. Delaware River Oral History Project [LDOHP], Independence Seaport Museum, Philadelphia.

Okavage, Krupsky, and Hopper. "Labor on the Delaware: The Longshore Experience." n.d. Delaware River Oral History Project [LDOHP], Independence Seaport Museum, Philadelphia.

Quinn, John. "Labor on the Delaware: The Longshore Experience." May 22, 1980. Delaware River Oral History Project [LDOHP], Independence Seaport Museum, Philadelphia.

Thompson, F. W. Oral history. Walter P. Reuther Library, Archives of Labor and Urban Affairs, Wayne State University, Detroit.

Tobbs, Arthur "Bobby." "Labor on the Delaware: The Longshore Experience." May 23, 1980. Delaware River Oral History Project [LDOHP], Independence Seaport Museum, Philadelphia.

Ushka, John. "Labor on the Delaware: The Longshore Experience." July 1, 1980. Delaware River Oral History Project [LDOHP], Independence Seaport Museum, Philadelphia.

Varlack, Henry. "Labor on the Delaware: The Longshore Experience." May 6, 1980. Delaware River Oral History Project [LDOHP], Independence Seaport Museum, Philadelphia.

Books

Allen, Keiran. *The Politics of James Connolly.* Winchester, Mass.: Pluto, 1990.

Arnesen, Eric. *Waterfront Workers of New Orleans: Race, Class, and Politics, 1863–1923.* Urbana: University of Illinois Press, 1991.

Avrich, Paul. *Anarchist Voices: An Oral History of Anarchism in America.* Princeton: Princeton University Press, 1995.

Ayers, Edward L. *The Promise of the New South: Life after Reconstruction.* New York: Oxford University Press, 1992.

Bailey, Bill. *The Kid from Hoboken: An Autobiography.* Edited by Lynn Damme. San Francisco: Circus Lithographic, 1993.

Barnes, Charles B. *The Longshoremen.* New York: Survey Associates, 1915.

Barrett, James R. *William Z. Foster and the Tragedy of American Radicalism.* Urbana: University of Illinois Press, 1999.

———. *Work and Community in the Jungle: Chicago's Packinghouse Workers, 1894–1922.* Urbana: University of Illinois Press, 1987.

Bell, Thomas. *Out of This Furnace.* 1941. Reprinted Pittsburgh: University of Pittsburgh Press, 1981.

Bernstein, Irving. *The Lean Years: A History of the American Worker, 1920–1933.* Boston: Houghton Mifflin, 1960.

Biagi, Ernest L. *Italians of Philadelphia.* New York: Carlton, 1967.

Bird, Stewart, Dan Georgakas, and Deborah Shaffer. *Solidarity Forever: An Oral History of the IWW.* Chicago: Lake View, 1985.

Bodnar, John. *The Transplanted: A History of Immigrants in Urban America.* Bloomington: Indiana University Press, 1985.

———. *Workers' World: Kinship, Community, and Protest in an Industrial Society, 1900–1940.* Baltimore: Johns Hopkins University Press, 1982.

Bonnett, Clarence. *Employers' Associations in the United States: A Study of Typical Associations.* New York: Macmillan, 1922.

———. *History of Employers' Associations in the United States.* New York: Vantage, 1956.

Brandes, Stuart D. *American Welfare Capitalism, 1880–1940.* Chicago: University of Chicago Press, 1970.

Brecher, Jeremy. *Strike!* Revised edition. Boston: South End Press, 1997.

Brissenden, Paul F. *The I.W.W.: A Study in American Syndicalism.* 1919. Reprinted New York: Russell & Russell, 1957.

Brooks, Thomas R. *Clint: A Biography of a Labor Intellectual.* New York: Atheneum, 1978.

Brundage, David. *The Making of Western Labor Radicalism: Denver's Organized Workers, 1878–1905.* Urbana: University of Illinois Press, 1994.

Budd, Henry. *The Charge to the Triers: The Richmond Ecclesiastical Trial.* Philadelphia: n.p., 1917.

Buhle, Mari Jo, Paul Buhle, and Harvey J. Kaye, eds. *The American Radical.* New York: Routledge, 1994.

Burkett, Randall K. *Black Redemption: Churchmen Speak for the Garvey Movement.* Philadelphia: Temple University Press, 1978.

Chaplin, Ralph. *Wobbly: The Rough-and-Tumble Story of an American Radical.* Chicago: University of Chicago Press, 1948.

Clark, Dennis. *Erin's Heirs: Irish Bonds of Community.* Lexington: University Press of Kentucky, 1991.

———. *The Irish in Philadelphia: Ten Generations of Urban Experience.* Philadelphia: Temple University Press, 1973.

———. *The Irish Relations: Trials of an Immigrant Tradition.* East Brunswick, N.J.: Associated University Press, 1982.

Clark, Norman H. *Mill Town: A Social History of Everett, Washington, from Its Earliest Beginnings on the Shores of Puget Sound to the Tragic and Infamous Event Known as the Everett Massacre.* Seattle: University of Washington Press, 1970.

Cohen, Lizabeth. *Making a New Deal: Industrial Workers in Chicago, 1919–1939.* New York: Cambridge University Press, 1990.

Cole, Peter. *Ben Fletcher: The Life and Times of a Black Wobbly.* Chicago: Kerr, 2007.

Collins, Herman LeRoy. *Philadelphia: A Story of Progress,* vol. 2. New York: Lewis Historical Publishing, 1941.

Conlin, Joseph Robert. *Big Bill Haywood and the Radical Union Movement*. Syracuse: Syracuse University Press, 1969.

———. *Bread and Roses Too: Studies of the Wobblies*. Westport, Conn.: Greenwood, 1980.

———, ed. *At the Point of Production: The Local History of the I.W.W.* Contributions in Labor History, no. 10. Westport, Conn.: Greenwood, 1981.

Cronon, David. *Black Moses: The Story of Marcus Garvey and the Universal Negro Improvement Association*. Madison: University of Wisconsin Press, 1955.

Cutler, William W., III, and Howard Gillette Jr., eds. *The Divided Metropolis: Social and Spatial Dimensions of Philadelphia, 1800–1975*. Westport, Conn.: Greenwood, 1980.

Daniel, Cletus E. *Bitter Harvest: A History of California Farm Workers, 1870–1941*. Ithaca, N.Y.: Cornell University Press, 1981.

Davis, Colin. *Waterfront Revolts: New York and London Dockworkers, 1946–61*. Urbana: University of Illinois Press, 2003.

Davis, Susan G. *Parades and Power: Street Theatre in Nineteenth-Century Philadelphia*. Philadelphia: Temple University Press, 1986.

De Caux, Len. *Labor Radical—From the Wobblies to the CIO: A Personal History*. Boston: Beacon, 1970.

Donner, Frank. *Protectors of Privilege: Red Squads and Police Repression in Urban America*. Berkeley: University of California Press, 1990.

Drake, St. Clair, and Horace R. Cayton. *Black Metropolis: A Study of Negro Life in a Northern City*. New York: Harcourt, Brace, 1945.

Draper, Theodore. *American Communism and Soviet Russia*. New York: Viking, 1960.

———. *The Roots of American Communism*. New York: Viking, 1957.

Dubofsky, Melvyn. *The State and Labor in Modern America*. Chapel Hill: University of North Carolina Press, 1994.

———. *We Shall Be All: A History of the Industrial Workers of the World*. 2nd edition. Urbana: University of Illinois Press, 1988.

———. *We Shall Be All: A History of the Industrial Workers of the World*. Abridged edition. Edited by Joseph A. McCartin. Urbana: University of Illinois Press, 2000.

Du Bois, W. E. B. *Black Reconstruction in America, 1860–1880*. 1935. Reprinted New York: Free Press, 1998.

———. *The Philadelphia Negro: A Social Study*. Philadelphia: University of Pennsylvania Press, 1899.

Dulles, Foster Rhea, and Melvyn Dubofsky. *Labor in America: A History*. 4th edition. Arlington Heights, Ill.: Harlan Davidson, 1984.

Ellis, Mark. *Race, War, and Surveillance: African Americans and the United States Government during World War I*. Bloomington: Indiana University Press, 2001.

Feldberg, Michael. *The Philadelphia Riots of 1844: A Study of Ethnic Conflict*. Westport, Conn.: Greenwood, 1975.

Fenton, Edwin. *Immigrants and Unions: A Case Study: Italians and American Labor, 1870–1920*. 1957. Reprinted New York: Arno, 1975.

Fine, Sidney. *"Without Blare of Trumpets": Walter Drew, the National Erectors'*

Association, and the Open Shop Movement, 1903–57. Ann Arbor: University of Michigan Press, 1995.

Fink, Leon. *Workingmen's Democracy: The Knights of Labor and American Politics.* Urbana: University of Illinois Press, 1983.

Flynn, Elizabeth Gurley. *I Speak My Own Piece: Autobiography of "the Rebel Girl."* New York: Masses & Mainstream, 1955.

Foglesong, David S. *America's Secret War against Bolshevism: U.S. Intervention in the Russian Civil War, 1917–1920.* Chapel Hill: University of North Carolina Press, 1995.

Foner, Eric. *Tom Paine and Revolutionary America.* New York: Oxford University Press, 1976.

Foner, Philip S. *The Bolshevik Revolution: Its Impact on American Radicals, Liberals, and Labor: A Documentary Study.* New York: International Publishers, 1967.

———. *History of the Labor Movement in the United States,* vol. 3: *The Policies and Practices of the American Federation of Labor, 1900–1909.* New York: International Publishers, 1964.

———. *History of the Labor Movement in the United States,* vol. 4: *The Industrial Workers of the World, 1905–1917.* New York: International Publishers, 1965.

———. *Organized Labor and the Black Worker, 1619–1981.* New York: International Publishers, 1981.

Fones-Wolf, Ken. *Trade Union Gospel: Christianity and Labor in Industrial Philadelphia, 1865–1915.* Philadelphia: Temple University Press, 1989.

Foster, William Z. *From Bryan to Stalin.* New York: International Publishers, 1937.

———. *Pages from a Worker's Life.* New York: International Publishers, 1939.

Frank, Dana. *Purchasing Power: Consumer Organizing, Gender, and the Seattle Labor Movement, 1919–1929.* New York: Cambridge University Press, 1994.

Franklin, John Hope. *From Slavery to Freedom: A History of Negro Americans.* 3rd edition. New York: Vintage, 1969.

Franklin, Vincent P. *The Education of Black Philadelphia: The Social and Educational History of a Minority Community, 1900–1950.* Philadelphia: University of Pennsylvania Press, 1979.

Fraser, Steven, and Joshua B. Freeman, eds. *Audacious Democracy: Labor, Intellectuals, and the Social Reconstruction of America.* Boston: Mariner, 1997.

Freeman, Joshua. *In Transit: The Transport Workers Union in New York City, 1933–1966.* New York: Oxford University Press, 1989.

Freeman, Moses. *Fifty Years of Jewish Life in Philadelphia.* Philadelphia: n.p., 1929.

Friedheim, Robert L. *The Seattle General Strike.* Seattle: University of Washington Press, 1964.

Gallagher, Dorothy. *All the Right Enemies: The Life and Murder of Carlo Tresca.* New Brunswick: Rutgers University Press, 1988.

Gambs, John S. *The Decline of the I.W.W., 1917–1931.* New York: Columbia University Press, 1932.

Garlock, Jonathan. *Guide to the Local Assemblies of the Knights of Labor.* Westport, Conn.: Greenwood, 1982.

George, Harrison. *Those Stormy Years: Memories of the Fight for Freedom on Five Continents.* London: Lawrence & Wishart, 1956.

Gerstle, Gary. *Working-Class Americanism: The Politics of Labor in a Textile City, 1914–1960.* New York: Cambridge University Press, 1989.

Golab, Caroline. *Immigrant Destinations.* Philadelphia: Temple University Press, 1977.

Goldberg, Joseph P. *The Maritime Story: A Study in Labor-Management Relations.* Cambridge: Harvard University Press, 1958.

Golin, Steve. *The Fragile Bridge: Paterson Silk Strike.* Philadelphia: Temple University Press, 1988.

Gompers, Samuel. *Seventy Years of Life and Labor: An Autobiography.* New York: Dutton, 1925.

Gray, John. *City in Revolt: James Larkin and the Belfast Dock Strike of 1907.* Belfast: Blackstaff, 1985.

Greaves, Desmond C. *The Life and Times of James Connolly.* London: Lawrence & Wishart, 1961.

Green, James R. *The World of the Worker: Labor in Twentieth-Century America.* New York: Hill & Wang, 1980.

Green, Venus. *Race on the Line: Gender, Labor, and Technology in the Bell System.* Durham: Duke University Press, 2001.

Greene, Lorenzo J., and Carter G. Woodson. *The Negro Wage Earner.* New York: Russell & Russell, 1930.

Gregg, Robert. *Sparks from the Anvil of Oppression: Philadelphia's African Methodists and Southern Migrants, 1890–1940.* Philadelphia: Temple University Press, 1993.

Grossman, James R. *Land of Hope: Chicago, Black Southerners, and the Great Migration.* Chicago: University of Chicago Press, 1989.

Guglielmo, Thomas. *White on Arrival: Italians, Race, Color, and Power in Chicago, 1890–1945.* New York: Oxford University Press, 2003.

Hall, Greg. *Harvest Wobblies: The Industrial Workers of the World and Agricultural Laborers in the American West, 1905–1930.* Corvallis: Oregon State University Press, 2001.

Halpern, Rick. *Down on the Killing Floor: Black and White Workers in Chicago's Packinghouses, 1904–54.* Urbana: University of Illinois Press, 1997.

Halpern, Rick, and Roger Horowitz. *Meatpackers: An Oral History of Black Packinghouse Workers and Their Struggle for Racial and Economic Equality.* New York: Twayne, 1996.

Harris, Howell John. *Bloodless Victories: The Rise and Fall of the Open Shop in the Philadelphia Metal Trades, 1890–1940.* New York: Cambridge University Press, 2000.

Harris, William H. *Keeping the Faith: A. Philip Randolph and Milton P. Webster and the Brotherhood of Sleeping Car Porters.* Urbana: University of Illinois Press, 1977.

Haywood, Harry. *Autobiography of an Afro-American Communist.* Chicago: Liberator, 1977.

Haywood, William D. *Bill Haywood's Book: The Autobiography of William D. Haywood.* New York: International Publishers, 1929.

Heinrich, Thomas R. *Ships for the Seven Seas: Philadelphia Shipbuilding in the Age of Industrial Capitalism.* Baltimore: Johns Hopkins University Press, 1997.

Higbie, Frank Tobias. *Indispensable Outcasts: Hobo Workers and Community in the American Midwest, 1880–1930*. Urbana: University of Illinois Press, 2003.

Higham, John. *Strangers in the Land: Patterns of American Nativism, 1865–1925*. 1955. Reprinted New York: Atheneum, 1981.

Hill, Herbert. *Black Labor and the American Legal System: Race, Work, and the Law*. 1977. Reprinted Madison: University of Wisconsin Press, 1985.

Hill, Robert A., ed. *The Marcus Garvey and Universal Negro Improvement Papers*, vol. 1: *1826–August 1919*. Berkeley: University of California Press, 1983.

———. *The Marcus Garvey and Universal Negro Improvement Papers*, vol. 2: 27 *August 1919–31 August 1920*. Berkeley: University of California Press, 1983.

Hobsbawm, Eric. *Labouring Men: Studies in the History of Labour*. New York: Basic Books, 1964.

Hoffman, Miles E. *A Contemporary Analysis of a Labor Union: International Longshoremen's Association AFL-CIO*. Labour Monograph, no. 7. N.P.: Labour Congress, n.d.

Horowitz, Roger. *Black and White, United and Fight! A Social History of Industrial Unionism in Meatpacking, 1939–90*. Urbana: University of Illinois Press, 1997.

Howe, Irving, Lewis Coser, and Julius Jacobson. *The American Communist Party: A Critical History*. New York: Praeger, 1962.

Huberman, Leo. *The Labor Spy Racket*. New York: Modern Age, 1937.

Hugill, Stan. *Sailortown*. New York: Dutton, 1967.

Ignatiev, Noel. *How the Irish Became White*. New York: Routledge, 1996.

Jackson, Kenneth T. *The Ku Klux Klan in the City, 1915–1930*. New York: Oxford University Press, 1967.

James, Winston. *Holding Aloft the Banner of Ethiopia: Caribbean Radicalism in Early Twentieth-Century America*. London: Verso, 1997.

Jenkins, Philip. *Hoods and Shirts: The Extreme Right in Pennsylvania, 1925–1950*. Chapel Hill: University of North Carolina Press, 1997.

Johanningsmeier, Edward P. *Forging American Communism: The Life of William Z. Foster*. Princeton: Princeton University Press, 1994.

Johnson, Daniel M., and Rex R. Campbell. *Black Migration in America: A Social Demographic History*. Durham: Duke University Press, 1981.

Joyce, J. St. George, ed. *Story of Philadelphia*. N.P.: Harry B. Joseph, 1919.

Kaplan, Temma. *Red City, Blue Period: Social Movements in Picasso's Barcelona*. Berkeley: University of California Press, 1992.

Kazin, Michael. *Barons of Labor: The San Francisco Building Trades and Union Power in the Progressive Era*. Urbana: University of Illinois Press, 1987.

Kelley, Robin D. G. *Hammer and Hoe: Alabama Communists during the Great Depression*. Chapel Hill: University of North Carolina Press, 1990.

———. *Race Rebels: Culture, Politics, and the Black Working Class*. New York: Free Press, 1994.

Kelly, Brian. *Race, Class, and Power in the Alabama Coalfields, 1908–1921*. Urbana: University of Illinois Press, 2001.

Kennedy, David M. *Over Here: The First World War and American Society*. New York: Oxford University Press, 1980.

Kimeldorf, Howard. *Battling for American Labor: Wobblies, Craft Workers, and the Making of the Union Movement*. Berkeley: University of California Press, 1999.

———. *Reds or Rackets? The Making of Radical and Conservative Unions on the Waterfront*. Berkeley: University of California Press, 1988.

Kohn, Stephen M. *American Political Prisoners: Prosecutions under the Espionage and Sedition Acts*. Westport, Conn.: Praeger, 1994.

Kornweibel, Theodore, Jr. *No Crystal Stair: Black Life and the Messenger, 1917–1928*. Westport, Conn.: Greenwood, 1975.

Kowaleski, Edmond. *Deaf Walls*. Philadelphia: Symphonist Press, 1933.

LaMar, Elden. *The Clothing Workers of Philadelphia: History of Their Struggles for Union and Security*. Edited by J. B. S. Hardman. Philadelphia: Philadelphia Joint Board, Amalgamated Clothing Workers of America, 1940.

Lane, Roger. *The Roots of Violence in Black Philadelphia, 1860–1900*. Cambridge: Harvard University Press, 1986.

———. *William Dorsey's Philadelphia and Ours: On the Past and Future of the Black City in America*. New York: Oxford University Press, 1991.

Larrowe, Charles P. *Maritime Labor Relations on the Great Lakes*. East Lansing: Michigan State University Press, 1959.

———. *Shape-Up and Hiring Hall: A Comparison of Hiring Methods and Labor Relations on the New York and Seattle Waterfronts*. Berkeley: University of California Press, 1955.

Laurie, Bruce. *Working People of Philadelphia, 1800–1850*. Philadelphia: Temple University Press, 1981.

Lenin, V. I. *"Left-Wing" Communism: An Infantile Disorder*. New York: International Publishers, 1934.

Letwin, Daniel. *The Challenge of Interracial Unionism: Alabama Coal Miners, 1878–1921*. Chapel Hill: University of North Carolina Press, 1998.

Leuchtenburg, William E. *The Perils of Prosperity, 1914–32*. Chicago: University of Chicago Press, 1958.

Lewis, David Levering. *W. E. B. Du Bois: Biography of a Race, 1868–1919*. New York: Henry Holt, 1993.

Lewis, Earl. *In Their Own Interests: Race, Class, and Power in Twentieth Century Norfolk, Virginia*. Berkeley: University of California Press, 1991.

Lewis, Sinclair. *Babbitt*. New York: Harcourt, Brace, 1922.

Licht, Walter. *Getting Work: Philadelphia, 1840–1950*. Cambridge: Harvard University Press, 1992.

Linebaugh, Peter. *The London Hanged: Crime and Civil Society in the Eighteenth Century*. London: Penguin, 1991.

Litwack, Leon. *Trouble in Mind: Black Southerners in the Age of Jim Crow*. New York: Knopf, 1998.

Lorence, James J. *The Suppression of Salt of the Earth: How Hollywood, Big Labor, and Politicians Blacklisted a Movie in Cold War America*. Albuquerque: University of New Mexico Press, 1999.

MacElwee, Roy S., and Thomas R. Taylor. *Wharf Management: Stevedoring and Storage*. New York: Appleton, 1921.

MacFarlane, John J. *Manufacturing in Philadelphia, 1683–1912*. Philadelphia: Philadelphia Commercial Museum, 1912.

[Mann, Tom]. *Tom Mann's Memoirs*. With a preface by Ken Coates. 1923. Reprinted London: MacGibbon & Kee, 1967.

Mawdsley, Evan. *The Russian Civil War*. Boston: Allen & Unwin, 1987.

McCartin, Joseph A. *Labor's Great War: The Struggle for Industrial Democracy and the Origins of Modern American Labor Relations, 1912–1921.* Chapel Hill: University of North Carolina Press, 1997.

McElvaine, Robert S. *The Great Depression: America, 1929–1941.* New York: Times Books, 1984.

McKay, Claude. *Home to Harlem.* 1928. Reprinted Boston: Northeastern University Press, 1987.

———. *The Negroes in America.* Edited by Alan L. McLeod. Translated by Robert J. Winter. Port Washington, N.Y.: National University Publications, 1979.

Mers, Gilbert. *Working the Waterfront: The Ups and Downs of a Rebel.* Austin: University of Texas Press, 1988.

Miles, Dione. *Something in Common: An IWW Bibliography.* Detroit: Wayne State University Press, 1986.

Montgomery, David. *The Fall of the House of Labor: The Workplace, the State, and American Labor Activism, 1865–1925.* New York: Cambridge University Press, 1987.

———. *Workers' Control in America: Studies in the History of Work, Technology, and Labor Struggles.* New York: Cambridge University Press, 1979.

Morgan, Austen. *James Connolly: A Political Biography.* Manchester: Manchester University Press, 1988.

Murray, Robert K. *Red Scare: A Study in National Hysteria, 1919–1920.* Minneapolis: University of Minnesota Press, 1955.

Naison, Mark. *Communists in Harlem during the Depression.* Urbana: University of Illinois Press, 1983.

Negro Population in the United States, 1790–1915. New York: Arno/New York Times, 1968.

Nelson, Bruce. *Divided We Stand: American Workers and the Struggle for Black Equality.* Princeton: Princeton University Press, 2001.

———. *Workers on the Waterfront: Seamen, Longshoremen, and Unionism in the 1930s.* Urbana: University of Illinois Press, 1990.

Norris, George W. *Ended Episodes.* Philadelphia: Winston, 1937.

Northrup, Herbert C. *Organized Labor and the Negro Worker.* New York: Harper, 1944. Reprinted New York: Kraus, 1971.

Norwood, Stephen H. *Strikebreaking and Intimidation: Mercenaries and Masculinity in Twentieth-Century America.* Chapel Hill: University of North Carolina Press, 2002.

O'Connor, Harvey. *Revolution in Seattle: A Memoir.* New York: Monthly Review, 1964.

Pacyga, Dominic A. *Polish Immigrants and Industrial Chicago: Workers on the South Side, 1880–1922.* Columbus: Ohio State University Press, 1991.

Palmer, Gladys L. *Philadelphia Workers in a Changing Economy.* Philadelphia: University of Pennsylvania Press, 1956.

Parker, Carleton H. *The Casual Laborer and Other Essays.* 1920. Reprinted Seattle: University of Washington Press, 1972.

Perlman, Selig, and Philip Taft. *History of Labor in the United States,* vol. 4: *Labor Movements.* New York: Macmillan, 1935.

Perry, Jeffrey B., ed. *A Hubert Harrison Reader.* Middletown, Conn.: Wesleyan University Press, 2001.

Pfeffer, Paula F. *A. Philip Randolph: Pioneer of the Civil Rights Movement.* Baton Rouge: Louisiana State University Press, 1996.

Phillips, Kimberley L. *AlabamaNorth: African-American Migrants, Community, and Working-Class Activism in Cleveland, 1915–45.* Urbana: University of Illinois Press, 1999.

Poole, Ernest. *The Harbor.* New York: Macmillan, 1915. Reprinted New York: Sagamore, 1957.

Post, Louis F. *The Deportations Delirium of Nineteen-Twenty.* Chicago: Kerr, 1923.

Preston, William. *Aliens and Dissenters: Federal Suppression of Radicals, 1903–1933.* Cambridge: Harvard University Press, 1963.

Rachleff, Peter. *Black Labor in Richmond, 1865–1890.* Urbana: University of Illinois Press, 1988.

Ramirez, Bruno. *When Workers Fight: The Politics of Industrial Relations in the Progressive Era, 1898–1916.* Westport, Conn.: Greenwood, 1978.

Rediker, Marcus. *Between the Devil and the Deep Blue Sea: Merchant Seamen, Pirates, and the Anglo-American Maritime World, 1700–1750.* New York: Cambridge University Press, 1987.

Reid, Ira De A. *Negro Membership in American Labor Unions.* 1930. Reprinted New York: Negro Universities Press, 1969.

Reynolds, Lloyd G., and Charles C. Killingsworth. *Trade Union Publications: The Official Journals, Convention Proceedings, and Constitutions of International Unions and Federations, 1850–1941.* 3 vols. Baltimore: Johns Hopkins University Press, 1944.

Richmond, Al. *Long View from the Left: Memoirs of an American Revolutionary.* Boston: Houghton Mifflin, 1973.

Roediger, David R. *Towards the Abolition of Whiteness: Essays on Race, Politics, and Working Class History.* London: Verso, 1994.

———. *The Wages of Whiteness: Race and the Making of the American Working Class.* London: Verso, 1991.

Roediger, David R., and Philip S. Foner. *Our Own Time: A History of American Labor and the Working Day.* Contributions in Labor Studies, no. 23. Westport, Conn.: Greenwood, 1989.

Rosen, Ellen Doree. *A Wobbly Life: IWW Organizer E. F. Doree.* Detroit: Wayne State University Press, 2004.

Rosenberg, Daniel. *New Orleans Dockworkers: Race, Labor, and Unionism, 1892–1923.* Albany: State University of New York Press, 1988.

Rosman, M. J. *The Lords' Jews: Magnate-Jewish Relations in the Polish-Lithuanian Commonwealth during the Eighteenth Century.* Cambridge: Harvard Ukranian Research Institute and the Center for Jewish Studies, Harvard University, 1990.

Rossi, A. *The Rise of Italian Fascism, 1918–1922.* Translated by Peter Wait and Dorothy Wait. 1938. Reprinted New York: Howard Fertig, 1966.

Rubin, Charles. *The Log of Rubin the Sailor.* New York: International Publishers, 1973.

Rubin, Lester, William S. Swift, and Herbert R. Northrup. *Negro Employment in the Maritime Industries.* Philadelphia: University of Pennsylvania Press, 1974. Part 2: *The Negro in the Longshore Industry,* by Lester Rubin and William S. Swift.

Russell, Maud. *Men along the Shore.* New York: Brussel & Brussel, 1966.

Salter, J. A. *Allied Shipping Control: An Experiment in International Administration.* Oxford: Clarendon, 1921.

Saposs, David J. *Left Wing Unionism: A Study of Radical Policies and Tactics.* 1926. Reprinted New York: Russell & Russell, 1967.

Schwantes, Carlos A. *Radical Heritage: Labor, Socialism, and Reform in Washington and British Columbia, 1885–1917.* Seattle: University of Washington Press, 1979.

Scranton, Philip. *Figured Tapestry: Production, Markets, and Power in Philadelphia Textiles, 1885–1941.* New York: Cambridge University Press, 1989.

Sellars, Nigel Anthony. *Oil, Wheat, and Wobblies: The Industrial Workers of the World in Oklahoma, 1905–1930.* Norman: University of Oklahoma Press, 1998.

Sexton, Patricia Cayo. *The War on Labor and the Left: Understanding America's Unique Conservatism.* Boulder, Colo.: Westview, 1991.

Smith, J. Russell. *Influence of the Great War upon Shipping.* Preliminary Economic Studies of the War, no. 9. New York: Oxford University Press, 1919.

Spero, Sterling D., and Abram L. Harris. *The Black Worker: The Negro and the Labor Movement.* 1931. Reprinted New York: Atheneum, 1968.

Steffens, Lincoln. *The Shame of the Cities.* 1904. Reprinted New York: Hill & Wang, 1957.

Stein, Judith. *The World of Marcus Garvey: Race and Class in Modern Society.* Baton Rouge: Louisiana State University Press, 1986.

Stern, Boris. *Cargo Handling and Longshore Labor Conditions.* Bulletin of U.S. Bureau of Labor Studies, no. 550. Washington, D.C.: Government Printing Office, 1932.

Taylor, Quintard. *The Forging of a Black Community: Seattle's Central District from 1870 through the Civil Rights Era.* Seattle: University of Washington Press, 1994.

Thomas, Richard W. *Life for Us Is What We Make It: Building Black Community in Detroit, 1915–1945.* Bloomington: Indiana University Press, 1992.

Thompson, E. P. *The Making of the English Working Class.* New York: Pantheon, 1963.

Thompson, Fred W., and Patrick Murfin. *The I.W.W.: Its First Seventy Years.* Chicago: Industrial Workers of the World, 1976.

Thorpe, Wayne. *The Workers Themselves: Revolutionary Syndicalism and International Labour, 1913–1923.* Amsterdam: Kluwer/International Institute of Social History, 1989.

Tripp, Anne Huber. *The I.W.W. and the Paterson Silk Strike of 1913.* Urbana: University of Illinois Press, 1987.

Trotter, Joe William, Jr. *Black Milwaukee: The Making of an Industrial Proletariat, 1915–45.* Urbana: University of Illinois Press, 1985.

———, ed. *The Great Migration in Historical Perspective: New Dimensions of Race, Class, and Gender.* Bloomington: Indiana University Press, 1991.

Tuttle, William M., Jr. *Race Riot: Chicago in the Red Summer of 1919.* New York: Atheneum, 1970.

Tyler, Robert L. *Rebels of the Woods: The I.W.W. in the Pacific Northwest.* Eugene: University of Oregon Press, 1967.

Warner, Sam Bass, Jr. *The Private City: Philadelphia in Three Periods of Its Growth.* Philadelphia: University of Pennsylvania Press, 1968.

Weintraub, Hyman. *Andrew Furuseth: Emancipator of the Seamen.* Berkeley: University of California Press, 1959.

Weir, Robert E. *Beyond Labor's Veil: The Culture of the Knights of Labor.* University Park: Pennsylvania State University Press, 1996.

White, Joseph. *Tom Mann.* Manchester: Manchester University Press, 1991.

Willentz, Sean. *Chants Democratic: New York City and the Rise of the American Working Class, 1788–1850.* New York: Oxford University Press, 1984.

Williams, James H., and Warren F. Kuehl, eds. *Blow the Man Down: A Yankee Seamen's Adventures.* New York: Dutton, 1959.

Winslow, Calvin, ed. *Waterfront Workers: New Perspectives on Race and Class.* Urbana: University of Illinois Press, 1998.

Wolman, Leo. *The Growth of American Trade Unions, 1880–1923.* New York: National Bureau of Economic Research, 1924.

Wortman, Roy T. *From Syndicalism to Trade Unionism: The IWW in Ohio, 1905–1950.* New York: Garland, 1985.

Wright, Richard R., Jr. *The Negro in Pennsylvania: A Study in Economic History.* 1912. Reprinted New York: Arno/New York Times, 1969.

Pamphlets

Doree, E. F., and Nef, Walter T. *The Philadelphia Controversy: Being a Complete and Detailed Statement of All That Has Occurred.*

George, Harrison. *Is Freedom Dead? Sequel to the Suppressed Pamphlet Shall Freedom Die.* Chicago: I.W.W., 1918.

———. *The I.W.W. Trial: Story of the Greatest Trial in Labor's History by One of the Defendants.* Chicago: I.W.W., n.d.

Industrial Workers of the World. *Exposed by the Marine Transport Workers Industrial Union no. 510 of the I.W.W.* Chicago: I. W. of the W., [1922?].

[———]. *I.W.W. Songs: To Fan the Flames of Discontent. A Facsimile Reprint of the Popular Nineteenth Edition, 1923.* Chicago: Kerr, 1989.

[———]. *To Colored Working Men and Women.*

[———]. *Twenty Five Years of Industrial Unionism.* Chicago: I.W.W., 1930.

Wedge, Fredrick R. *Inside the I.W.W.: A Study of the Behavior of the I.W.W., with Reference to Primary Causes.* Berkeley: Wedge, 1924.

Articles and Essays

Abernethy, Lloyd M. "Progressivism, 1905–1919." In *Philadelphia: A 300-Year History,* edited by Russell F. Weigley, 524–65. New York: Norton, 1982.

Alisauskas, Arunas. "Lithuanians." In *Harvard Encyclopedia of American Ethnic Groups,* edited by Stephen Thernstrom, 665–76. Cambridge: Harvard University Press, 1970.

Arnesen, Eric. "Following the Color Line of Labor: Black Workers and the Labor Movement before 1930." *Radical History Review* 55 (Winter 1993): 53–87.

———. "'It Aint Like They Do in New Orleans': Race Relations, Labor Markets, and Waterfront Labor Movements in the American South, 1880–1923." In *Racism and the Labour Market: Historical Studies*, edited by Marcel van der Linden and Jan Lucassen, 57–100. Bern/New York: Peter Lang, 1995.

Barrett, James R., and David Roediger. "Inbetween Peoples: Race, Nationality, and the 'New Immigrant' Working Class." *Journal of American Ethnic History* 16 (1997): 3–44.

Bekken, Jon. "Marine Transport Workers IU 510 (IWW): Direct Action Unionism." *Libertarian Labor Review* 18 (1995): 12–25.

Berger, Max. "The Irish Emigrant and American Nativism as Seen by British Visitors, 1836–1860." *Pennsylvania Magazine of History and Biography* 70 (1946): 146–48.

Bernstein, Leonard. "The Working People of Philadelphia from Colonial Times to the General Strike of 1835." *Pennsylvania Magazine of History and Biography* 74 (1950): 322–39.

Bruere, Robert W. "The Industrial Workers of the World: An Interpretation." *Harper's Magazine* 137 (1918): 250–57.

Burt, Nathaniel, and Wallace E. Davies. "The Iron Age, 1876–1905." In *Philadelphia: A 300-Year History*, edited by Russell F. Weigley, 471–523. New York: Norton, 1982.

Caulfield, Norman. "Wobblies and Mexicans in Mining and Petroleum, 1905–1924." *International Review of Social History* 40 (1995): 51–75.

Clark, Dennis. "Urban Blacks and Irishmen." In *Black Politics in Philadelphia*, edited by Miriam Ershkowitz and Joseph Zikmund II, 15–30. New York: Basic Books, 1973.

Cleland, Hugh G. "The Effects of Radical Groups on the Labor Movement." *Pennsylvania History* 26 (April 1959): 119–32.

Cole, Peter. "Andrew Furuseth." In *American National Biography*, edited by John A. Garraty and Mark C. Carnes, 8:591–92. New York: Oxford University Press, 1999.

———. "Philadelphia's Lords of the Docks: Interracial Unionism Wobbly-Style," *Journal of Gilded Age and Progressive Era*.

———. "Quakertown Blues: Philadelphia's Longshoremen and the Decline of the IWW," *Left History* 8:2 (Spring 2003): 39–70.

Critchlow, Donald T. "Communist Unions and Racism: A Comparative Study of the Responses of the United Electrical Radio and Machine Workers and the National Maritime Union to the Black Question during World War II." *Labor History* 17 (Spring 1976): 230–44.

Davis, Mike. "The Stop Watch and the Wooden Shoe: Scientific Management and the Industrial Workers of the World." *Radical America* 9 (January–February 1975): 69–95.

Disbrow, Donald W. "Reform in Philadelphia under Mayor Blankenburg, 1912–1916." *Pennsylvania History* 27 (1960): 379–96.

Doree, E. F. "Ham-stringing the Sugar Hogs." *International Socialist Review* 17 (April 1917): 615–17.

———. "Here's What Happened." *Solidarity*, January 1, 1921, 3–4.

Dubofsky, Melvyn. "The Radicalism of the Dispossessed: William Haywood and the IWW." In *Dissent: Explorations in the History of American Radicalism*, edited by Alfred F. Young, 177–213. DeKalb: Northern Illinois University Press, 1968.

216   *Bibliography*

—. "The Rise and Fall of Revolutionary Syndicalism in the United States." In *Revolutionary Syndicalism: An International Perspective*, edited by Marcel van der Linden and Wayne Thorpe, 203–20. Hants, England: Scolar Press, 1990.
Du Bois, W. E. B. "I.W.W." *Crisis* 18 (1919): 60.
Durham, John Stephens. "The Labor Unions and the Negro." *Atlantic Monthly*, February 1898, 222–31.
Elkins, W. F. "Black Power in the British West Indies: The Trinidad Longshoremen's Strike of 1919." *Science and Society* 33 (Winter 1969): 71–75.
Emlen, John T. "The Movement for the Betterment of the Negro in Philadelphia." *Annals of the American Academy* 49 (September 1913): 81–92.
Erwin, Claude. "Philadelphia." *General Office Bulletin*, January 1925, 7–9.
Fern, John. "Good Man Gone." *The Dispatcher* 54 (December 1996): 11.
Ferrell, Jeff, and Kevin Ryan. "The Brotherhood of Timber Workers and the Southern Lumber Trust: Legal Repression and Worker Response." *Radical America* 19 (1985): 55–74.
Fields, Barbara J. "Race and Ideology in American History." In *Region, Race, and Reconstruction: Essays in Honor of C. Vann Woodward*, edited by James M. McPherson and J. Morgan Kousser, 143–77. New York: Oxford University Press, 1982.
Fletcher, Ben. "Philadelphia Waterfront Unionism." *Messenger* 5 (June 1923): 740–41.
Foner, Philip. "The IWW and the Black Worker." *Journal of Negro History* 55 (January 1970): 45–64.
Fones-Wolf, Ken. "Employer Unity and the Crisis of the Craftsman." *Pennsylvania Magazine of History and Biography* 107 (July 1983): 449–55.
Francis, Robert C. "Longshoremen in New Orleans." *Opportunity*, March 1936, 82–85, 93.
—. "The Negro and Industrial Unionism." *Social Forces* 15 (December 1936): 272–75.
Franklin, Vincent P. "The Philadelphia Race Riot of 1918." *Pennsylvania Magazine of History and Biography* 99 (1975): 336–50.
Gabaccia, Donna R. "Worker Internationalism and Italian Labor Migration, 1870–1914." *International Labor and Working-Class History* 45 (Spring 1994): 63–79.
Geffen, Elizabeth M. "Violence in Philadelphia in the 1840's and 1850's." *Pennsylvania History* 36 (October 1969): 381–410.
Gertrude, M. Agnes, "Italian Immigration into Philadelphia." *Records of the American Catholic Historical Society of Philadelphia* 58 (June 1947): 133–43.
Golab, Caroline. "The Immigrant and the City: Poles, Italians, and Jews in Philadelphia, 1870–1920." In *The Peoples of Philadelphia: A History of Ethnic and Lower-Class Life, 1790–1940*, edited by Allen F. Davis and Mark H. Haller, 203–30. Philadelphia: Temple University Press, 1973.
—. "The Polish Experience in Philadelphia: The Migrant Laborers Who Did Not Come." In *The Ethnic Experience in Pennsylvania*, edited by John Bodnar, 39–73. Lewisburg, Penn.: Bucknell University Press, 1973.
Goldfield, Michael. "Race and the CIO: The Possibilities for Racial Egalitarianism during the 1930s and 1940s." *International Labor and Working-Class History* 44 (Fall 1993): 1–32.

———. "Response to Controversy: Race and the CIO." *International Labor and Working-Class History* 46 (Fall 1994): 142–60.

Green, James. "The Brotherhood of Timber Workers, 1910–1913: A Radical Response to Industrial Capitalism in the Southern U.S.A." *Past and Present* 60 (1973): 161–200.

Gutman, Herbert. "The Negro and the United Mine Workers of America: The Career and Letters of Richard L. Davis and Something of Their Meaning, 1890–1900." In *The Negro and the American Labor Movement*, edited by Julius Jacobson, 49–127. New York: Doubleday, 1968.

Halpern, Rick. "Organized Labor, Black Workers and the Twentieth Century South: The Emerging Revision." In *Race and Class in the American South*, edited by Melvyn Stokes and Rick Halpern, 43–76. Oxford: Berg, 1994.

———. "Race, Ethnicity, and Union in the Chicago Stockyards, 1917–1922." *International Review of Social History* 37 (1992): 25–58.

Haywood, William D. "An Appeal for Industrial Solidarity." *International Socialist Review* 14 (1914): 392–94.

Hershberg, Theodore. "Free Blacks in Antebellum Philadelphia: A Study of Ex-Slaves, Freeborn, and Socioeconomic Decline." In *Philadelphia: Work, Space, Family, and Group Experience in the Nineteenth Century: Essays toward an Interdisciplinary History of the City*, edited by Theodore Hershberg, 368–91. New York: Oxford University Press, 1981.

Hershberg, Theodore, S. W. Greenberg, A. N. Burnstein, W. L. Yancey, and E. P. Erickesen. "A Tale of Three Cities: Blacks, Immigrants, and Opportunity in Philadelphia, 1850–1880, 1930, 1970." In *Philadelphia: Work, Space, Family, and Group Experience in the Nineteenth Century: Essays toward an Interdisciplinary History of the City*, edited by Theodore Hershberg, 461–91. New York: Oxford University Press, 1981.

Hewitt, Nancy A. "'The Voice of Virile Labor': Labor Militancy, Community Solidarity, and Gender Identity among Tampa's Latin Workers, 1880–1921." In *Work Engendered: Toward a New History of American Labor*, edited by Ava Baron, 142–67. Ithaca, N.Y.: Cornell University Press, 1991.

Hill, Herbert. "Myth-Making as Labor History: Herbert Gutman and the United Mine Workers of America." *Journal of Politics, Culture, and Society* 2 (Winter 1988): 132–200.

———. "The Problem of Race in American Labor History." *Reviews in American History* 24 (1996): 189–208.

———. "The Racial Practices of Organized Labor: The Age of Gompers and After." In *Employment, Race, and Poverty*, edited by Arthur M. Ross and Herbert Hill, 365–402. New York: Harcourt, Brace & World, 1967.

Hohman, Elmo Paul. "Maritime Labour in the United States, I: The Seamen's Act and Its Historical Background." *International Labor Review* 38 (August 1938): 190–218.

———. "Maritime Labour in the United States, II: Since the Seamen's Act." *International Labor Review* 38 (September 1938): 376–403.

Jenkins, Philip. "'Spy Mad'? Investigating Subversion in Pennsylvania, 1917–1918." *Pennsylvania History* 63 (1996): 204–31.

Jones, William D. "The Mixed Union: Merits and Demerits." *Messenger* 5 (1923): 812.

Juliani, Richard N. "The Italian Community in Philadelphia." In *The Ethnic Experience in Philadelphia*, edited by John Bodnar, 233–62. Lewisburg, Penn.: Bucknell University Press, 1973.

Kelley, Robin D. G. "'We Are Not What We Seem': Rethinking Black Working-Class Opposition in the Jim Crow South." *Journal of American History* 80 (1993): 75–112.

Kimeldorf, Howard. "Bringing Unions Back In (or, Why We Need a New Old Labor History)." *Labor History* 32 (1991): 91–129.

———. "Radical Possibilities? The Rise and Fall of Wobbly Unionism on the Philadelphia Docks." In *Waterfront Workers: New Perspectives on Race and Class*, edited by Calvin Winslow, 97–130. Urbana: University of Illinois Press, 1998.

Kimeldorf, Howard, and Robert Penney. "'Excluded' by Choice: Dynamics of Interracial Unionism on the Philadelphia Waterfront, 1910–1930." *International Labor and Working-Class History* 51 (Spring 1997): 50–71.

Letwin, Dan. "Interracial Unionism, Gender, and 'Social Equality' in the Alabama Coal Fields, 1878–1908." *Journal of Southern History* 61 (1995): 519–54.

Lewandowka, M. Theodosetta. "The Polish Immigrant in Philadelphia to 1914." *Records of the American Catholic Historical Society* 65 (June 1954): 67–101, 131–41.

Linden, Marcel van der. "On the Importance of Crossing Borders." *Labor History* 40 (1999): 362–64.

"Longshore Labor Conditions in the United States—Part I." *Monthly Labor Review* 31 (October 1930): 1–20.

"Longshore Labor Conditions in the United States—Part II." *Monthly Labor Review* 31 (November 1930): 11–25.

"Longshoremen—Atlantic and Gulf Ports." *Monthly Labor Review* 18 (1924): 128–29.

Manly, A. L. "Where Negroes Live in Philadelphia." *Opportunity*, May 1923, 10–15.

Mann, Tom. "A Plea for Solidarity." *International Socialist Review* 14 (1914): 544–46.

Marcus, Irwin M. "Benjamin Fletcher: Black Labor Leader." *Negro History Bulletin* 35 (1972): 138–40.

———. "Fletcher, Benjamin Harrison." In *Dictionary of American Negro Biography*, edited by Rayford W. Logan and Michael R. Winston, 225–26. New York: Norton, 1982.

McGirr, Lisa. "Black and White Longshoremen in the IWW: A History of the Philadelphia Marine Transport Workers Industrial Union Local 8." *Labor History* 36 (1995): 377–402.

Miller, Fredric. "The Black Migration to Philadelphia: A 1924 Profile." *Pennsylvania Magazine of History and Biography* 108 (July 1984): 315–50.

Miller, Raymond Charles. "The Dockworker Subculture and Some Problems in Cross-Cultural and Cross-Time Generalizations." *Comparative Studies in Society and History* 11 (June 1969): 302–14.

Montgomery, David. "The Shuttle and the Cross: Weavers and Artisans in the Kensington Riots of 1844." *Journal of Social History* 5 (1972): 411–46.

———. "What More to Be Done?" *Labor History* 40 (August 1999): 356–61.

Neill, Richard D. "Passing through the Port of Philadelphia." *The Hawsepipe* 8 (February–March 1989): 1, 13–15.

Nelson, Bruce. "Class and Race In the Crescent City: The ILWU, from San Francisco to New Orleans." In *The CIO's Left-Led Unions*, edited by Steve Rosswurm, 19–45. New Brunswick: Rutgers University Press, 1992.

——. "Organized Labor and the Struggle for Black Equality in Mobile during World War II." *Journal of American History* 80 (December 1993): 952–88.

Nelson, Daniel. "The Company Union Movement, 1900–1937: A Reexamination." *Business History Review* 56 (1982): 335–57.

Paget, Blanche J. "The Plight of the Pennsylvania Negro." *Opportunity*, October 1936, 309–11.

Painter, Nell Irvin. "The New Labor History and the Historical Moment." *Journal of Politics, Culture, and Society* 2 (Spring 1989): 367–70.

Perry, Grover H. "Transport Workers Join I.W.W." *International Socialist Review* 13 (May 1913): 812.

Peterson, Larry. "The One Big Union in International Perspective: Revolutionary Industrial Unionism, 1900–1925." *Labour/Le Travailleur* 7 (1981): 41–66.

Poole, Ernest. "The Men on the Docks." *Outlook* 164 (May 25, 1907): 142–44.

——. "The Ship Must Sail on Time." *Everybody's Magazine* 19 (August 1908): 176–86.

——. "The World of Wharves: Queer Trades and Denizens of the Water-front." *Harper's Weekly*, April 23, 1910, 15–16.

Preston, William. "Shall This Be All? U.S. Historians Versus William D. Haywood et al." *Labor History* 12 (Summer 1971): 435–53.

Radzialowski, Thaddeus. "The Competition for Jobs and Racial Stereotypes: Poles and Blacks in Chicago." *Polish American Studies* 33 (1976): 5–19.

Renshaw, Patrick. "The IWW and the Red Scare, 1917–24." *Journal of Contemporary History* 3 (1968): 63–72.

Runcie, John M. "'Hunting the Nigs' in Philadelphia: The Race Riot of 1834." *Pennsylvania History* 39 (April 1972): 187–218.

Salinger, Sharon V. "Artisans, Journeymen, and the Transformation of Labor in Late Eighteenth-Century Philadelphia." *William and Mary Quarterly* 3rd series, 40 (1983): 62–84.

Scott, Emmit J. "Additional Letters of Negro Migrants, 1916–1918." *Journal of Negro History* 4 (1918): 412–65.

Seraile, William. "Ben Fletcher: I.W.W. Organizer." *Pennsylvania History* 46 (1979): 213–32.

Shor, Francis. "The IWW and Oppositional Politics in World War I: Pushing the System beyond Its Limits," *Radical History Review* 64 (1996): 75–94.

——. "'Virile Syndicalism' in Comparative Perspective: A Gender Analysis of the IWW in the United States and Australia." *International Labor and Working-Class History* 56 (1999): 65–77.

Simpson, George E. "Social Changes in the Negro Population of Philadelphia since 1908." *Opportunity*, December 1936, 375–77.

Slater, Joseph. "Public Workers: Labor and the Boston Police Strike of 1919." *Labor History* 38 (1997): 7–27.

Stein, Jeff. "Ben Fletcher: Portrait of a Black Syndicalist." *Libertarian Labor Review* 3 (1987): 30–33.

Taft, Philip. "Strife in the Maritime History." *Political Science Quarterly* 54 (June 1939): 216–36.

220   *Bibliography*

Wakstein, Allen. "Origins of the Open Shop Movement." *Journal of American History* 51 (1964): 460–75.
Washington, Booker T. "The Negro and the Labor Unions." *Atlantic Monthly,* June 1913, 756–67.
Westergard-Thorpe, Wayne. "Towards a Syndicalist International: The 1913 London Conference." *International Review of Social History* 23 (1978): 33–78.
Whatley, Warren C. "African-American Strikebreaking from the Civil War to the New Deal." *Social Science History* 17 (Winter 1993): 525–58.
Whiteman, Maxwell. "The East European Jew Comes to Philadelphia." In *The Ethnic Experience in Pennsylvania,* edited by John Bodnar, 287–308. Lewisburg, Penn.: Bucknell University Press, 1973.
Winslow, Calvin. "On the Waterfront: Black, Italian, and Irish Longshoremen in the New York Harbour Strike of 1919." In *Protest and Survival: Essays for E. P. Thompson,* edited by John Rule and Robert Malcolmson, 355–93. London: Merlin, 1993.
Wortman, Roy T. "The I.W.W. and the Akron Rubber Strike of 1913." In *At the Point of Production: The Local History of the I.W.W.,* edited by Joseph R. Conlin, 49–60. Contributions in Labor History, no. 10. Westport, Conn.: Greenwood, 1981.
Wright, R. R., Jr. "The Negro in Unskilled Labor." *Annals of the American Academy* 49 (September 1913): 19–27.

Dissertations and Theses

Brown, Myland R. "The I.W.W. and the Negro Worker." PhD diss., Ball State University, 1969.
Cole, Peter. "Shaping Up and Shipping Out: The Philadelphia Waterfront during and after the IWW Years, 1913–1940." PhD diss., Georgetown University, 1997.
Disbrow, Donald W. "The Progressive Movement in Philadelphia, 1910–16." PhD diss., University of Rochester, 1956.
Dutcher, Dean. "The Negro in Modern Industrial Society: An Analysis of Changes in the Occupations of Negro Workers, 1910–1920." PhD diss., Columbia University, 1930.
Finney, John, Jr. "A Study of Negro Labor during World War I." PhD diss., Georgetown University, 1967.
Hardin, Clara A. "The Negroes of Philadelphia: The Cultural Adjustment of a Minority Group." PhD diss., Bryn Mawr College, 1945.
Hardy, Charles Ashley, III. "Race and Opportunity: Black Philadelphia during the Era of the Great Migration, 1916–1930." PhD diss., Temple University, 1989.
Levinson, Esther. "A History of the Hampton Roads Longshoreman's Association." MA thesis, Old Dominion College, 1968.
Mossell, Sadie Tanner. "The Standard of Living among One Hundred Negro Migrant Families in Philadelphia." PhD diss., University of Pennsylvania, 1921.
Nelson, H. Viscount, Jr. "Race and Class Consciousness of Philadelphia Negroes with Special Emphasis on the Years between 1927 and 1940." PhD diss., University of Pennsylvania, 1970.

Rumm, John Charles. "Mutual Interests: Managers and Workers at the Du Pont Company, 1802–1915." PhD diss., University of Delaware, 1990.

Topp, Michael Arthur Miller. "Immigrant Culture and the Politics of Identity: Italian-American Syndicalists in the U.S., 1911–1927." PhD diss., Brown University, 1992.

Weintraub, Hyman. "The I.W.W. in California, 1905–1931." MA thesis, University of California, Los Angeles, 1947.

Unpublished Manuscripts and Papers

Rosenthal, Anton. "The Other Wobblies: The I.W.W. Press in Latin America." Paper delivered at the annual meeting of the Social Science History Association, New Orleans, October 1996.

Web Sites

Anderson, Colin M. "The Industrial Workers of the World in the Seattle General Strike." http://faculty.washington.edu/gregoryj/strike/anderson.htm (accessed April 25, 2000).

Wright, Jon. "Organized Labor and Seattle's African American Community: 1916–1920." http://faculty.washington.edu/gregoryj/strike/wright.htm (accessed April 25, 2000).

INDEX

AFL: competition with IWW, 2, 4, 36, 39–40, 58, 67–68, 81, 103, 176; Gompers, Samuel, 85, 87; race relations, 51–52, 145; World War I, 81, 85–86. *See also* International Longshoremen's Association

ALU. *See* American Longshoremen's Union

African Americans: communism, 138; Great Migration, 27, 80, 96–98, 125, 148–50, 163; housing, 25, 70; job discrimination, 1, 27; replacement workers, 35, 43–45, 118, 120, 149–50, 161–62, 172; unions, 13, 22, 97. *See also* Carter, Charles; Du Bois, W. E. B.; Fair, James; Fletcher, Benjamin; International Longshoremen's Association; Local 8; longshoremen; Moses, Abe; National Urban League; Philadelphia; Richards, Alonzo; Universal Negro Improvement Association

American Federation of Labor. *See* AFL

Americanization, 102–3, 109, 150

American Longshoremen's Union, 33–35, 57–58

anarcho-syndicalism, 53, 66

Arnesen, Eric, 35–36, 48, 52, 134, 178n10

Baker, Paul "Polly": ILA, 170–72; 1920 strike, 120, 126; 1922 lockout, 151, 154–59, 163, 167; organizing workers, 68, 71, 106, 143; World War I, 82–83, 92, 94–95. *See also* International Longshoremen's Association; Local 8; 1922 lockout

Baldwin Locomotive Works, 11, 37, 121

Baltimore, 18, 35, 42, 45, 48, 77, 154

Barnes, Charles, 15–18, 35

Barrett, James, 169

British Shop Stewards Movement, 115, 137, 143

Brotherhood of Timber Workers, 38, 40, 52

Carter, Charles, 72, 100, 105, 108, 120, 126, 132. *See also* Local 8

CIO, 6, 171–72, 176

communism: Marine Workers Industrial Union, 172; vs. syndicalism, 128, 136–38. *See also* IWW; Philadelphia Controversy

Congress of Industrial Organizations. *See* CIO

Cramp's Shipyard, 11, 103, 164

Dempsey, William, 35, 44, 52–55, 58, 62, 71–72. *See also* ILA

Doree, Edwin F.: Agricultural Workers Organization, 133; arrest, trial, prison, and pardon, 87–90, 108–9, 126, 159; biography, 76; Brotherhood of Timber Workers, 54, 76; Local 8, 78–79; Philadelphia Controversy, 132–34, 142; World War I, 82. *See also* Fletcher, Benjamin; IWW; Local 8; Nef, Walter

Dubofsky, Melvyn, 51, 135–36, 146–47, 176

Du Bois, W. E. B.: IWW, 52, 173; job discrimination, 1, 14, 51–52; Philadelphia Negro, 21–22, 26, 180n8; World War I, 83

National Adjustment Commission,
85–86, 104, 113, 123
National Association for the Advancement of Colored People. *See*
NAACP
National Industrial Union of Marine
Transport Workers, 39–40, 59
National Urban League (Armstrong
Association of Philadelphia), 29,
161–62, 169, 171
Nef, Walter: Agricultural Workers Organization, 75; arrest, trial, prison,
and pardon, 87–92, 94, 104, 107–8,
120, 126, 159; biography, 75–76;
Marine Transport Workers Industrial Union, 75–78, 82; World War
I, 82–84. *See also* Doree, Edwin F.;
IWW; Local 8, Philadelphia Controversy
Nelson, Bruce, 141, 169
"new" labor history, 2–6, 177n7
New Orleans, 11, 36, 117, 148–49
New York City, 11, 33–36, 42, 94,
148, 154
1922 lockout: leadership, 153; race
relations, 148–49, 156–60; replacement workers, 154. *See also* Baker,
Paul; International Longshoremen's
Association; Richards, Alonzo;
United States Shipping Board
Norfolk, 35, 52, 86, 105, 154

O'Connor, T. V.: International
Longshoremen's Association, 36,
65, 85–86; United States Shipping
Board, 144. *See also* International
Longshoremen's Association;
United States Shipping Board
Office of Naval Intelligence, 86–87,
91–92, 94–95, 104
ONI. *See* Office of Naval Intelligence
Open Shop, 36, 65, 103, 112, 120–21,
150
Owen, Chandler. *See Messenger*

Pazos, Genaro, 91, 104–5, 108, 120.
See also Marine Transport Workers

Perrymore, Glenn, 60, 71, 97, 144–45.
See also Local 8
Philadelphia: African Americans, 19–
22, 24; antebellum riots, 10, 25–26;
demographics, 20–21; Department
of Wharves, Docks, and Ferries,
71, 114; economy, 10–12, 80–83,
111–14, 122, 124; ethnicity and
immigration, 23; neighborhoods,
20; 1918 riot, 18, 97; politics, 43;
port of, 28, 61, 63, 69, 100–101,
114–16, 144, 150–54, 164–68; race
relations, 19, 24, 70, 96, 169–70;
unions, 36–37; World War I, 65,
74–75. *See also* African Americans;
Irish; Italians; Jews; Lithuanians;
Poles
Philadelphia Chamber of Commerce,
11, 63, 74–75, 103. *See also* employers; open shop
Philadelphia Controversy: centralization, 141, 146–47; General
Executive Board, 131–32, 135–36;
initiation fees, 132–34, 142, 146;
Russian Civil War, 129–32, 137.
See also Doree, Edwin F.; Dubofsky, Melvyn; Fletcher, Benjamin;
IWW; Scott, James; Speed, George;
Thompson, Fred
Philadelphia Longshoremen's Union,
170
Poles: immigration to Philadelphia,
22–23, 53; longshoremen, 28–29,
51–53, 62, 77, 118; relations with
African Americans, 29, 53, 80, 169;
sugar refineries, 13, 40, 77. *See
also* Knebel, Simon; Local 8; sugar
refineries
Poole, Ernest, 12–14, 16–17

Randolph, A. Philip, 3, 105–6, 108–9,
145. *See also Messenger*
Red Scare, 102–3
Rey, Manuel: anarchism, 66–67; arrest, trial, prison, and pardon, 87,
90–92, 107, 119–20. *See also* Marine
Transport Workers; Spanish

PETER COLE is an associate professor of history at Western Illinois University. He received his BA from Columbia University and PhD from Georgetown University. He is the author of *Ben Fletcher: The Life and Times of a Black Wobbly* (Charles H. Kerr) and has had articles published in *Left History* and the *Journal of the Gilded Age and Progressive Era*. He is an avid rock climber, cyclist, backpacker, traveler, and vegan cook.

Workers on the Waterfront: Seamen, Longshoremen, and Unionism
in the 1930s *Bruce Nelson*

German Workers in Chicago: A Documentary History of Working-Class
Culture from 1850 to World War I *Edited by Hartmut Keil and
John B. Jentz*

On the Line: Essays in the History of Auto Work *Edited by
Nelson Lichtenstein and Stephen Meyer III*

Upheaval in the Quiet Zone: A History of Hospital Workers' Union, Local
1199 *Leon Fink and Brian Greenberg*

Labor's Flaming Youth: Telephone Operators and Worker Militancy,
1878–1923 *Stephen H. Norwood*

Another Civil War: Labor, Capital, and the State in the Anthracite Regions
of Pennsylvania, 1840–68 *Grace Palladino*

Coal, Class, and Color: Blacks in Southern West Virginia, 1915–32
Joe William Trotter Jr.

For Democracy, Workers, and God: Labor Song-Poems and Labor Protest,
1865–95 *Clark D. Halker*

Dishing It Out: Waitresses and Their Unions in the Twentieth
Century *Dorothy Sue Cobble*

The Spirit of 1848: German Immigrants, Labor Conflict, and the Coming
of the Civil War *Bruce Levine*

Working Women of Collar City: Gender, Class, and Community in Troy,
New York, 1864–86 *Carole Turbin*

Southern Labor and Black Civil Rights: Organizing Memphis Workers
Michael K. Honey

Radicals of the Worst Sort: Laboring Women in Lawrence, Massachusetts,
1860–1912 *Ardis Cameron*

Producers, Proletarians, and Politicians: Workers and Party Politics in
Evansville and New Albany, Indiana, 1850–87 *Lawrence M. Lipin*

The New Left and Labor in the 1960s *Peter B. Levy*

The Making of Western Labor Radicalism: Denver's Organized Workers,
1878–1905 *David Brundage*

In Search of the Working Class: Essays in American Labor History and
Political Culture *Leon Fink*

Lawyers against Labor: From Individual Rights to Corporate Liberalism *Daniel R. Ernst*

"We Are All Leaders": The Alternative Unionism of the Early 1930s
Edited by Staughton Lynd

The Female Economy: The Millinery and Dressmaking Trades, 1860–
1930 *Wendy Gamber*

"Negro and White, Unite and Fight!": A Social History of Industrial
Unionism in Meatpacking, 1930–90 *Roger Horowitz*

Power at Odds: The 1922 National Railroad Shopmen's Strike
Colin J. Davis

The Common Ground of Womanhood: Class, Gender, and Working Girls'
Clubs, 1884–1928 *Priscilla Murolo*

Marching Together: Women of the Brotherhood of Sleeping Car
Porters   *Melinda Chateauvert*
Down on the Killing Floor: Black and White Workers in Chicago's
Packinghouses, 1904–54   *Rick Halpern*
Labor and Urban Politics: Class Conflict and the Origins of Modern
Liberalism in Chicago, 1864–97   *Richard Schneirov*
All That Glitters: Class, Conflict, and Community in Cripple Creek
Elizabeth Jameson
Waterfront Workers: New Perspectives on Race and Class   *Edited by
Calvin Winslow*
Labor Histories: Class, Politics, and the Working-Class Experience   *Edited
by Eric Arnesen, Julie Greene, and Bruce Laurie*
The Pullman Strike and the Crisis of the 1890s: Essays on Labor and
Politics   *Edited by Richard Schneirov, Shelton Stromquist, and
Nick Salvatore*
AlabamaNorth: African-American Migrants, Community, and Working-
Class Activism in Cleveland, 1914–45   *Kimberley L. Phillips*
Imagining Internationalism in American and British Labor, 1939–49
Victor Silverman
William Z. Foster and the Tragedy of American Radicalism
James R. Barrett
Colliers across the Sea: A Comparative Study of Class Formation in
Scotland and the American Midwest, 1830–1924   *John H. M. Laslett*
"Rights, Not Roses": Unions and the Rise of Working-Class Feminism,
1945–80   *Dennis A. Deslippe*
Testing the New Deal: The General Textile Strike of 1934 in the
American South   *Janet Irons*
Hard Work: The Making of Labor History   *Melvyn Dubofsky*
Southern Workers and the Search for Community: Spartanburg County,
South Carolina   *G. C. Waldrep III*
We Shall Be All: A History of the Industrial Workers of the World (abridged
edition)   *Melvyn Dubofsky, ed. Joseph A. McCartin*
Race, Class, and Power in the Alabama Coalfields, 1908–21   *Brian Kelly*
Duquesne and the Rise of Steel Unionism   *James D. Rose*
Anaconda: Labor, Community, and Culture in Montana's Smelter
City   *Laurie Mercier*
Bridgeport's Socialist New Deal, 1915–36   *Cecelia Bucki*
Indispensable Outcasts: Hobo Workers and Community in the American
Midwest, 1880–1930   *Frank Tobias Higbie*
After the Strike: A Century of Labor Struggle at Pullman
Susan Eleanor Hirsch
Corruption and Reform in the Teamsters Union   *David Witwer*
Waterfront Revolts: New York and London Dockworkers, 1946–61
Colin J. Davis
Black Workers' Struggle for Equality in Birmingham   *Horace Huntley and
David Montgomery*

The University of Illinois Press
is a founding member of the
Association of American University Presses.

Composed in 9.5/12.5 Trump Mediaeval
at the University of Illinois Press
Manufactured by Thomson-Shore, Inc.

University of Illinois Press
1325 South Oak Street
Champaign, IL 61820-6903
www.press.uillinois.edu